CRITICAL ACCLAIM FOR RASCALS, RUFFIANS, AND REBELS

Forney brings to life some of Montana Territory's more infamous characters and sheds light on some lesser known originals who called Montana
home. If you like stories about women and men of grit, with motives both
pure and evil, you will find someone to love or hate between these pages.
In a series of profiles, he follows the tumultuous lives of legends like Martha Canary (Calamity Jane) and Thomas Francis Meagher, as well as the
adventures of some of the not-so- famous, who contributed to early settler
society. Forney's passion for Montana history is evident in every page of
Rascals, Ruffians, and Rebels.
— Diana L. Di Stefano, Editor, *Montana The Magazine of Western History*

"Rascals, Ruffians, and Rebels transports readers back in time to explore
Montana's rough, dangerous and chaotic early history. From spunky Sarah Forbis to the legendary Jack Slade, author Gary Forney's meticulous
research brings these vibrant, history-shaping Montana men and women
to life. Highly recommended reading for all lovers of Montana history."
— Rachel Philips, author of *Legendary Locals of Bozeman* and Research
Coordinator at the Gallatin History Museum in Bozeman.

In *Rascals, Ruffians, and Rebels*, author Gary Forney juxtaposes the eclectic profiles of twelve unique men and women—some admirable, some
contemptible, all fascinating—who helped shaped Montana's early history. Forney crafts these profiles with impressive detail and exhaustive
scholarship, helping readers more clearly understand some of the distinct
personalities and events at the heart of many of Montana's formative moments. Anyone who is interested in Montana history will discover new
and illuminating facts about even the most familiar figures, and a rich
introduction to some early Montanans worthy of discovery.
— Bob Brown, former Montana Secretary of State, State Senate President,
and long-time Montana historian.

With in-depth research and a subtle wit, Gary gives us a sense of what life
in early Virginia City and Montana was really like. Through the well-told
stories of twelve "noteworthy" and very different individuals, we learn

how they contributed to the basis and character of Montana. Born a slave, Sarah Gammon Bickford realized her mark in history by owning a public utility, the Virgina city Water Company. A spirited lawyer and Vigilante, Wilbur Fisk Sanders also became instrumental in creating the Montana Historical Society, Which convened in Virginia City in March 1865, with sanders serving as President for over 25 years. Political activist and statesman, Thomas Francis Meagher, served Montana as Territorial Secretary and Active Governor, established the Territorial Executive Office in Virginia City, "and immersed himself in the turbulent waters of Montana politics and the wildly eclectic mass of humanity which called the Territory their home." Everyone in Montana should read this informative and enjoyable book. This is a must in our museum bookstore! — Elijah Allen, Ph.D Executive Director, The Montana Heritage Commission and Marge Antolik, Curator, The Montana Heritage Commission

"None of the twelve individuals described in *Rascals, Ruffians, and Rebels* were villains, none were saints. But they were people who were there when the great State of Montana began to take shape out of the chaos of the mining camps. And Forney tells their stories with verve in a clear, direct, engaging prose. Once I began reading, one history led to another, and I could not put it down." — Lee Robison, Former President, Madison Valley History Association

The title of this interesting book is an accurate summation of Gary Forney's coverage and presentation of a dozen biographies from the 1800s in Montana history. The reasons for his choices for inclusion and how they fit together are well detailed in his introduction. In wide ranging and readable style, personal details, facts, accomplishments (of all sorts), and even myths about these "characters" bring a lively history to readers. This book will add well to Forney's impressive body of work. — Marcia Melton, author *Joe Henry's Journey, Joe Henry's Return*, and *The Boarding House*, all historical fiction for young adults

Rascals, Ruffians, and Rebels

Profiles from early Montana

Gary R. Forney

Raven Publishing, Inc.
Norris, MT

Rascals, Ruffians, and Rebels
Profiles from Early Montana
Copyright © 2020 Gary R. Forney
Cover Photo by Ken Parent, April, 1909
Ravenswood Ranch cabin of Joseph "Jack" Slade
Men identified as (L-R): Sterling Findley, Dave Davis, and Jim Gunn

Raven Publishing, Inc. PO Box 2866, Norris, MT 59745

www.ravenpublishing.net

ISBN: 978-1-937849-63-4

Printed in the United States

Library of Congress Cataloging-in-Publication Data

Names: Forney, Gary R., author.
Title: Rebels, rascals, and ruffians : profiles from early Montana / Gary R. Forney.
Description: Norris, MT : Raven Publishing, Inc., [2020] | Includes bibliographical references. | Summary: "By 1863, rich discoveries of gold in what would become a part of the Montana Territory brought a flood of immigrants to the area. The twelve individuals from early Montana history included in this book represent the generation that created the trails which have become the highways we travel. They built Montana's first schools, churches, farms, ranches, mines and businesses, established law and civil order, and lay the foundations of our state government. Their lives touch those who call Montana home. "-- Provided by publisher.
Identifiers: LCCN 2020005117 | ISBN   (paperback) | ISBN 9781937849641 (ebook)
Subjects: LCSH: Pioneers--Montana--Biography. | Frontier and pioneer life--Montana. | Montana--History--19th century. | Gold miners--Montana--Biography. | Montana--Gold discoveries. | Gold mines and mining--Montana--History--19th century. | Vigilantes--Montana--History--19th century.
Classification: LCC F731 .F67 2020 | DDC 978.6/01--dc23
LC record available at https://lccn.loc.gov/2020005117

To Cathy, my family, and many friends who have given me a hand-up and helped me to find my way on the long trail from Woodside to Ennis.

ACKNOWLEDGMENTS

I am very grateful to all of those who have been so helpful to me in bringing the stories of these wonderful characters from Montana's early days to realization. Their contributions and encouragement have made this a great journey.

Among those to whom I am indebted would be: the library staff of the Montana Historical Society, particularly Zoe Stolz; the staff of the Thompson-Hickman Madison County Library & Pace Archives, Jack Albrecht, Christina Koch, Jane Bacon and Evelyn Johnson; Kathleen Mumme and her wonderfully helpful staff in the Madison County Clerk & Recorder's Office; Kathy Ketchu and staff of the Madison Valley Library; and Rachael Phillips and the staff of the Gallatin Historical Museum. All of these good people went above and beyond in their efforts to be of help to me and their patience in assisting my search among books, boxes and files for esoteric bits of information.

Likewise, I must express my appreciation to all those who took the time to read my work and make helpful suggestions; to Loren Tucker, Jane Williams Yecny, and Bill Tate for sharing their knowledge of local history; and Sam Maloney for graciously allowing me access to his historic property.

And to those a bit farther afield, my great friend and fraternity brother, Clark Guy, and Edith Antoline of the Derry County (PA) Historical Society for their work to obtain details on the early life of Neil Howie.

Finally, to my publisher, Janet Hill, I offer my deep appreciation for your advice, encouragement, and professional skills in bringing this work to life.

Introduction

The land known as Montana has been blessed with incredible natural beauty, bountiful resources, and—since its earliest years—a wealth of daring men and women who have helped to shape this land in many ways. For some time now, I have been an eager student of Montana's history, and have found myself charmed, curious, amused, and often-times, in awe, as I've read stories of those pioneers who dared to make this place their home. I've found, to borrow a phrase from Jimmy Buffet, we can learn much from both heroes and crooks.

By 1863, there was a rapidly spreading awareness of the incredibly rich discoveries of gold in what would become a part of the Montana Territory. This news became the primary impetus for the first major wave of immigration of Whites (as well as some Blacks and Chinese) into the area. It was a land which was previously known only to those who may have read accounts of the Lewis & Clark Corps of Discovery, some fur trappers, a few Jesuit missionaries, and several tribes of Native Americans who had known this place since time immemorial.

Not to be overlooked in any consideration of early Montana is the phenomenally disruptive economic, social, and cultural impact of the Civil War. Suddenly, those who had been merchants, farmers, school teachers, lawyers, or practicing virtually any other imaginable occupation of that time were in search of a place where they could have a new beginning. Montana's gold and untamed land became a magnet for people from not only the Northern and Southern states of American, but from dozens of countries. Montana became a collision point of people with different political beliefs, different social and cultural customs, and different languages, but all with a common dream. Regardless of the means by which these people chose to achieve their goal, I find myself in admiration of the determination and courage which was required of those to strike out for a place unlike anything most had ever seen, with nothing more than what they could transport in a wagon or carry on their backs, and with their life savings in a currency which they would find to be devalued by 50% upon arrival. The title of J.W. Rawlston's painting of an emigrant train, "The weak ones turned back, the cowards never started," aptly captures the essence of the courage and perseverance required of all those who would be Montana pioneers.

In this work I have striven to present a balanced and accurate profile of the lives of some famous, some infamous, and some barely known men and women whom it has been my good fortune to become acquainted with as I've read Montana history. I want to lift up these people so as to preserve the stories of how an eclectic cross-section of men and women pursued their dream of a better life in early Montana. Of course, it is also my hope that through these profiles, I may also "set the hook." Which is to say, that readers will become interested enough in some—or several—of those I've selected for this anthology that they may seek to read in greater depth from the excellent sources which are cited at the end of each chapter. Each of the lives of these men and women are significant in term of what they did—for better or for worse—to shape and define the structure and character of Montana.

While not each of those profiled in this work is necessarily worthy of emulation, they do represent examples of the generation that would create the trails which have become the highways we travel. They built Montana's first schools, churches, farms, ranches, mines and businesses. They would establish law and civil order, and lay the foundations of our state government. Every day, their lives touch those of us who call Montana home. We stand upon their shoulders.

Gary R. Forney
Ennis, Montana

TABLE OF CONTENTS

Sarah Gammon Bickford
Triumph over Tragedy

Success in life can be measured in many ways: number of home runs hit, the value of one's personal fortune, degrees earned, awards received, etc., etc. Perhaps there's no success more impressive, however, than that of those people who rise by virtue of indefatigable determination from modest—even tragic—circumstances to become devoted parents and respected leaders of their communities. And, if one accepts that standard, there's no doubt that Sarah Bickford deserves recognition as having lived a very successful life.

Sarah began her life as a slave. She was born on Christmas Day in 1852, on the Blair family plantation, near the town of Jonesboro, in the southeastern corner of Tennessee. It would seem most likely that Sarah's mother was known as Mary, but there is some question regarding who her father may have been. Although there was a slave identified

1

as "George" in residence at the plantation of an appropriate age to have been her father, Sarah was identified as a "Mulatto," on later census reports indicating some Caucasian heritage in her family tree.[1]

John Blair, III, was patriarch of the family plantation at the time of Sarah's birth. Blair was educated at Washington College as an attorney, but he had found his primary source of wealth through a successful mining claim during the California gold strike in 1849. Upon his return to Tennessee, Blair nominally practiced law, owned a hotel in Jonesboro, and was active in politics; identifying as "Jacksonian Republican." Blair served multiple terms as a state Senator and Representative, and as U.S. Representative from 1823-1835. Despite owning slaves, the Blair family was considered to be "pro-Union" in their political sympathies. It is presumed that Sarah may have spent some time working at Blair's hotel, which would not only give her experience which may have later proven useful, but more importantly may have provided a very helpful contact.[2]

Built in 1814 by slave brick masons, the Blair mansion still stands as a testament to their skill.

Slave quarters, Blair Mansion

One of the mysteries of Sarah's early life is that of her education. As would later become obvious, Sarah could read, write, and had at least basic arithmetic skills. How and when she obtained these important skills is not only uncertain, but a bit of a marvel considering the common practice of withholding education from slaves.

John Blair died in July of 1863, at the age of 72, just a few months after the Proclamation of Emancipation—which exempted Tennessee—was issued. It appears that Blair's family needed to raise funds to settle debts connected with his estate, however, and perhaps they were further motivated by the probability of an extension of Emancipation. Nevertheless, the decision was made to sell some of the family slaves at this time; including Sarah's mother whom Sarah would never see again. When the State of Tennessee declared the abolishment of slavery in January of 1865, Sarah, now 12 years old, left the Blair Plantation and made her way to Knoxville to seek out Nancy Gammon; a woman she would later refer to as her "aunt." It seems virtually certain that Sarah

3

had met Nancy in Jonesboro (during her time at Blair's hotel), at which time Nancy was known to be a "free black."[3]

Sarah was taken into the home of Nancy and her husband, Isaac, and also assumed the family name of "Gammon." Sarah soon found employment as a housekeeper in Knoxville with the family of John and Viola Murphy. Mr. Murphy, educated as an attorney, had served in the Union Army with the rank of Major and commander of four companies (A, B, C, D) of the 60th Regiment of African Infantry. As with other such units, it was a command position which few sought and which was literally a death sentence for any White officer captured by the enemy. Perhaps it was his willingness to take on such challenging and potentially dangerous assignments which led Murphy to accept an appointment by President Grant in January of 1871, to serve as Federal Justice for the fledgling Territory of Montana.[4]

Young Sarah Gammon

In what had to have been an incredibly daring, life-changing decision, Sarah Gammon accepted Mr. Murphy's invitation to accompany his family to Montana, serving in the dual role of housekeeper and nanny for their two children. For a young woman whose world had been only as large as the space between Jonesboro and Knoxville, this was a grand opportunity. On the other hand, what may have been the Murphy family's vision of an exciting opportunity was soon to fade.

Although it was the epicenter of one of North America's richest gold discoveries and the territorial capital of Montana, by the time Sarah and the Murphy family arrived in Virginia City (via wagon train) in the late Summer of 1871, they found a town that was a shadow of its former glory. Once boasting an eclectic population of approximately 10,000, the city had been a cacophonous blend of a rough, bawdy mining camp with a generous portion of cultural groups, churches, and schools, and where the residents lived in domiciles ranging from wicki-ups to elegant Victorian homes. But by 1871, the Alder Gulch and town of Virginia City was in a slow but very obvious decline from its zenith, and certainly lacked many of the amenities and refinements which the Murphy family may have reasonably expected to find.

For all that it may have lacked, however, Virginia City was an inviting environment in at least one respect: it lacked much of the ethnic prejudice found in the eastern cities. Although things would change, the Montana Territory was a place of emigrants from many states and many countries, and—with the exception of Chinese—it was a place where hard work and honesty carried more weight than social position, ethnicity, or family name. It was a place where someone like Sarah Gammon could make a good life for herself. After just over a year in service, John Murphy resigned as Federal Justice and moved his family to Bozeman where he went into private legal practice. Sarah remained in Virginia City.

Sarah found work as a housekeeper at the Madison House Hotel and, by 1872, Sarah had been discovered by John Brown. Regrettably, we know little about Brown's background other than he was an African-American, he was working as a miner, and that he successfully courted Sarah. Brown and Sarah were married and, in fairly quick succession, the couple had three children: two boys (William and Leonard) and a girl (Eva). It isn't certain as to exactly when it began, but Sarah became the target of physical abuse by Brown. In court testimony, it was disclosed that Brown repeatedly beat Sarah "with his fists and a wooden broom handle" and threatened her with knife and gun.[6]

As if her life was not already difficult, Sarah had to endure further heartbreak when her two young boys died of diphtheria. Their deaths may have been the proverbial "last straw" for Sarah. She obtained a divorce from Brown and, taking Eva, went to work as a live-in housekeeper and nanny for Jean Baptiste Laurin and his wife, Adeline. Jean Baptiste and Adeline were natives of Quebec and had become prominent residents of the community known as Cicero (present-day Laurin). This setting seems to have provided Sarah a safe, healing environment where she also quickly acquired a fluency in speaking French.[7]

With the encouragement (and perhaps the financial support) of the Laurins, Sarah returned to Virginia City and went into business for herself. She opened the New City Bakery and Restaurant in late 1881, "two doors up" from her former employer, the Madison House Hotel. Her advertisement for the bakery illustrates the effort Sarah put into the enterprise: "meals and lunches at all hours" "fresh bread, cakes, pies and confectionery constantly on hand." Sarah was not only successful in her business, but also attracted the attention of Stephen Bickford—a regular diner who soon became a suitor.[8]

Stephen Bickford

Stephen Eben ("Dick") Bickford was a native of Saco, Maine, where he was born December 4, 1835, the first of two children in the family. He briefly spent time as a miner in Colorado before heading for the new gold fields of the Idaho Territory, "with E.F. Johnson," in early 1863. It would be his good fortune to arrive at Bannack soon after the discovery of gold in the Alder Gulch. Stephen was among the earliest men to have arrived in the Alder Gulch in June of 1863, and may have been in the group of miners led to the site by the original discovery men. He was a hard-working man who had avoided the common pitfalls of most miners (alcohol and gambling). Stephen wisely invested some of his earnings from mining into farming, a telegraph company, and would also be involved in cattle ranching in the Madison Valley for fifteen years.[9]

Sarah and Stephen were married in 1883, and lived in the home which he had built on Granite Creek (approximately 5 miles west of Virginia City). Sarah would give birth to four children in this home: Stephen Elmer in 1884, Harriet Virginia in 1887, Hellena in 1890, and Mabel in 1892. Tragically, daughter Eva would die in 1885, but memories of the bright little girl would live on in Sarah's heart.

In 1888, Stephen became the managing partner—and held a 2/3 ownership—in the Virginia City Water Company. The family moved to Virginia City in 1893, and made their home at the eastern edge of town (a site known as "Romey's Farm"). Sarah managed the water company's financial records, operated a vegetable farm, and mothered four active children. Already well known, Stephen and Sarah—and their mixed-race children--quickly became popular members of the community. Ella Mountjoy would later recall how thrilled she was to be selected to share a school desk with Mabel Bickford who was the "brightest student in school."[10]

Following a long illness, Stephen Bickford died of dropsy (edema) and pneumonia on March 22, 1900, leaving his estate to Sarah; whom he also appointed executor. She immediately assumed the management of the Water Company (as well as Stephen's mining interests) and, within a few months, purchased the additional 1/3 share of the water company; likely becoming the first woman—and the first person of African-American descent—to own a public utility in the United States. She also acquired the "Hangman's Building," one of the original buildings of Virginia City, for use as an office space. Sarah astutely remodeled the building in order to provide two separate offices—and an additional source of rental revenue.[11]

An Exterior view of the original entryway of the
Hangman's building prior to 1930 renovation.

Sarah sought to become as solidly prepared as possible for her new
role by earning a correspondence course degree in business management and establishing a reputation in Virginia City—and with the state
utility commission--as a firm, but fair business woman. Although her
son, Elmer, would assist as the company's maintenance person, and
daughter Harriet would briefly assist with the bookkeeping, Sarah handled all other responsibilities of operating the water company for the
next 31 years.

Sarah's example for hard work, her determination in the ability of
women to achieve professional success, and her value of education was
obviously passed along to her daughters. Each of her girls would earn
Bachelor degrees and Mabel, after earning her Bachelor of Arts degree
from Columbia, would go on to earn a doctorate degree from Chicago
University.

As was her custom, Sarah would spend Sunday evenings working
in her garden, and on July 19, 1931, it was in her garden that Elmer
found his mother, who had suffered a heart attack. She would die at
10:45 that night. In yet another example of the community's respect for
this remarkable lady, Sarah was buried beside Stephen in Virginia City's
Hillside Cemetery and her funeral was attended by hundreds. Sarah's
daughters, Hellena and Mabel would remember that, at the time of her
mother's death, a small photograph of Eva was on a table beside her

bed; where it had been since Eva's death. The shared headstone of Sarah and Stephen is simply engraved "Bickford."[12]

Regrettably, as is oftentimes the case in other families, there was conflict regarding Sarah's estate management between Elmer and his sisters. In a Quit Claim Deed which Sarah had executed in April of 1927, she gave each of the girls 1/3 of the properties known as "Romey's Garden" and "Fisher's Garden" (site of the Bickford home property), as well as 1/3 each of the Virginia City Water Company and its property. She also would name her daughter, Mabel, as administrator of the estate. Nearly ten years following his mother's death, Elmer filed a petition in Madison County to be appointed as administrator for Sarah's estate. Despite their physical separation from one another, the girls quickly responded with a joint petition in opposition. Elmer's petition was denied by the court on July 14, 1941. Apparently, there was no lingering animosity, however, inasmuch as Elmer would later move to New York where he would live with Mabel and her husband until his death.[13]

One of Sarah's biographers has written: "Mrs. Bickford was a loving mother, an exceptional business woman, and needs to be remembered. Her story has taught me to never give up, even when the going gets tough." If one were looking for an epitaph to inscribe upon the Bickford headstone, one could do a lot worse.[14]

Notes:

1. Washington Country, Tennessee.

2. Peterson. Congressional Directory.

3. Hampton.

4. Appointed by Grant, January 27, 1871. 60th Regiment organized at Keokuk, Iowa on October 15, 1863. J. Murphy aged 22 at time of appointment, a resident of Kentucky but native of Tennessee. Resigned commission at Little Rock, May 25, 1863.

5. H.F. Sanders, Vol. 1. Murphy resigned September 21, 1872, would later move to San Francisco.

6. Name also appears as <u>William</u> Brown in some sources.

7. Sarah appears on 1880 Census in Laurin household. Mabel Bickford later wrote that the boys, and Eva, were buried in the Virginia City cemetery. *Pioneer Trails and Trials:* daughters Hellena and Mable recalled Sarah singing lullabies and reciting nursery rhymes in French.

8. Madison House was located between present-day sites of Hangman's Building and the Madison County Courthouse annex.

9. "with E.F. Johnson," *Madisonian,* March 22, 1900. Bickford worked the Shoo Fly and Last Chance placer claims in Alder Gulch, and held claims on the Belmont, Old Baldy, and Way Up lodes per *Pioneer Trails and Trials.*

10. Water Company originally established in January 1865, per *PT&T.* "brightest student…," Wiley & Ella Mountjoy mss, SC 545, MHS.

11. Obituary in *Alder Gulch Times,* March 23, 1900. Stephen prepared his Will on October 27, 1927.

12. Obituary in *Madisonian* of July 24, 1931. Grave site plot presumed to also be site of Eva's grave as well as that of Sarah's boys, per letter of Mabel Bickford (April 28, 1953, in Leeson. "photo" story per *P T&T.*

13. District Court Records, Pace Archives, "Sarah Bickford" notebook.

14. Unidentified quote in Pace archives, op cit.

Sources:

African American Registry

Alder Gulch Times (Virginia City, Montana)

Hampton, Kate. "Sarah Bickford: Pioneer," *Virginia City Nugget* Vol. 18, no. 2,

Virginia City Preservation Alliance.

Leeson, Michael. *The History of Montana 1739-1885.*

Madison County Clerk & Recorder's Archives.

Madisonian (Virginia City, Montana)

Olsen, Lauri. *Whispers on the Wind.*

Pace Archives, Thompson-Hickman Madison County Library, Virginia City, MT.

Peterson, Dr. William. "Finding Sarah Bickford," *Virginia City Nugget,* Vol. 15, no. 2.

Pioneer Trails & Trials. Madison County History Association, 1976.

Sanders, Helen F. *History of Montana, Vol. I.*

Photo credits:

Portrait of Sarah; Wikipedia

Blair mansion & slave quarters; Dr. Bill Peterson.

Young Sarah; African American Registry.

Stephen Bickford; <u>Madison County Trails & Trials</u>.

Hangman's Building: Pace Archives

Bickford cemetery plot; author.

JOHN M. BOZEMAN
Legendary Trailblazer...and Rascal

He was born a rebel, but his natural character was that of a rascal. Like his father, he seems to have chafed at the notion of domestic encumbrances and eagerly sought to live life on his own terms and in search of some elusive measure of financial success. Unlike his father, John Bozeman's name lives on in a much grander scale than either could have ever imagined.

John Merin Bozeman was born in the family cabin in, what at the time, was Cherokee County, Georgia, in January of 1835, to William and Delila (nee Sims). John would reportedly have four siblings; George, Phoebe, Mary, and Nancy. Although the 1850 Federal Census does not show any schools in Cherokee County at that time, it does appear as if John did acquire some—albeit very basic—level of literacy. In 1850, William left his family with the stated intent of finding his fortune in the California gold rush. However, he never returned to his

home nor was he ever in contact with his family following his departure. John, age 15 at this time, undoubtedly assumed a greater share of
responsibility for scratching out a living from the family farm.[1]

On January 9, 1856, John married Catherine Ingram, also of Cherokee County, who was 19 years old. In relatively short order, the couple
would become parents to three daughters; Lila, Martha, and Melinda.
During those years, John most likely continued to work as a farmer to
provide for his growing family. By the Spring of 1860, John would learn
of the recent gold strikes in Colorado, and the dream would infect
him—as it had his father—with a case of "gold fever." He soon packed
what was almost certainly some modest belongings and headed west,
leaving Catherine and his mother for what they must have suspected
could be the last time they would see him.[2]

Catherine Bozeman (c1890)

Bozeman's daughters: Lila, Martha, and
Melinda (L-R middle row in white blouses)

Bozeman would not find his fortune in Colorado, but he did find what
may have suited him as pleasant substitutes: freedom from responsibilities and a cadre of other young men who shared the joy of an unfet-
tered life. Among those whom he befriended was Thomas Stuart, the
younger brother to James and Granville who were making a name for
themselves—and good money—in a settlement alluringly known as
Gold Creek. Stuart's brothers wrote glowingly of their life and encouraged Thomas to join them, which he did, along with 16 of his closest
friends; including John Bozeman. Thomas and his entourage arrived at

Gold Creek, Idaho Territory, on June 24, 1862.

Soon after their arrival, Tom Stuart and friends learned that while James and Granville may have exaggerated the quality of gold prospects in the Gold Creek area, there was a legitimate new gold strike which had been recently discovered some 130 miles to the south at a site known as Grasshopper Creek. John Bozeman didn't wait long before he was en route to the "Grasshopper diggings" and the principal camp of the mining district, Bannack; which quickly became a difficult place for a man to stay alive. Author Tom Stout would opine that "It is probable that there never was a mining town of the same size that contained more desperados and lawless characters than did Bannack during the winter of 1862-63." Emily Meredith, one of the relatively few female residents of Bannack at the time, wrote in a letter to her father: "I don't know how many deaths have occurred this winter, but that there have not been twice as many is entirely owing to the fact that drunken men do not shoot well." The new town took its name—and arguably the land itself—from the Bannock Indians who inhabited this region. Legend has it that it was a matter of poor penmanship that resulted in the town being registered as "Bannack" rather than Bannock." Regardless of how it was known, or its fearsome reputation, it proved to be the first major gold strike in the land which would become Montana.[3]

It isn't certain whether Bozeman had his own claim in Bannack, or whether he was working as a laborer for someone who held a claim. Certainly, the population of the area had grown so quickly that it wasn't possible that all those arriving were going to find a good paying claim. In any event, he certainly didn't find his fortune and was very willing to consider other options. In November, Bozeman would accompany three other men to scout an area which was thought to be a promising new gold strike 15 miles north of Bannack, but found "everything exaggerated" and soon returned to Bannack.[4]

By early January of 1863, the snow was more than 30 inches deep in Bannack and the ice on Grasshopper Creek was thick enough that mining operations had closed. Most of Bannack's residents were spending their days and nights huddled in their dingy cabins or crowded into the unstable environment of the camp's saloons dreaming of their plans for the next season while nursing glasses of a volatile concoction generously called whiskey. Many of the men (and likely all of the women) were probably thinking of going home, while others—including James Stuart—were considering prospecting expeditions into new areas. John Bozeman was considering yet another option.[5]

The exact details have escaped being recorded, but Bozeman formed a partnership with John Jacobs, a man whom he met in Bannack, who was—in terms of personality—his exact opposite. While Bozeman was described by most as personable and gregarious, Jacobs was taciturn, grizzled, and foul-tempered…but he knew the land. Jacobs had spent most of his years living in the Rocky Mountains working as a trapper. He had also married a woman from the Flathead Nation who was another likely source of his familiarity of the region. The two men determined that as soon as weather conditions permitted, they would explore a route Jacobs knew to have been commonly used by Indians as a trail to hunting grounds. Although it does not appear as if he had actually traveled the route, and may have had only general knowledge of the area, Jacobs told Bozeman that much of the trail (which lay to the east of Bannack) followed the Yellowstone River. Jacobs believed it should provide for easy travel by the wagons of settlers and freighters which they expected would be trying to reach the new gold camps and, moreover, would be a significantly shorter route than those commonly in use. Bozeman quickly calculated that travelers would undoubtedly be willing to pay for the privilege of being guided over such a route and concluded that it could be a very successful enterprise. How much Jacobs knew, or told Bozeman, about the one major disadvantage of the route is another lingering question.[6]

John Bozeman, John Jacobs, and Jacobs's daughter, Emma, left Bannack in the early Spring of 1863 to explore the possible new route to Grasshopper Creek from the east, probably close to the same time as James Stuart departed with his "Yellowstone Expedition." The two men platted a trail east from the present-day town of Three Forks, across the valley of the Gallatin River, crossed over a pass through the Bridger range into the Yellowstone valley, and turned south to meet the Oregon Trail.

As Jacobs had predicted, the route they followed featured good grazing for the livestock that would pull or accompany the wagons of emigrants, good access to water, and was plentiful with wild game over much of the route. Unfortunately, however, the trail crossed the traditional lands of at least six tribes of Indians. And if there was any doubt in their minds of just how strongly that the Indians felt about intrusions across their traditional hunting lands, it was soon answered. As they were traveling southeastward on their new trail, Bozeman and Jacobs encountered a party of 75-80 Crow warriors. The Crows took most of the trailblazers' supplies, forcibly "traded" horses (leaving Bozeman and Jacobs with much weaker horses) and they severely beat Emma; no doubt because, as part-Flathead, she was regarded as a traditional enemy.

Perhaps Bozeman and Jacobs believed that a large party of emigrants would lessen the chance of an Indian attack, or that their encounter with the Crow was an isolated incident. In any event, they subsequently neglected to tell their prospective clients about their encounter with the Crow. This "oversight" would seem consistent with the opinion one old pioneer expressed regarding Bozeman's ethical code: "His sense of honor in some directions was terribly sensitive, while in other directions his conscience was very elastic. He never posed as a saint, but it would have been a very dangerous experiment to call him a liar."[7]

After their meeting with the Crow, the men would spend several days of uncertain travel (during which time they subsided largely on roots which Emma would gather and prepare), before arriving at a little settlement known as Deer Creek Station in mid-May. Deer Creek was a "fort and military station" on the Oregon Trail, just east of present-day Casper, Wyoming. Oscar Collister, a telegraph operator at Deer Creek, would recall that: "in the summer of 1863 a man named Bozeman, accompanied by an old-time mountaineer and guide, whose name I have forgotten…staked out a trail…that would shorten the distance of the then existing route. They established a camp and began diverting emigrants [and] were not long in gathering a sufficient number of wagons to make a good-sized party…." One of the men who joined the inaugural wagon train remembered John Bozeman as, "a tall, fine looking Georgian [and] not as voluble as Jacobs."[8]

After several days of travel (nearly 120 miles) from Deer Creek Station, the Bozeman-Jacobs train of forty-four wagons reached Willow Creek; near present-day Buffalo, Wyoming. As they established their campsite on July 20, the travelers were suddenly surprised to find themselves confronted by approximately 150 Cheyenne and Sioux Indians. Through a parlay, the Indians made it clear they did not want the wagon train to go any further north, and warned of dire consequences should the emigrants ignore their request.

Instead of immediately turning back, however, the emigrants spent three days in deliberations among themselves. As a part of the party's fact-finding efforts they sent riders back over the trail to see if any additional wagons were following; there weren't. Finally convinced they had no better options, the wagon train, led by Jacobs, dejectedly retreated. Rather than exactly retrace their previous route, however, Jacobs led them on a southwesterly course, striking the Oregon Trail approximately forty miles west of Deer Creek. As soon as they reached the established trail, Jacobs abandoned the pilgrims and headed east; reportedly spending the winter in Denver. It isn't certain whether Emma accompanied Jacobs to Denver or remained with the train to make her own way home.

Meanwhile, John Bozeman, accompanied by nine volunteers on good horses, continued north along the route that he and Jacobs had scouted. While en route, the men paused briefly to admire the spectacular vista as they crossed from the Yellowstone Valley into the Gallatin River valley. One of the party, George Irvin, suggested that it would be appropriate to name the pass in honor of their guide, and thus Bozeman Pass was christened. After a ride of twenty-one days, with much of their travel during nighttime, the determined men arrived at the Three Forks. While camped there, the party met two men who had recently left Bannack. These men informed Bozeman's group that Bannack was rapidly being deserted, as people were daily moving to a big new strike to the east of Bannack. Armed with this new information, the Bozeman party eagerly altered their intended destination and John

Bozeman arrived in time to join those filing mining claims along an area known as the Alder Gulch.[9]

"Truly truth is more wonderful than fiction, and excels in marvelousness even the Arabian Nights' Entertainments, but truth and marvelous go hand in hand when Young America finds a good gold gulch."

John Bozeman filed two mining claims in Bachelor's Gulch, located near the top and entering on the east side of Alder Gulch. Despite the enormous amount of gold being taken from the Alder Gulch and its branches, Bozeman—whether through lack of effort or poor judgment in terms of the location of his claims—wasn't able to have any significant success at mining. It was probably by virtue of spending a good deal of time in Virginia City, however, that he was able to make some contacts which would have long-term consequences.

In early January of 1864, Bozeman was hired as a "packer" to accompany a train of three wagons from Virginia City to Salt Lake City to acquire merchandise and food supplies. Known as the "Moody train" for its leader, Milton Moody, the party was carrying more than $80,000 in gold dust (approximate present-day equivalent of $5,780,000) and $1,500.00 in currency for the purchase of supplies as well as to place on deposit on behalf of some Virginia City miners and merchants. While en route, two men (suspected to have been "Dutch John" Wagner and Steve Marshland) attempted to rob the train while the packers were well out in advance of the wagons scouting for a campsite. The wagon crew managed to fend off the robbers, wounding both, who escaped... for the time being.[10]

At some point during the winter of 1863-64, Bozeman also encountered William McKinzie in Virginia City. The two men had previously met in May, when Bozeman was working with Jacobs, platting their trail, and McKinzie was en route to Bannack, but it is possible they had known one another in Georgia inasmuch as McKinzie was also a native of Cherokee County. Nevertheless, they obviously spent time together in the bustling new camp, and it seems McKinzie may have shared

Bozeman's lack of enthusiasm for gold mining as he would soon pull up stakes for work as a ranch hand.[11]

One of the "high profile" contacts which Bozeman made in Virginia City was with Thomas Cover. Bozeman could have met Tom Cover in either Gold Creek or Bannack, since their time in both camps overlapped, but seems more probable that their acquaintance was made in Virginia City—and may have been initiated by Bozeman. Thomas Cover was one of the six original "discovery men" who had made the discovery of gold at Alder Gulch, and had wisely invested his newfound wealth into property and successful business ventures. It is easy for one to imagine that, rather than any genuine friendship existing between the men, Bozeman sought to gain a place within Cover's orbit; hopeful to gather some "crumbs" which may fall from his table. It certainly doesn't seem as if Cover and Bozeman had any common ground or shared interests, but it became an association which would irrevocably link them together in Montana history.

Perhaps one of the most significant contributions which Bozeman made during his association with Cover during this time was to urge him to consider the possibilities which the Gallatin River Valley provided in terms of agricultural potential. Bozeman may have also reasonably suggested there would be good commercial prospects as well for that location, enthusiastically anticipating there would soon be hundreds of new immigrants passing through on the trail which he and Jacobs had established. Cover, who was already somewhat familiar with the area during his own travels, was motivated to take a thorough look at the area and began to realize the possibilities. This potential was further enhanced in May of 1864, when the U.S. Congress established the Territory of Montana and created a long-term foundation for the area's development. While some embraced this potential, others were less eager to be embraced by "Uncle Samuel." Granville Stuart simply groused that instead of "Montana" the Shoshone term "To Yabe Shock-up" (meaning "Country of the Mountains") should have been the choice of Congress as the name of the new territory.[12]

Seemingly with Cover's encouragement, several men followed his

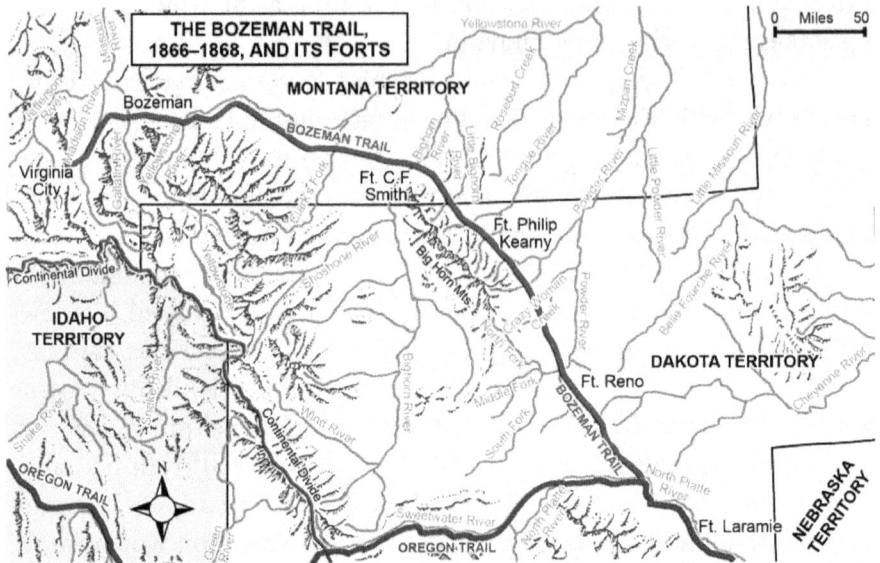

THE BOZEMAN TRAIL,
1866–1868, AND ITS FORTS

lead to the Gallatin Valley in the Spring of 1864; including: Daniel
Rouse, Nelson Story, William Beall, Rev. William and John Alderson,
Elliott Rouse, John Stafford, Bud McAdow, and John "Jack" Mendenhall; who had the distinction of opening the first saloon. Tom Cover filed claims on several parcels of land, started farming operations,
and with McAdow, quickly set about building a grist mill and preparing land for grain production. And Cover, true to his word, also
filed claims on behalf of Bozeman for some land as well. Informally
known as both "Jacob's Crossing," and "Farmington," the new settlement quickly began to take shape (albeit a bit crudely) in the absence
of Bozeman--who was leading the first train of immigrants along his
trail into the newly established Montana Territory.

Against a back-drop of dramatic vigilante activity during the winter
of 1863-64, many were busy just trying to make their fortune. Among
the hundreds of new enterprises launched in Virginia City during that
winter was the Missouri River & Rocky Mountain Wagon Road and
Telegraph Company. The company's directors were a "Who's Who"
in early Montana, including: Samuel Hauser, Walter Dance, Samuel
Word, Nathaniel Langford, Anson Potter, and Hezekiah Hosmer. In
order to determine what would likely be the most popular, ie: faster,

immigrant route to Virginia City, the directors determine to have a "race." Jim Bridger (the well-known guide/mountain man) was hired to lead a train over a route which he had proposed, and Bozeman was hired to bring a train over the route which he and Jacobs established— with a branch to Virginia City rather than to the Three Forks. Both trains were to leave from Fort Laramie; a distance of 608 miles.[13]

Bozeman, without incident, led a train of 150 wagons along his route and despite Bridger's head-start "of several weeks," rolled into Virginia City without any fanfare on August 1, 1864, a few hours ahead of his rival. Although some would refer to Bozeman's route as the Bozeman Cut-off, the Virginia City Road, or the Bighorn Road, the "accepted appellation" would thereafter be the Bozeman Trail. Although to the directors of the Missouri River & Rocky Mountain Wagon Road Company, it was considered "our road." For Bozeman, it would be the last time he would guide a train.[14]

The territory's first newspaper, the *Montana Post*, was in operation at Virginia City by the late autumn of 1864, and was regularly featuring news of conflicts—or reported conflicts—between Whites and Indians. The newly appointed Governor of the territory, Sidney Edgerton, finally responded to the perceived threat of war by issuing a proclamation calling for the establishment of a territorial militia. The *Post*'s issue of November 19th reported that "Captain Bozeman," who had been authorized by the governor to raise a company of cavalry, would be at the Virginia Hotel in Virginia City to receive volunteers "to pursue marauding Indians." The request of Bozeman and Edgerton for volunteers was, however, widely ignored and neither the militia nor the militia cavalry materialized as a viable force.

In December, the First Session of the Territorial Legislature would go into session at Bannack. Although sometimes raucous, and often at odds with the Governor, the legislature would achieve an impressive record of accomplishments; including selecting Virginia City as the first territorial capital. Emma Jacobs, the frequently abused daughter of John, probably wasn't aware that the legislature was in session, nor is it likely that she would have understood much of their proceedings. But as the legislators were closing their historic chapter of Montana's history, Emma's life story also came to a close. Not far south from the new diggings at Last Chance Gulch (near present-day Clancy), thirteen-year-old Emma was buried in an unmarked grave. Her role in the unfolding grand drama of Montana was as unknown to herself as it would be to the thousands who would travel the Bozeman Trail. What Emma had tragically known, however, and what many of the White emigrants would come to learn, is that life could be very harsh in To Yabe Shock-up.[15]

The Bozeman Trail quickly became a popular immigrant route— much to the bitter resentment of several tribes of Native Americans. In the Spring of 1866, through the chicanery of a "peace treaty," the U.S. government assumed the right to establish three forts along the Trail to keep the peace and to protect immigrants and commerce. Primarily led by Red Cloud of the Lakota, an unrelenting war was unleashed, which would include such notable battles as the "Fetterman Massacre" and the "Wagon Box Fight." It soon became difficult for the Army to protect itself, much less provide protection to immigrant trains. By the time the trail was "officially" closed (March 2, 1868) it had served as the highway for several thousand hopeful pilgrims and thousands of tons of equipment and supplies. Traces of the trail can still be seen today, including, perhaps, none more clearly than along the final grade down into Virginia City. From this hillside venue the immigrant, who had been traveling for approximately four months (and most of whom had walked the entire route), caught their first view of the new El Dorado. For most, it was less than awe-inspiring. Ellen Fletcher perhaps best captured the moment as she would write in her diary: "The outside streets consisted entirely of log cabins, some of them the littlest bits of houses that I ever saw…it reminded me more of a row of hen coops." Nevertheless, despite all its blemishes, it was a place for new beginnings, new dreams, and refuge.[16]

"We passed a half-dozen huts dignified with the name of Bozeman City…I saw the great man, [Bozeman] with one foot moccassioned [sic]and the other as Nature made it, [he was] giving opinions to a crowd of miners

as to the location of the mythical mines."
Edward B. Neally (9/64)

Soon after his victory over Bridger, Bozeman had returned to the new settlement in the Gallatin Valley where he was present for an organizational meeting of the area's residents, held on August 9th. The new settlers voted—upon the motion of Rev. William Alderson—to name the aspiring settlement "Bozeman City," and also elected John Bozeman as City Recorder. In a remarkable coincidence, the leader of the first emigrant train to arrive in the newly christened settlement was led by none other than John Jacobs. It is perhaps indicative of his irascible reputation that Jacobs was denied any lasting memorial for his role in establishing the trail that played such an important part in founding the city. In the fall of 1865, an election was held for Gallatin County officials, and Bozeman City was well-represented. Tom Cover was elected County Clerk; P.W. McAdow, County Treasurer, Jack Mendenhall, County Sheriff; and John Bozeman, Probate Judge.[17]

It does not appear as if Bozeman made any effort to resume attempts to become a miner, nor actively take up farming as several area residents, nor, as previously mentioned, to serve as a guide on his namesake trail. Rather, it seems, he was content to live life less encumbered and enjoy the role of local celebrity. Described by Walter Davies at the time as "several inches over 6' tall...and probably 225 pounds... all bone and muscle," combined with his joie de vivre personality, Bozeman would have been a prominent figure dressed, as described by Bill McKenzie: *"Bozeman never wore buckskin or a bead. He had a small sandy mustache.* [author's emphasis]. Customarily he wore a black beaver cloth suit, his coat of the frock style and a black slouch hat—never tucked his trousers into boots as some frontiersmen wore then." His typical nonchalance toward gainful employment was also noted by Davies: "[Bozeman] had no use for money except to bet with, and the most congenial place to him on earth was the saloon, with a few boon companions at a table, playing a game of draw." Davies additionally noted that Bozeman was "quite a favorite with women."[18]

Bozeman was an active promoter of his namesake town. He became a partner in the City Hotel with a recent immigrant couple from McLeansboro, Illinois, George and Elmyra Frazier. And although he had a small cabin in the settlement, Bozeman would thereafter spend most nights at the hotel; which was undoubtedly more comfortable— and cleaner—than his cabin. Bozeman also contributed $25 to the building fund of the local Methodist Church (which Tom Cover also supported), and became a member of the newly established Masonic Lodge #6; which was "more or less restricted to those men or their sons with Confederate ties." He also made it a point to stay in contact with Tom Cover, proposing business enterprises of various sorts though none of which seemed to gain support from Cover. Bozeman also regularly contacted Nathaniel P. Langford, who was the managing director of the Virginia City Wagon Road Company. By the Spring of 1866, Bozeman had established a ferry service on behalf of the VCWR Company across the Yellowstone River, at a site known as Hunter's Hot Springs (near present-day Springdale). He reported to Langford that: "on the 25th I crost [sic] 45 wagons and had no bad luck. Emigrants well pleased."[19]

Bozeman took time to occasionally write to his mother. In a couple of surviving examples one notes that he (probably intentionally) doesn't provide much detail as to his enterprises, and it would appear that Catherine was most likely illiterate inasmuch as he obviously directed comments to her through his mother. Bozeman wrote:

"I am yet on the land and among the living...up and down rich and poor several times. I have a good start now again and I can not see what will hinder me from making all the money I want in 2 or 3 years more. Tell Catherine I would like to pay her and the children a visit but I do not know when I can as my Business is in this country and I cannot leave it very well...Dear Mother Brother and Sisters I am well at present and I hope these phew lines will find you all the same...your affectionate Sone and Brother."

A few months later, Bozeman again wrote his mother:

"I received your loving letter the other day, which gave me much pleasure...but it was very mortifying to me to hear that times are so hard

there…how [sic] Catherine and the children getting along. I will pay you a visit in a year or two, but do not expect me to come there to live any more. I have made a great amount of money in this country but have had some bad luck and spent a great deal. I am [in] partnership with a man by the name of Frazier in a Hotel and some groceries…his wife name was Bozeman before she was married. I don't know whether we are any relation or not….

P.S. I will send you a piece of chiney money as it will be an oddity in that country…your affectionate Son until death."[20]

One may assume from these letters that Bozeman had not lost all affection for his family, but—at some level—both he and they must have recognized the reality was that he would never return to Georgia. And they would have been right.

Although Bozeman had enjoyed his notoriety, the pedestal upon which he had rested seems to have become less secure and he felt a growing uncertainty as to his future role in his namesake community—and the community felt a growing discomfort for his presence. Phyllis Smith would write: "John Bozeman was still casting about, searching for his niche in the growing settlement. He farmed a bit, got into a few fights, gambled a lot, [and] dreamed up a number of business schemes…." And, as previously noted, he enjoyed a flirtatious relationship with several of the town's women. All of which may have been factors leading to his declining popularity among most of the town's male population—and to one of the darkest episodes connected to John Bozeman.[21]

Sometime between mid-December of 1866 and early January of 1867, Rosa VanVlierden was awakened in the middle of the night by John Bozeman's knocking at her door. A very anxious Bozeman told Rosa that a woman was having a baby in his cabin, and pleaded that she help with the delivery. Rosa agreed to assist and the delivery went well for mother and baby, but she would later state she didn't know the identity, or ever again see, the woman or child. It isn't known whether Rosa shared this story with others at the time but, if so, it certainly would have done nothing to have enhanced Bozeman's reputation.[22]

25

"Bozeman never could see danger...."

As spring of 1867 arrived in the Montana Territory, acting governor Thomas Francis Meagher began to increasingly receive petitions from settlers requesting protection from anticipated Indian attacks...fears almost certain exacerbated by the "Fetterman Massacre" near Fort Kearny in December. As it had in 1864, the *Montana Post* quickly, passionately took up this torch and reported on the "incipient panic [which] exists among a large number of ranchers on the Gallatin." Among those who wrote to Meagher (almost certainly with some editing assistance and at the encouragement of others) was John Bozeman, whose letter was reproduced in the *Post* and ominously declared in part that: "We have reliable reports here that we are in imminent danger of hostile Indians."[23]

Meanwhile, whether it was due to the quality of the meals, the quality of conversation, or that the general ambience had significantly improved, Bozeman had become an increasingly frequent visitor to Cover's home since Cover's return to Montana with his young bride, Mary, in the early summer of 1866. Reportedly, some of these visits were unannounced and made at a time when Tom was not at home; which was an egregious breach of social decorum. Bozeman's reason, perhaps a bit contrived, for these visits was to promote new money-making ideas to Cover. It must be assumed, however, that these incidents further eroded the community's goodwill toward Bozeman...and became a source of deep embarrassment to Mr. Cover.

A genuine business associate of Cover was an interesting character by the name of John Richau. Richau was of French/Indian descent (reportedly a nephew of the Sioux chief Red Cloud), and an experienced guide and trapper who was familiar with the languages and customs of several Montana tribes. Richau was employed by Cover to serve as the guide for a supply train delivery from Bozeman City to Fort C. F. Smith in early January 1867. Fort Smith was one of the posts established on the Bozeman Trail, and was located approximately 200 miles east of Bozeman. On its return to Bozeman, the supply train had

Thomas W. Cover

been harassed and lost seven mules to Indian raiders. It is probable that Richau and those men accompanying the train were among the sources of information regarding Indian activity which fueled the anxiety of Gallatin Valley settlers. Additionally, Richau carried the news that ten wagons of flour were needed at Fort Smith. Author Dan Thrapp writes that Cover had also "received communication from Captain George B. Dandy, quartermaster at Fort Phil Kearny...that flour was needed equally that far down the Bozeman Trail."[24]

Despite the knowledge that there was an immediate demand for flour, Cover appears to have done nothing to respond throughout the remainder of January, February, and into March. Concerns among the area residents for their safety, however, had grown increasingly desperate. At a meeting held on March 18, the Gallatin Valley citizens determined to build a stockade at Cover's mill for the dual purpose of protecting the critical gristmill operation as well as providing a sanctuary in the event of a large-scale Indian attack. The meeting also resulted in a resolution, which Cover helped to draft and personally deliver, to acting governor Thomas Meagher. The resolution solicited Meagher to provide arms, ammunition, and a militia force to protect the Valley. Although Meagher was sympathetic to the delegation's concerns, he advised them there was no stockpile of arms and ammunition, or a viable militia force. Meagher would, however, undertake extraordinary efforts to obtain arms and the protection of regular U.S. Army forces, and was granted permission to form a territorial militia.[25]

Curiously, it was at the end of March, when rumors of impending Indian attacks were at their peak, that Tom Cover finally announced his intention to visit the military posts of the Bozeman Trail to determine their need for supplies—which anyone must reasonably expect would have become only more desperate since January. The circumstances became even more interesting, however, when Cover solicited John Bozeman to serve as his guide and sole companion for this trip. Even if one assumes that Cover felt two men could travel more quickly, and possibly be more likely to escape the attention of Indians than a larger party, it would seem that Richau would have been a more logical choice as a guide than Bozeman. Although he was certainly familiar with the route of his namesake trail, John Bozeman had not led a train across the route since 1864. Consequently, it is unlikely that Bozeman was personally acquainted with the personnel serving at the military posts, and he was certainly not as likely to be as skilled a negotiator—or fighter—as Richau would have been with any Indians who may have been encountered. Perhaps Cover simply wanted to make certain he knew the whereabouts of Mr. Bozeman, and to know he wasn't visiting his home.

John Bozeman was commonly regarded as a very self-confident man, but he had grave misgivings about the possible outcome of his trip with Cover. One may assume, however, that Bozeman felt this was an opportunity to earn favor with Cover for partnership in future projects. Nevertheless, before their departure on Wednesday, April 17, Bozeman recurrently expressed doubts about his safe return and left instructions to notify his family in Georgia if his premonitions were accurate. There were those who believed that Bozeman's impending misfortune was more of a foregone conclusion than mere chance. As

John Bozeman rode away from the City Hotel to meet Cover, Elmyra Frazier is said to have remarked, "Isn't he a handsome man?" To which her husband, George, replied, "Yes, and take a good look at the son-of-a-bitch as this is the last you are going to see of him."[26]

Tom Cover and John Bozeman spent the first night of their journey at a cow camp on the ranch of Nelson Story, near present-day Livingston. The day's events had done nothing but reinforce Bozeman's apprehension of this expedition. A small party of Blackfeet made a tentative and unsuccessful raid on the camp shortly after the arrival of Cover and Bozeman, which understandably stoked Bozeman's apprehensions and which may have provided Cover with a storyline. William McKinzie, the long-time friend of John Bozeman, was also bunking at the camp that night. McKinzie was struck by how the man he regarded as "game to the back-bone" and "could never see danger," was so unnerved that night. McKinzie recalled that, as the wind moaned in the late night's darkness, Bozeman not only confessed his fears but he offered McKinzie his "horse, saddle and outfit" if Bill would take his place. McKinzie, who had just completed a long ride himself and was anxious to get to Bozeman City to "get cleaned up a little," attempted to reassure his friend that he would probably be safer than anyone else passing through this territory. The next morning, Bozeman and Cover rode toward the rising sun…and into one of Montana's great mystery stories. One of the few things we know with certainty is that, in the early morning darkness of the following day, Tom Cover stumbled back into Story's cow camp, on foot, exhausted, wounded—and alone. As Cover received treatment for a bullet wound in his left shoulder, he breathlessly related that Indians had killed John Bozeman. One of the camp's cowhands immediately rode to Bozeman City to notify Nelson Story of the tragedy.[27]

Nelson Story quickly rode to the camp, where he examined Cover's wound and listened as he repeated his account of Bozeman's murder. Cover related that he and Bozeman had stopped about midday on April 18, at a site along the Yellowstone River known as Cady Coulee; approximately fourteen miles east of Story's camp. As he and Bozeman were preparing a meal, they observed five Indians approaching them

"Death of John Bozeman" by E.S. Paxson (Note depiction of
Bozeman's appearance: buckskin, moccasins and full beard)

and giving signs that they were peaceful. Cover said that Bozeman
thought the Indians to be of the Crow tribe, and therefore represented
no danger. As the Indians came into the campsite, they asked for something to eat and Bozeman agreed to share some food. Moments later,
however, Cover said that Bozeman whispered to him that the Indians
were not Crow but Blackfeet; a tribe well known—and much feared—
for their animosity towards whites. It seems a bit curious that Cover,
who had previously spent some significant up close and personal time
with the Crow, would not have also recognized this fact, or that Blackfeet would have approached so benignly. Nevertheless, Bozeman quietly directed that Cover slowly, but surely, go to where their horses were
tethered and prepare them for a quick departure.[28]

As he went to the horses, Cover said that he left his 16-shot Henry's
rifle lying beside Bozeman. Bozeman, who was kneeling by the campfire, already had his own Spencer's rifle at his side. Cover recounted

30

that he was walking to the horses, his back to the campfire, when he heard a gunshot. He spun around to see an Indian fire a second time at Bozeman, who dropped to the ground. Cover turned, ran to the horses, and had just retrieved a pistol from their packhorse when he was struck by a shot in his shoulder. Cover fired at the retreating Indians as he charged back to where Bozeman lay. Observing that Bozeman had received two wounds in his chest, Cover picked up his Henry's and attempted to fire at the Indians. The rifle, however, didn't initially fire, so Cover retreated approximately fifty yards before it began to function. Cover recounted that he killed one of the Indians and then he retreated another 300-400 yards to hide in some brush along the riverbank. Cover told Story that he hid in the brush for about an hour before the Indians rode away, taking their dead companion and the horses of Cover and Bozeman. Cover cautiously returned to the campsite and confirmed that Bozeman was dead, took his watch and Spencer rifle, covered his body with a blanket, and began walking to the cow camp. It was many years later before Nelson Story's son, Thomas Byron Story, told the editor of a Bozeman newspaper what his father had done after hearing Cover's version of events.[30]

While examining Cover, Story noticed that not only was there a powder burn around his wound, but it appeared that the entry of the bullet had been from the front rather than the back. This was obviously inconsistent with Cover's statement that he had been shot at a distance of several yards and with his back turned to the Indians. Story excused himself from Cover, and went to one of his most trusted ranch hands; a man known as "Spanish Joe." Joe was an experienced mountain man before being hired by Story to help drive cattle up from Texas. Story instructed Joe to immediately ride to the site of the attack, make a thorough examination of the area, and return to him as soon as possible. Story said he would organize a burial party that would follow, but that Joe should not talk with any member of the party, or anyone else, before reporting to him. Spanish Joe returned that evening to give his report to Nelson Story.[31]

Spanish Joe reported that Bozeman's body was lying near the site of a campfire, but that he could find only the signs of Bozeman's and

Cover's boot prints at the site. Joe had widened his circle of investigation from the campfire area, but was unable to find any signs of Indians or any traces of blood from the Indian which Cover indicated that he had killed. What Joe did find was the trail made by three shod horses—presumably Cover's and Bozeman's—leading away from the campsite. There were also signs that several stones had been thrown toward the direction of their travel, as if someone had deliberately chased the horses away from the campfire site. Joe said he had remained at the site until the burial party arrived with a roughly-made coffin, and watched as they dug John Bozeman's grave within a few yards of the Bozeman Trail. Armed with this vital information, Nelson Story appears to have remained silent.

Just over one year later, the Episcopalian Bishop, Daniel Tuttle, visited with Tom and Mary Cover at their home in Bozeman City. As the Bishop recounted to his wife, during the evening of his visit, Cover shared the story of the events surrounding Bozeman's death—and one finds some interesting disparities in the version as reported by the Bishop with the statement Cover had given to Nelson Story. Cover told Bishop Tuttle that he had been wounded with the second shot fired, and that Bozeman had received only one, fatal, wound. Cover also stated that, after repeatedly firing his pistol as he advanced to Bozeman's side, he picked up his Henry's rifle and immediately used it to kill one of the Indians. Cover also mentioned that the Indians had not used their guns again since wounding him but, instead, were shooting arrows at him during his charge to the campfire and during his retreat to the river. Cover further recounted that he remained in the brush by the river for only about five minutes, during which time he could not see the Indians, before coming out of hiding to find they were gone.[32]

In addition to the difference in the number and sequence of shots being fired, one is struck by the other discrepancies in Cover's version of events which he gave to Bishop Tuttle. Most notably, the performance of the Henry's rifle, the Indian's use of arrows (which would have been much too obvious to have been overlooked by Spanish Joe), and the significant difference with respect to the time Cover said he remained hidden along the river. Taken together, however, these de-

tails are troubling in how they conflict with both Cover's original statement to Nelson Story and the written account of the events that he sent
to Governor Meagher. One is also struck by the incongruity that, although the Indians presumably took time to gather the horses of Cover
and Bozeman, they did not take such a valuable prize as the Spencer
rifle lying beside Bozeman's lifeless body.

Shortly after Cover's return to Bozeman City, an auction of John
Bozeman's personal property was held in front of the Frazier Hotel, and
news of Bozeman's death was communicated to acting governor Meagher via a letter from Tom Cover; which was subsequently conveyed
throughout the territory by virtue of being reprinted in the *Montana
Post*. The result of this tragic news was a wide-spread call for general
retaliation against Indians. Generously overstated as the "Indian War
of 1867," a militia force that was short on enlisted men and heavy with
officers spent a few weeks (and a great deal of money) chasing shad-
ows. Even Meagher recognized the many shortcomings of the militia,
humorously referring to it as, "not an invincible, but invisible force."[33]

Why Nelson Story never made public the information from Spanish Joe's investigation of the murder site only compounds the uncertainty of events. There was never a formal investigation into Bozeman's
death, and the version(s) of Tom Cover apparently were readily accepted as fact...or at least what most were willing to accept as fact. It
does seem, however, as if Nelson Story was haunted by the thought of
Bozeman's remains lying in that lonely gulch along the Yellowstone. In
1870, Story finally made arrangements for Bozeman's remains to be recovered and brought to Bozeman for re-internment in the Story family
plot at Sunset Hills Cemetery. Bozeman's remains were transferred to
a new casket made of "native pine" and constructed by "W.J. Beall and
Judge A.D. McPherson." It was reported that the burial services, under
the direction of Rev. Matthew Bird of the Methodist Church, "drew
forth a larger concourse of people than any similar occasion that has
ever taken place in Gallatin County."[34]

Tom Cover was among several prominent merchants in the territory who fed deeply from the government's trough by providing supplies for the militia at greatly inflated prices. In October, Cover was

sufficiently recovered from his shoulder wound to lead a supply train of thirty-six wagons down the Bozeman Trail to Fort Smith. Cover's earlier misfortunes were apparently behind him by this time, as neither he nor his supply wagons encountered any further incidents of Indian attacks. In fact, it could be said that the only significant casualty that occurred during the "Indian War" was that of Thomas Francis Meagher…whose death provides its own very generous share of mystery to Montana's colorful history.

Thomas Cover sold all of his Montana interests and, with his wife, moved to Southern California in the autumn of 1868. Cover became a founding father of Riverside, California, and continued to have very significant financial success through land development and the production of oranges. Although, in what some may regard as delayed justice, Cover disappeared in 1884, while searching for the legendary gold field of "Peg-leg" Pete Smith in the Borrego Desert. His body was never recovered.[35]

Bozeman's good friend Bill McKinzie subsequently served as sheriff of Gallatin County, and for the remainder of his life he carried feelings of remorse regarding Bozeman's death. Almost certainly it seems he carried some guilt as to whether Bozeman's murder may have been avoided had he agreed to take his place; although it is also possible that act would have only temporarily delayed the demise of Mr. Bozeman. At the time of his death in 1913, McKinzie asked that he be buried next to Bozeman. His request was honored and the epitaph on the tombstone which marks the gravesite of McKinzie and Bozeman epitaph reads: "Here Lies Two Friends."

Monument at Bozeman/McKinzie gravesite

Notes:

1. Pickens County was established in December 1853, from a portion of Cherokee County; which included the Bozeman residence. Some sources cite John's middle name as "Marion." Siblings per Geni. com, Duckett Family site. Marilyn Drew writes that William Bozeman died en route to California on May 14, 1852, as he was swept overboard from the *Clarissa Andrews*.

2. Marriage certificate in Burlingame mss, folder 6945. Commonly known by her middle name, Catherine, her first name was actually Lucinda.

3. Stout, History of Montana. Camps of the Grasshopper Mining District included Marysville, Centerville, Bon Accord, and Jerusalem, in addition to Bannack. Meredith letter of April 30, 1863, in Frontier Omnibus. Bannack is operated as a Montana State Park, located in southwest Montana, and is a beautifully maintained "ghost town."

4. Contemporary estimates of the population of Bannack by November indicate 500-700, with 200-300 in each of the other camps. "everything...," Morley diary, November 22, 1862. There is no record of a mining claim at Bannack for Bozeman; he probably earned his way through day labor or gambling.

5. "snow" quote in Purple.

6. Some portion of the proposed route had been traveled by the expeditions of Lewis & Clark in 1806, and Captain William Raynolds in 1860 (whose guide was Jim Bridger).

7. "his sense of honor...," W.J. Davies, *Avant Courier*, December 19, 1891.

8. Emma's role per William McKinzie, *Avant Courier*, ibid. The exact trailhead would deviate slightly during the ensuing years, but the principal course of the trail would remain generally as established by Bozeman and Jacobs. Fort Ellis (near Bozeman) was established in late August of 1867.

Epigram: "Truly truth...," J.H.Morely diary, November 12, 1864.

9. Mining Claims, Fairweather District

10. Nathaniel Langford, Vigilante Days & Ways.

11. McKinzie a native of Georgia, per Hebbard & Brininstool.

12. Cover had passed through, or very near, this area during the journey of the original Alder Gulch discovery men. "To Yabe Shock-up" quote: Frontier Omnibus.

13. The company was granted incorporation status and exclusive rights by the First Legislative Session (12/27/1865), to create a road from Virginia City to a point of navigation on the Yellowstone River, to operate a toll gate every 40 miles of the route, and all land for five miles on either side of the road. Mileage based upon a later survey by Jim Bridger.

14. "150 wagons" and "accepted appellation" per Hebbard & Brininstool.

15. Edgerton selected Bannack as the site for the first session. Per the Organic Act which established the territory, the legislature had the responsibility to select the first capital.

16. The forts (from south-north) were: Reno (1865), Kearney (1866), and C.F. Smith (1866). An additional fort, Fort Ellis, was added in August of 1867; located just east of Bozeman. "the outside…," Fletcher mss.

Epigram: "We passed a half-dozen…," E.B. Neally, September 1864.

17. Jacobs arrival per Houston, who wrote that at a subsequent meeting a motion to change the town name to "Montana City," was introduced, but failed.

18. Quotes per "Reminisces of W.J. Davies," Burlingame Collection, folder #794.

19. Two rooms were regularly held at the two-story hotel; one for Bozeman and one for McKinzie. Bozeman was a third cousin to Elmyra, per Sketches of the Bozeman Family. "more or less…," per Smith. Bozeman to Langford, June 26, 1866. Langford was also serving at the time as Federal Collector of Revenue, and would later become the first Superintendent of Yellowstone National Park.

20. "I am yet…," John Bozeman to Delila Bozeman, July 11, 1866.

"I received...," ibid, December 4, 1866. Bozeman was a 3rd cousin to Elmyra per Rev. Joseph Bozeman. George and Elmyra later operated the Frazier House Hotel at the corner of Main & Bozeman Streets. Elmyra died in 1928, at the age of 92.

21. "Bozeman casting about," P. Smith.

22. Ibid, per interview of Dr. James Hamilton with Rosa Van-Vlierden Beall.

23. "incipient panic...," "we have...," *Montana Post*, March 30, 1867, April 6, 1867.

24. "received communication...," Thrapp. Forney, *Dawn in El Dorado*.

25. Forney, *Thomas Francis Meagher*.

26. "Isn't he...," P. Smith per interview with Roy Walton.

27. "Game to the..., "horse, saddle...," "get cleaned up...," William McKinzie per interview in *Avant Courier*, December 19, 1891.

28. Letter of T. Cover to T.F. Meagher, *Montana Post*, May 4, 1867.

29. "Murder of John Bozeman," Jefferson Jones and M. Burlingame presentations.

30. Ibid, Jones. Story became suspicious of wound as well as claim that only 5 Blackfeet would be traveling in Crow territory; their traditional enemies.

31. Ibid.

32. Tuttle.

33. Auction per "Reminisces of W.J. Davies," March 8, 1891. *Montana Post*, May 4, 1867. New casket per Davies "Reminiscences." "not an invincible...," J. Bruce, *Lectures*.

34. Nelson Story's version of events first publicly revealed by his son, Thomas Byron ("TB") Story in an interview with Jefferson Jones in 1946. Merrill Burlingame interviewed Lester Biersdorf, a confidant of Nelson, in 1954; shortly after T.B.'s death. Biersdorf related version of events he heard from Nelson in "near identical detail' to that which T.B. had told Jones. "drew forth...," *Missoula & Cedar Creek Pioneer*, October 20, 1870.

35. Forney. *Discovery Men*.

Sources:

Acts, Resolutions and Memorials of the First Session of the Montana Territory.

Avant Courier (Bozeman, MT)

Bozeman, Rev. Joseph W. Sketches of the Bozeman Family.

Bruce, John. Lectures of Thomas Francis Meagher in Montana.

Burlingame mss, Montana State University archives.

_____. "John Bozeman, Montana Trailmaker," Mississippi Valley Historical Review.

_____. "Murder of John Bozeman," presentation to the Quest for Knowledge Club (Bozeman), November 20, 1973.

Davies, W.J. "Reminiscences of W.J. Davies," Burlingame Collection, fldr. 794.

Drew, Marilyn J. "A Brief History of the Bozeman Trail," World History.org.

Fletcher, Ellen mss, Montana Historical Society, SC #78

Forney, Gary R. Dawn in El Dorado.

_____. Discovery Men.

_____. Thomas Francis Meagher.

Hakola, John W., editor, Frontier Omnibus.

Hebard, Grace and E.A. Brininstool, The Bozeman Trail, Vol. 1.

Houston, E. Lina "Early History of Gallatin County," in History of Montana, From Wilderness to Statehood, James Hamilton.

Jones, Jeffrey. "Murder of John Bozeman," address to the Quest of Knowledge Club (Bozeman),December 13, 1955.

Langford, Nathaniel. Vigilante Days and Ways.

McLemore, Clyde editor. Frontier Omnibus.

Missoula & Cedar Creek Pioneer (Missoula, MT)

Montana Post (Virginia City, MT)

Morley, James Henry diary. MHS, SC#533

Neally, Edward.B. "A Year in Montana," The Atlantic Monthly, Vol. 18, no. 2.

Purple, Edwin. Perilous Passage, edited by Kenneth Owens.

Smith, Phyllis, Bozeman and the Gallatin Valley.

Thrapp, Dan. Vengeance!

Photo credits

Portrait; Bozeman Chronicle
Catherine Bozeman; Bozeman and the Gallatin Valley.
Bozeman family; ibid.
Bozeman Trail; Wikipedia
Thomas W. Cover; Pace archives
"Death of John Bozeman;" by Paxson, Wikipedia.
Bozeman/McKinzie gravesite: author

JOHN P. BRUCE
A Most Eccentric Character

Although he was born in Philadelphia in 1811, John P. Bruce had deep roots—and strong sympathies—with the South. His family (which had Scottish heritage) spent much of John's childhood years in Virginia and later in Kentucky, which Bruce generally regarded as his home. The culture of the South would clearly shape his political views, many of his eccentric characteristics…and some of his demons.

Educated at Harvard University and trained as an attorney, Bruce was drawn to a career in journalism where, one suspects, he enjoyed the opportunity to utilize the "bully pulpit" to espouse his personal agenda and achieve some regional notoriety. Returning to Kentucky following graduation from Harvard, he would serve as editor for at least three Kentucky newspapers: the *Cynthiana News,* the *Somerset Gazette* (where he mentored his nephew, Joseph Wright), and the *Interior Journal.* Bruce was also granted license as a "Tavern Keeper" at Wordsville,

Kentucky; although there is no evidence that he actively managed the tavern. It appears he was also able to capitalize upon the recognition gained through these enterprises to earn election to Kentucky's House of Representatives in 1837 and to the Senate for the sessions of 1848 and 1850, representing the Knox County area.[1]

Bruce also certainly enhanced his social position by virtue of his marriage to Charity Word. The Word family (also of Scottish heritage) was prominent and well-established within the Kentucky aristocracy. Charity's father, John, and mother, China, would have six children; four sons and two daughters. Among Charity's several cousins was Samuel Word, who would briefly attend Bethany College (in present-day West Virginia) en route to a career in law, and who would also find his way to the Montana Territory.

Despite the outward appearances of social achievement and a successful career, however, Bruce found himself struggling to deal with personal issues. On two occasions during 1857, he was admitted to the Asylum for the Insane at Lexington for periods of treatment. Whatever the source of his mental health problems may have been, it would prove to be a continuing battle.[2]

Soon after the outbreak of the Civil War, Bruce and Charity moved to St. Joseph, Missouri, where they found a number of former Kentucky residents and Southern sympathizers in the vicinity. Bruce began working as an editor within the friendly confines of the *St. Joseph Gazette*. Paris F. Pfouts, the publisher of the *Gazette*, was another immigrant to Missouri and another unabashed proponent of the Confederacy who set the tone of the paper. Although popular with many of the local area residents, the *Gazette* became a continuing target of harassment by Federal troops. Pfouts, in particular, felt immense pressure and left St. Joseph in the Spring of 1861, apparently never personally meeting Bruce who arrived shortly afterwards. In addition to his duties with the paper, Bruce would also attempt to return to the political arena, but was twice an unsuccessful candidate for United States Representative. His defeats included the especially contentious election in 1862, when there were multiple instances of Union militia preventing "Bruce men" from voting and destroying polling books.[3]

In early 1865, no doubt seeking respite from the stress of war time harassment, Bruce and Charity left St. Joseph for Salt Lake City, which would be a relatively brief place of residence. Bruce attempted—unsuccessfully—to purchase the *Salt Lake Telegraph*, which was regarded as the "Jack-Mormon" newspaper. Bruce was, however, able to purchase press equipment necessary to produce a newspaper. Although rather than setting up shop in the Salt Lake area, he was lured to move to the Montana Territory, probably with encouragement from Charity's cousin, Sam Word (who had been among the early immigrants to the Alder Gulch). Perhaps Bruce also interpreted the name of the territory's capital city, Virginia City, as an omen of where he could find a comfortable environment for the re-birth of his personal and professional lives.[4]

Montana's streams were pouring forth wagon loads of gold, the territory was being flooded by waves of new immigrants, and there was only one other newspaper in existence, the *Montana Post,* which was unmistakably Republican in its political sympathies. Bruce eagerly seized upon the opportunity to serve as a torch-bearer of the Democratic Party's interest in Montana and boldly established his new paper in Virginia City…which was also home of the *Post.* Bruce launched the *Montana Democrat,* on November 1, 1865, from its offices on South Jackson Street, just a stone's throw from the office of the *Post,* located on North Jackson Street. Bruce also established his credentials as an attorney and was among the first men admitted to the Montana Bar.[5]

Thomas Josiah Dimsdale was editor of the *Montana Post*. A native

Thomas J. Dimsdale

of England, Dimsdale was an Oxford educated immigrant who had quickly become an outspoken proponent of all matters Republican, and who had become the confidant of many leading citizens; one of whom was his primary source for his recently published manuscript, *The Vigilantes of Montana*. Dimsdale possessed a wonderfully expansive vocabulary, a biting wit, and many of the cultural characteristics one expected to find in an Englishman of his era. He was commonly described by his contemporaries as "not a robust man," physically small, and bookish. He was active in the Masonic Lodge, delighted in watching horse racing and boxing matches, theatre, classical music, and poetry. He also suffered from the effects of "consumption" (tuberculosis).[6]

Although Bruce "had no trouble in securing substantial encouragement for the prosecution of his undertaking," he obviously had some trouble in securing personal friends. Even among the ample number of unique individuals in the Virginia City area, John Bruce attracted attention. One biographer acknowledged that, "the mass of the people were slow in taking kindly to him. He was, naturally, a kindly good-hearted gentleman, but he had been reared in an atmosphere of aristocracy foreign to the cosmopolitan crowds which made up the population of mining camps. The native hauteur and courtly dignity peculiar to the plantations of the South [were regarded in Virginia City] as 'putting on airs.'" At least in one respect, however, Bruce found common ground with the common man of Virginia City. It was noted that "[Bruce]… had all of a genuine Kentuckian's passion for gaming, and was often found deep in the dalliance with the mystic pasteboards in hand at poker or bucking the equally seductive 'tiger' [ie playing faro]."[7]

Although it would seem that the similarities in personality between Bruce and Dimsdale may have drawn them toward one another, the reality was quite the opposite. While both men were perhaps too well-bred to literally throw punches at one another, they seldom let an opportunity pass without challenging one another in print. As example, in one issue of the *Post*, Dimsdale mused that "our friend, Major Bruce, has a perfect right to inform the public that his brain is a pumpkin bed or a melon patch." Bruce responded to another perceived slur by declaring, "We would desire to avoid personalities with the *Post*... but if terms such as 'tussey-boy' are applied to use hereafter in the *Post*, we shall inquire who it is that chooses to use such terms in regard to ourselves." One may interpret Bruce's response as a thinly disguised implication that he felt the matter may need to be resolved by a duel.[8]

Although his aristocratic personality may have initially alienated him from the general population of the Alder Gulch, it may have actually assisted Bruce in establishing friendships with some of the influential men of the Territory. In what would seem an incongruous relationship between a devoted Southerner and a former general of the Union Army, Bruce quickly became acquainted with—and a great admirer of—the acting governor, Thomas Francis Meagher. Bruce was aware of Meagher's world-wide reputation as an orator, and preserved a critical part of early Montana history by publishing a book of the speeches made by Meagher in Montana. Bruce was also selected to introduce Montana's second governor, another former Union Army general, and native Kentuckian, Green Clay Smith at his first public address in Virginia City in October of 1866.[9]

Perhaps it was his association with Meagher and Smith that rekindled Bruce's political ambitions—much to the chagrin of Paris Pfouts, who referred to him as "an old broken down politician." In August of 1866, Thomas Francis Meagher publicly announced his intention to resign as Territorial Secretary, and Bruce attempted to secure the appointment to replace Meagher. Despite the support of some influential supporters which included Anson Potter, John Rockfellow, Dr. Levinus Daems, and Meagher, Bruce was unsuccessful in securing the appointment from President Johnson. Bruce also jockeyed for various leadership roles within Montana's Democratic Party, however, his ambitions were thwarted—and his ego badly bruised. The final blow appears to have been his loss at gaining the party's nomination for the coveted position of Territorial Delegate.[10]

Denied the opportunity to serve as Montana's official representative, Bruce took it upon himself to make an extended journalistic visit to Washington during the Spring of 1868. In one of the columns he filed for publication in the *Democrat*, Bruce reported upon the impending impeachment trial of President Johnson. Bruce, in obvious support of a fellow Southerner, reported that "the opinion [in Washington] is that the President will be removed...but time will prove all things. God grant that justice and right may prevail and our country be saved from the hand of the radicals who are seeking its overthrow and destruction."[11]

Bruce returned to Virginia City only to find himself embroiled in his own conflict at the _Democrat_. The paper's typesetters, along with those of the *Post*, had recently organized themselves as the "Virginia Typesetters Union" and were demanding higher wages. Ironically, it was Henry Blake—who had briefly served as editor of the *Post* and had returned to the practice of law—who had drafted the articles of organization for the union, and who would later opine that "like most strikes the demands [of the union] were unreasonable."[12]

Although John Bruce had been listed as "editor and proprietor" of the *Democrat* in the December 26, 1867 edition, by the first edition of February of 1868, Joseph Wright (maternal nephew of Bruce) and James Word (one of Charity's brothers) were listed as publishers and Samuel Word as editor. In fact, it was Wright and the Words who had truly managed the paper for most of the previous year. Clearly Bruce had lost interest in the rigors of operating a newspaper by the time he returned to Montana. Whether motivated by economic necessity or moral principle isn't certain, but Bruce refused to meet the demands of the union. Bruce ended publication of the *Democrat* in February of 1869, and left the Territory. Coincidentally, the thorn in the side of Bruce, the *Montana Post*, had closed its operation in Virginia City the previous April and relocated to Helena.[13]

Bruce initially traveled to San Francisco, but he only briefly stayed there before relocating to Washington, D.C., where he began work as a claims agent and "amassed money at a respectable rate." Bruce was lured back to Montana, however, in the Spring of 1872. His nephew, Joseph Wright, had established the *Avant Courier* in Bozeman in September of 1871, and although Bruce was ostensibly employed as an editor with the paper, it appears his primary interest was to revive his political aspirations.[14]

Bruce once again earnestly lobbied the Democratic Party for its nomination as Territorial Secretary and, once again, was unsuccessful. Soon afterwards, Bruce would move from Bozeman to Helena, where he served on the editorial staff of the *Rocky Mountain Gazette*. Here again, it seems reasonable to assume that Bruce was primarily motivated more by the opportunity to be near the seat of political power than any serious desire to serve as a journalist. Nevertheless, it was his contributions to Montana journalism which resulted in Bruce actually winning an election to the Montana Historical Society. Among the men in the membership class elected in October of 1873 were other pioneer journalists: Peter Ronan, Robert Fisk, Daniel Tilton, Horatio Maguire, and James Mills. Following the destruction of the *Gazette* offices in the great Helena fire of January 1874, Bruce returned to Bozeman.[15]

Perhaps finally recognizing that his political ambitions were also charred ground, Bruce stepped back from an active role in politics upon his return to Bozeman and focused his energies on establishing commercial interests and his legal practice. He was a founding director of the First National Bank of Bozeman, established a grist mill and grocery, and served as the District Attorney for Gallatin County.

One of Bruce's most interesting enterprises was as chairman of the Yellowstone Wagon Road and Prospecting Expedition, whose other organizers included such prominent Bozeman residents as Nelson Story, Peter McAdow, Daniel Rouse, Lester S. Willson, and Peter Koch. The expedition force included 140 well-equipped men (none of the organizing directors), which remained in the field for three months in early 1874. It was the hopeful intention this expedition would "establish a free wagon road" to the Tongue River, and make discoveries of "rich mineral deposits [which] are believed to exist in the region...." Not only did the expedition fail to establish any commercial success, it was regularly harassed by Indian attacks.[16]

Regrettably, the entrepreneurial efforts of Bruce were generally not much more successful than his political career had been. The First National Bank failed in August of 1878, the Yellowstone Expedition was perhaps generously summarized as: "[it] did not fulfill the expectations of the promoters," and the grist mill and grocery operations could also be said to have not fulfilled expectations. The despondency of his professional life had been further exacerbated with the very heavy blow delivered by the sudden, unexpected death of nephew Joseph Wright. Thomas Baker recalled afterwards that: "The waning of [Bruce's] powers was sadly noticed by his friends…and he presented but the shadow of his old-time virility." In June of 1879, Bruce was elected as a Trustee of Bozeman's Presbyterian Church in what appears to have been an honorific exercise. It is possible that Bruce had actually left Bozeman prior to his election as Trustee, for shortly afterwards an open letter appeared in the *Avant Courier* (which indicated it had been received from Kentucky) in which Bruce acknowledged he was in poor health—physically and mentally—and that he deeply regretted leaving Montana. Bruce had returned to Kentucky with Clara and Nellie Wright, two of Wright's five orphaned children, and a very troubled mind.[17]

In early August of 1880, the *Madisonian* would report that "The Hon. John P. Bruce of Stanford, Kentucky, was tried for lunacy on July 17, 1880, and committed to the asylum in Lexington." The paper opined that it was "severe financial losses [in Montana] which probably caused his illness." The *Avant Courier* would expand upon this report in its columns, noting that "Major John P. Bruce has become hopelessly insane…this sorrowful event, though not altogether a surprise to the people of Bozeman and vicinity, is universally regretted, not only on the Major's account, but also on account of Mrs. Bruce, who is recognized a most estimable lady by all who know her." Just three weeks later, the *Madisonian* reported that "Mrs. John P. Bruce, accompanied by Nellie Wright, had arrived by coach [in Virginia City] and is staying at the Rodgers House." Presumably the purpose of Mrs. Bruce's return was to settle affairs related to the family's financial and property interests. John Bruce would remain confined at the Eastern Kentucky Asylum until his death in 1882.[18]

In a biographical sketch written by Thomas Baker, he eulogized John Bruce as "doubtless the most eccentric character that ever toiled in the newspaper field of the territory. He was, naturally, a kindly, good-hearted gentleman, but he had been reared in an atmosphere of aristocracy foreign to the cosmopolitan crowds which made up the

Eastern Kentucky Asylum for the Insane (Lexington)

population of mining camps in the Rockies." When one considers the collection of colorful and eccentric characters that played upon the field of early Montana journalism, to rank John Bruce as "the most eccentric" may be considered as a bit over-reaching. But if it was Baker's intention to single out Bruce as a man determined to walk his own path, then it would seem he certainly hit the mark. [19]

Notes:

1. "Tavern Keeper," Knox County, Kentucky. Wright would subsequently serve as editor of paper at Stanford, KY before moving west.

2. Bruce was committed in May and September of 1857.

3. The 1862 election for the 7th Congressional District of Missouri was investigated and the majority report of the Committee recommended the neither Bruce nor his opponent (Republican Benjamin Loan) be seated, but the House voted to seat Loan. Samuel moved to

Missouri and studied law under Silas Woodson (later Governor of Missouri), and went into law partnership with James Foster. Pfouts left Missouri in the Summer of 1861, and apparently did not meet JPB until his arrival in Montana; per <u>Four Firsts.</u> Two other prominent figures in St. Joseph at this time, both of whom would also become prominent in Montana, were Alexander Davis and Thomas Thoroughman, both of whom would serve with the Missouri State Guard. An interesting bit of historical trivia, the *Gazette* was the only newspaper to have been carried on the inaugural Pony Express ride between St. Joseph and Sacramento, CA on April 3, 1860.

4. "Jack-Mormon," per Tom Baker (Bancroft). Baker wrote that Bruce purchased equipment for the *Valley Tan*, whose recently departed editor, Horatio Maguire, would later find his way to Montana. Per Word mss (SC #284) he arrived in Alder Gulch September 27, 1863.

5. Various sources indicate the offices of the *Democrat* were located "opposite the Catholic Church."

6. First installment of Vigilantes appeared in the August 26m 1865 issue of the *Montana Post*. "Not robust..." G. Stuart, Forty Years.

7. Quotes per T. Baker, who also wrote that he witnessed Bruce losing $200 in one night's gambling (a present-day equivalent of $13,000 +/-).

8. "our friend...," *Montana Post*, April 7, 1866. "we would desire...," *Montana Democrat*, August 30, 1866. Although Bruce is frequently referred to with the title/rank of "Major," this author has been unable to learn when/how this title was earned. There is no evidence Bruce ever served with a military unit, so one must assume the title was an honorary appointment.

9. Lectures of Gov. Thomas Francis Meagher in Montana.

10. "an old...," Pfouts. Upon the request of Gov. Green Clay Smith, Meagher's resignation was not accepted. Joseph Cavanagh would win nomination and election in March 1867.

11. "the opinion...," *Montana Democrat*, March 28, 1868.

12. Blake served as editor during the final period of Dimsdale's illness.

13. Bruce's personal cash position or profit from the operations

of the *Democrat* is uncertain; Blake would write that the paper was "losing money." The 1869 Madison County tax assessment of Bruce's property cited: Lot 13, Block 190: $1,500; 1 horse at $75; 1 cow at $50; household furnishing at $550; watches & jewelry at $250; and all other property at $4,000. All together, a fairly significant financial portfolio. Charity Bruce is listed as owner of Lot 34 in Block 196.

14. "amassed...," per Baker. Baker also writes that Bruce founded a short-lived paper in San Francisco prior to his departure for DC, but this author cannot verify.

15. Leeson.

16. Quotes from advertisement (photo in Bozeman and the Gallatin Valley. Leeson also includes an account of the expedition.

17. "did not fufill...," Leeson. "the waning...," Baker. Death of J. Wright per Leeson (December 29, 1876).

18. *Madisonian*, August 7 & 21, 1880. *Avant Courier*, August 12, 1880.

19. "doubtless...," Baker, "Major John P. Bruce," *Rocky Mountain Magazine*, March 1901.

Sources:

Avant Courier (Bozeman, Montana).

Assessor's Ledger, 1869, Virginia City, Montana.

Baker, Thomas. "Major John P. Bruce," *Rocky Mountain Magazine*, March 1901.

Blake, Henry. "The First Newspaper of Montana," Contributions to the Montana Historical Society, Vol. V (1905)

"Henry N. Blake: Proper Bostonian, Purposeful Pioneer." Edited by Vivian Paladin, *Montana Magazine of Western History*, Vol. 14, no. 4.

John P. Bruce mss. Montana Historical Society, SC #917.

Collins, Lewis. Collins' *Historical Sketches of Kentucky, Vol. 2*.

Contested Elections in Congress 1834-1865, D.W. Bartlett, Clerk. Govt. Printing Office 1865.

Leeson, Michael A. History of Montana 1739-1885. Chicago: Warner, Beers & Co., 1885.

Madisonian (Virginia City, Montana).

"Major John P. Bruce." Vertical file, Montana Historical Society.

"Reminisences of an Editor," James Mills. Contributions, Vol. 5.

Montana Democrat (Virginia City, Montana).

The Montana Post (Virginia City, Montana).

Pfouts, Paris S. Four Firsts for a Modest Hero.

Senate Journal of the Commonwealth of Kentucky, Sessions of 1848 & 1850.

Stuart, Granville. Forty Years on the Frontier, Vol. 2.

Samuel Word mss (SC 284) MHS

Tap, Bruce. "Union Men to the Polls and Rebels to Their Holes," Civil War History, Vol. 46, number 1 (March 2000)

Photo Credits

Portrait; Pace Archives

Thomas J. Dimsdale; Pace Archives

Eastern Kentucky Asylum; Lexington (KY) History Museum.

Martha Canary
A life of pure calamity

"My maiden name was Marthy Cannary...born in Princeton, Missourri, May 1, 1852." Thus begins the autobiography of Martha Canary and thus began the life of a woman who would become one of the most familiar characters throughout the United States—at a time when it was uncommon for a woman to be recognized beyond the church which she attended and the neighborhood in which she lived. The fact that Martha misstated her birth year (1856) may also be a clue as to the torturous journey she made to earn such notoriety in her life.[1]

Located in north-central Missouri, adjacent to the Iowa border, Mercer County was established in 1845 and would be embroiled in controversy regarding its exact border with Iowa well into the 1890's. The community of Princeton (located in the approximate center of the county) was platted in 1846, and designated as the County Seat in 1847; an honor it still carries. Most of the early settlers of the Princeton area were natives of "Virginia, North Carolina, Tennessee, and Kentucky." Not surprisingly, many of those early settlers held strong Southern loyalties although very few were actually slaveholders. The 1860 Federal Census shows a population of 249 in Princeton, and 9,225 people in Mercer County (including 2 "Free Blacks" and 24 slaves). It was, to be sure, an area of tough living, few luxuries and where the chief commodities of exchange were "pelts, beeswax and wolf scalps."[2]

Martha Canary was the first child born to Robert and Charlotte (Burge); who were both natives of Ohio. The couple met and married in Polk County, Iowa, on June 14, 1855, before moving to Missouri. At the time of their marriage Charlotte (the 5th of 6 siblings) was 15 years old and Robert aged 30. By all accounts, despite their age difference, Charlotte appears to have been the more dominant partner by the force of her lively personality. The couple would make their home on 180 acres of farm land outside of Princeton which Robert's father, James, had sold to them for $500.[3]

Although Robert would declare his occupation as "Farmer" at the time of the 1860 Census, virtually all of his acquaintances would declare that he made a very poor attempt at earning that title and had an aversion to work in general. Robert's "laid-back" approach to life was in sharp contrast, however, to the force of nature that was his wife. Charlotte "bruised the social expectations of Princeton" with her free-spirited behavior which included the frequent and liberal use of profanity, cigar smoking, and frequent (often excessive) drinking. To top things off, Charlotte was also openly "Secesh" [pro- Confederacy] in her political stance and took every opportunity to loudly express those feelings—which most area residents feared was an invitation to Federal troops to pay a visit to the county. Martha appears to have (at times) attended a local school and also made an impression upon the locals at a relatively tender age; though not as a promising scholar. Martha seemed to be following in the footsteps of her mother and was remembered as a very high-spirited girl and, in the vernacular of the time, a "tomboy."[4]

With the death of Robert's father in 1862, and the subsequent financial issues attendant to his death, Robert and Charlotte decided it was time to find greener pastures for their family. The couple moved to Iowa, where it is believed they lived with relatives for approximately a year before deciding that those greener pastures actually laid near the newly established gold mining camps of the Alder Gulch. By the late Spring of 1864, the Canary family—with twelve-year-old Martha— were on their way west.[5]

Details of the Canary family's trip west are few and far between. It does appear that they immigrated to Montana via the Bozeman Trail (presumably as part of a wagon train) and that the experience was a grand adventure for young Martha. It could be said that it was also something of an internship to prepare Martha for her life in the Rocky Mountains. As she wrote in her autobiography: "By the time we reached Virginia City I was considered a remarkable good shot and a fearless rider for a girl of my age." One can easily imagine the experience was less a grand adventure and more of an ordeal for Charlotte, who had three younger children to care for during a trip of approximately four months.[6]

Although the date of their arrival in the Alder Gulch isn't certain (probably in mid-summer), it is known that Robert and Charlotte made their home—of an uncertain nature—in or near Nevada City; approximately one mile from Virginia City. Rather than attempt to make a living panning gold, which would have been an anathema to Robert, the couple apparently decided it would be easier to "pan the miners." Based upon an article which appeared in the local newspaper at the end of December, however, it appears that they also struggled with this ambition:

"A most flagrant and wanton instance of unnatural conduct on the part of parents to their children, came under our notice today. Three little girls, who state their name to be Canary, appeared at the door of Mr. Fergus, on Idaho street, soliciting charity. The ages of the two elder ones were about ten and twelve, respectively. The eldest girl carried in her arms her infant sister, a baby of about 12 months of age. Canary, the father, it seems, is a gambler in Nevada [City]. The mother is a woman of the lowest grade, and was last seen in town at Dr. Byam's office a day or two since. A calico slip without any additional clothing was all that defended the poor children from the inclemency of the weather. Mrs. Fergus, Mrs. Castner, and Mrs. Moon kindly provided them with food and some cloth-

ing. 'Blessed are the merciful.'

As for the inhuman brutes who have deserted their poor, unfortunate children, the Divine anger will overtake them sooner or later; but meanwhile, the laws of man, which they have so audaciously violated, should be applied to their case, and stern justice meted out to the offenders. We understand that the little ones returned to Nevada, where they have existed for some time."[7]

The reference to Charlotte as "a woman of the lowest grade" leaves open to interpretation whether the editor is expressing an opinion of her maternal abilities, reiterates her previously cited unladylike behavior, or alludes to the possibility that she was now pursuing a career of negotiable virtue. In any event, there is no indication that the "laws of man" were applied to Robert or Charlotte, but it could be said that they would soon feel some "divine anger."

Several of the miners and camp followers in the Alder Gulch camps, including Robert and Charlotte Canary and family, packed up and quickly headed north when news of a new gold strike at Ophir Gulch became known in early 1865. By late 1865, Robert was involved in operating a saloon known as the "Bird Cage," located in the camp of Blackfoot City. Again, details of this time seem virtually nonexistent despite the fact it became so significant in the trajectory of the Canary family; it was after only a few months in Blackfoot, that Charlotte died.

At some point in the summer of 1866, following Charlotte's death, Robert decided to leave Montana and take his children to Salt Lake City. It has been suggested that he did so with the intention of finding homes for his children (and perhaps help for himself?) among the Mormon families of that area. Before the end of 1867, however, Robert died in Salt Lake City, leaving Martha to care for her siblings. There is considerable uncertainty regarding Martha's siblings. It does appear certain that she had two sisters, Lena and Isabelle, and a brother, Elijah, who were known to have come to Montana from Missouri and arrived in Salt Lake. There may have also been another boy, Silas, who died in Missouri at the age of 3 (1862). Finally, in 1866, Charlotte may have also given birth to a daughter named Sarah; who died at or soon after her birth. And although this author has found no absolute evidence of such, one must assume that Charlotte died during or soon after the birth of Sarah.[8]

It appears that the younger Canary children were taken in by families in the Salt Lake area soon after Robert's death. Martha subsequently left Salt Lake and was at Fort Bridger (WY) by early May of 1868; perhaps accompanied by sister Lena and her brother Elijah. Now 16 years-old, Martha had grown to be approximately six-feet tall, with long brown hair. She had worked at a variety of menial jobs before being hired as a hunter in 1869 for the Union Pacific Railway; no doubt attributable to her skill as a marksman. Although Elijah would occasionally be with Martha in subsequent years, it seems as if he and Lena were also placed with families.

Between 1870 and the early summer of 1876, Martha traveled much of Wyoming and the western Dakota territories in the employ of the United States Cavalry. As she would later recount, her responsibility on the various cavalry expeditions was to serve as a "Scout." It seems more probable, however, that she actually served as a teamster for the supply trains which accompanied the cavalry. In any event, she certainly did acquire a good knowledge of the territory, adopted the custom of frequently wearing "man's clothing" (a practice which was illegal in many communities), had developed a fondness for rot-gut whiskey, and had become "an unrepentant swearer of world-class caliber" (a trait common among teamsters). It was also noted that she had "no high regard for truth...."[9]

Jesse Brown, who also worked as a freight teamster, recalled his first meeting with Martha in the Spring of 1876, as she arrived at Fort Custer driving a wagon team of "government mules." Brown's first impression was that she was "about the toughest looking human that I had ever seen" and that "the first place that attracted her attention was a saloon, where she was soon made blind as a bat from looking through the bottom of a glass." Undoubtedly, Brown had already heard of her and tales of her exploits before she came rolling into Fort Custer that day, but it's unlikely he would have known her as Martha Canary. Brown, as most others in the territory, knew her as "Calamity Jane."[10]

Exactly how and when Martha acquired the sobriquet "Calamity

Jane" is not at all certain. Versions of how she was christened with this frontier identity range from an act of bravery during a skirmish with Indians (her version), to a version which implies promiscuity; another claim which has been widely discounted. Nevertheless, it was to be an identity which she accepted, especially once it would prove to be highly marketable. At the end, however, it was not how she wished to be remembered. Perhaps one of the most significant, albeit relatively brief, chapters in the life of Martha Canary (and the legend of "Calamity Jane") has a very unpromising beginning. In mid-June of 1876, Martha went on another "bender" of epic proportions at Fort Laramie. Outraged by her behavior—and the accompanying property destruction—the fort's commanding officer directed a cleansing of the undesirable elements of the community, with Martha at the top of the list. Coincidentally, just at the time the purge of Ft. Laramie began, a train of 30 wagons under the direction of "Colorado Charlie" Utter arrived.

**James Butler
"Wild Bill" Hickok**

Charlie Utter's train included freight wagons and hopeful new settlers bound for the gold camps of the Black Hills; specifically, the metropolis of Deadwood. Among those traveling with the train was a man whose reputation was well-known throughout the West, James Butler "Wild Bill" Hickok. Hickok, who had recently married, was ostensibly going to Deadwood to make his fortune as a gold miner. Whether it was Laramie's commanding officer or a junior officer isn't certain, but it was an officer of Ft. Laramie who convinced (commanded?) that

Charlie take on some additional passengers; including: "Madame Mustache," "Dirty Em," and 10-12 of their working girls—and Martha Canary; who had spent the previous 24 hours in the fort's jail, drying out from a spectacle of drunken debauchery.

Once sober, Martha reportedly proved to be very helpful addition to Utter in handling camp chores and assisting some of the "pilgrims" in the train. One of the fellow travelers seemed especially impressed with her marksmanship, and related that one day several men—using rifles—were unsuccessfully shooting at a coyote "more than 100 yards distant." Martha stepped forward and—with a pistol—made the shot. She also was an entertaining story-teller around the evening campfires as she told, in undoubtedly wildly exaggerated and colorful terms, tales of her adventures. Hickok was among those who enjoyed Martha's stories and she, in turn, was unashamedly star-struck by his presence. Despite some stories to the contrary, virtually all reliable sources concur that their relationship never went beyond this point of mutual acquaintance.[11]

Utter's train arrived in Deadwood on or about July 12, 1876. While the sights and sounds of that camp must have been startling to any pilgrim, it was familiar ground to Martha. After probably making an in-depth inspection of some of the several saloons, Martha was employed as a Pony Express rider between Deadwood and the camp of Custer; a stretch of approximately 50—very dangerous—miles to ride, which she did very reliably. And although she would later claim otherwise, Martha does not appear to have been in Deadwood on August 2, 1876, the day that James Butler Hickok was murdered.

As most readers would likely be familiar, Hickok was shot in the back of his head by Jack McCall while playing cards at the Saloon No. 10, and holding a hand of aces and eights; ever after known as the "Dead Man's Hand." Martha would go so far as to claim that she single-handedly captured McCall, but this story is an unmistakable fabrication. While very possible she would have told this story as simply inebriated bragging and self-aggrandizement, one may also consider that it was told as a means of personal healing. By all accounts, when Martha was in Deadwood she would "follow Hickok like a puppy." Perhaps, in her mind, she believed that had she been with Hickok on that fateful day that she could have prevented his murder.[12]

Martha would spend most of the five years following Hickok's death in Deadwood and other camps in the Black Hills. One of the well documented incidents which revealed a side of her character not often exposed was during an outbreak of smallpox in Deadwood when she served tirelessly as a volunteer nurse to those infected. It has been reported that she also recited a prayer over the graves of those who succumbed; the only prayer she said she knew: "Now I lay me down to sleep...." Considering her family background, it seems especially worth considering the comment which appeared in the *Black Hills Daily Times*: "it didn't matter to [Martha] whether a person was rich or poor, white or black. Or what their circumstances were, Calamity Jane was just the same to all."[13]

Most of her employment in Deadwood does appear to have been working at saloons as a hostess or card dealer. Thanks to her growing notoriety, Martha was becoming something of an attraction which saloon owners were anxious to capitalize upon—even if it meant supporting her insatiable drinking habit "on the house." The Gem Theatre was a frequent venue of Martha's, which suggests she would have been very familiar with the scurrilous manager of the Gem, Al Swearingen; also, something of a Deadwood legend. Some writers have speculated that Martha was also actively engaged as a prostitute during this time, or even earlier. Most, however, seem to question any such claims and point out that those stories are unfounded.

One of the most influential men Martha met in Deadwood (in late 1876 or early 1877) was another immigrant from Montana by the name of Horatio Nelson Maguire. Maguire was a well-traveled newspaper editor who was now publishing the *Black Hills Pioneer*. Maguire was an excellent writer, loved the spirit and natural beauty of the West, and was a man willing to not let the truth get in the way of a good story from time to time. In 1877, Maguire published the book The Black Hills and American Wonderland which extolled the beauty and opportunities awaiting new immigrants which would be beyond the fondest dream of a present-day Chamber of Commerce. Obviously charmed by Martha's colorful stories and personality, Maguire includes in the book an imaginative portrait of "Calamity Jane" which includes mention that she came from "a family of respectability" and concludes by observing that "She is still in early womanhood, and her rough and dissipated career has not altogether swept away the lines where beauty lingers." Maguire followed that piece up with another publication, The Coming Empire, in 1878, in which he further embellished upon his earlier profile with more tales of Calamity Jane's daring adventures and her heart of gold.

Other writers, none of whom had met Martha, were eager to make some money on this colorful character Maguire had introduced to the world and quickly began to churn out their own—totally fabricated—stories of her exploits. Most notably among these writers was Edward L. Wheeler, who created the dime novel series "Deadwood Dick" which regularly featured the beautiful and daring Calamity Jane. One of the early writers who took an entirely different approach was Dr. A. R. Hendricks. Upon learning of Hendricks' account, Martha hunted down Maguire and angrily expressed her outrage that she had been labeled by Hendricks as "a horse thief, highway-woman [robber], card sharp, and a minister's daughter." Martha adamantly declared to Maguire that "these [accusations] are false, the last especially." The combined effect of Maguire, Wheeler, and all those who wrote of "Calamity Jane" was to give Martha virtually a nation-wide recognition…and that was something which she probably wasn't able to truly understand, appreciate, or with which she was able to cope.[14]

In the Summer of 1881, Martha left Deadwood to begin an odyssey lasting 23 years. The Sidney Telegraph noted her departure: "Her husband [presumably George Cosgrove] is not a violent mourner…If she has any conscience, she took it with her, and if she had any virtue her husband didn't know it." During those years Martha would travel widely, marry or live with at least four men, and give birth to two children. While there are few details of this time (and those often in conflict with her own version of events), the following account attempts to summarize the myriad of events, men, and calamities which would play a part in the drama of Martha's life.[15]

Martha spent some of her early post-Deadwood years in Eastern Montana. In 1882, the *Yellowstone Journal* of Miles City would note that "Calamity Jane has been heard from again. This time she bobbed up serenely at Ratlines, got drunk and knocked a frail sister out of time for which she was arrested and fined ten dollars and costs." In November of 1882, the *Journal* would report that "Calamity Jane has settled down to domestic life on a ranch in Yellowstone Valley, below Miles City. She lives with her husband and a fine baby boy she calls 'little Calamity.'" Sadly, the baby died soon after this article appeared, and her husband (presumed to be Frank King) received no further mention. A dated photograph of Martha suggests she remained in the area at least into 1885.[16]

"Calamity Jane" (c1885)

Following the death of her child, Martha moved to the Coeur d'Alene mining district in northern Idaho, where she spent some time, as in Deadwood, working at various saloons and unsuccessfully attempting to organize an entertainment troupe. We next find Martha wandering around Wyoming in the company of the much younger and volatile William Steers. Reports of their frequently turbulent co-existence were noted in newspapers along the route of their travels, with one journalist offering the opinion that Steers was "one of the most worthless curs unhung." In October of 1887, Martha gave birth to a girl whom she named Jessie Elizabeth, Six months later (May 30, 1888) Martha and Steers were married at Pocatello, Idaho, in what one may assume was a "shot-gun wedding"—with Martha holding the gun. Soon after their marriage, however, Steers disappears from the story line and Martha is in company with Clinton Burk; ironically, the son of a Methodist minister.[17]

Martha's time with Burk was a nomadic experience. The couple (presumably with Jessie Elizabeth, whom Martha would introduce as her child by Burk) traveled throughout Montana, Wyoming and South Dakota from approximately 1890 until 1895. Burk would find part-time employment at a farm or ranch for a few weeks or months, then the couple would pack up and move on. Details of this time are very slight, which perhaps is a signal that it was a time of relative calm and happiness in Martha's life. And, based upon later events, may be evidence of her genuine affection for Mr. Burk.[18]

In the Summer of 1895, Martha returned to Deadwood with Jessie and Clinton Burk. Martha was anxious that Jessie would have the opportunity for a good education, and several of her friends agreed to sponsor a benefit for the purpose of sending Jessie to the St. Martin's Convent School at Sturgis. The benefit was held at the Green Front Saloon and was an unqualified success until, much to the shock of the event organizers, Martha announced that she was buying drinks for the gathering in appreciation. It does appear as if friends were able to cut off her largesse in time for the proceeds to not be totally expended and that Jessie did—although perhaps briefly—attend the convent school.[19]

It was also while at Deadwood that Martha was recruited to perform with the Kohl & Middleton "wild-west" show in Minneapolis during the winter of 1895-96. Accompanied by Burk, Martha reportedly remained reasonably sober and gave well-reviewed presentations of her "heroic adventures." Before the scheduled exhibition was completed, however, Martha received word that the Jessie had fallen ill. Martha immediately returned to be with her daughter—who recovered—but there is some question as to whether Clinton Burk ever returned to the Black Hills. In any event, Martha picked up Jessie at Sturgis and Mr. Burk is no longer part of Martha's life story beyond this point. By early 1898, Martha was back in Eastern Montana and in company with a new paramour, Bob Dorsett.

During 1898 and through the Summer of 1899, Martha and Dorsett (again with Jessie in tow) traveled around Montana. Noted among their stops are Billings, Lewistown, and Utica. Martha's life trail had turned steeply downhill during this time, as she was falling back into a bottle with alarming frequency. It may have been as a result of one of these benders that Dorsett abandoned Martha, and took Jessie to his mother's home in Livingston. Martha managed to find and reclaim custody of Jessie, but that incident marked the end of her relationship with Bob Dorsett. It also appears to have provided Martha with a new home base.

Martha would spend most of the next two years in the Livingston area, making her way by working as cook and laundress for various establishments and by selling her little autobiographical pamphlets and posing for photographs with Yellowstone tourists. Sadly, much of what she did earn was quickly spent on her bar bills and, at one point in 1901, she was residing at the Gallatin County Poor Farm. Yet, while Martha was becoming widely known as a common drunk in Montana, the legend of "Calamity Jane" as a daring heroine remained a popular—and positive—image among the general public.[20]

The news story of Martha living in the county poor house and being "broken in spirit" attracted national attention and sympathy. In what appears to have been a well-intended effort to rehabilitate Martha, journalist Josephine Brake traveled to Montana in early July of 1901, and found Martha—drunk—south of Livingston in a mining camp known as Horr. Brake successfully convinced Martha to return east to appear as a Midway attraction at the Pan-American Exposition in Buffalo, New York. Brake was able to get Martha cleaned up and escorted her on the trip to Buffalo. The journey may have stretched the limits of what Ms. Brake could endure, however, inasmuch as Martha insisted upon being well "medicated" throughout much of the trip.[21]

Soon after Martha's arrival in Buffalo she was offered a contract to appear as a performer with Colonel Fred Cummins and his Indian Congress, a Wild West show appearing at the Exposition, and which featured the well-known Sioux leader, Red Cloud. Ms. Brake served as Martha's agent in negotiating her contract, which included a stipulation that she would receive the majority of Martha's pay to cover room and boarding expenses. Martha chafed at this arrangement and soon re-negotiated her contract with Mr. Cummins with the proviso that all payments be made directly to her…which greatly enhanced her available "discretionary funds." Predictably, Martha was soon spending generously at local bars and, just as predictably, she soon found trouble.[22]

On the night of August 9, Martha was found by a Buffalo policeman staggering down Amherst Street, "reeling from side to side". Whether or not she actually assaulted the officer is questionable, but she was arrested on charges of Drunk and Disorderly Behavior and spent the remainder of the night in jail. At her court hearing the next day, Martha was released on a suspended sentence, which even she must have realized was not likely to be suspended for long. Martha sought out Bill Cody, who had recently arrived with his Wild West show, and begged him for enough money to get back to Montana. Bill very generously gave her some cash and bought a train ticket. When later asked about his role in aiding Martha's departure, Cody merely stated: "I expect she was no more tired of Buffalo than the Buffalo police were of her." Of course nothing could be quite as simple as just putting Martha—without a chaperone—on a train back to Montana.[23]

William F. "Buffalo Bill" Cody

Martha would make several unscheduled stops, of various durations, during her return trip, the longest of which was in Pierre, South Dakota, where she spent the winter months of 1901-02. The common denominator among those towns blessed with her presence, whether for a few days or a few weeks, is that the residents were uniformly grateful when Martha left—and in some cases assisted in her departure. When she finally arrived back in Livingston (in April 1902) she quickly set about renewing acquaintances at all her favorite Livingston haunts—and was arrested for Drunk and Disorderly Behavior on her first night. It appears that soon after her homecoming night's festivities that Martha reached perhaps the nadir of her time in Livingston, when she was literally thrown from the Bucket of Blood saloon by "Madam Bulldog" for her objectionable behavior. It staggers the imagination to consider what may have crossed the line of objectionable behavior at an establishment known as the Bucket of Blood.[24]

Martha spent the summer of 1902 once again hawking her autobiography to Yellowstone tourists and living in a bottle. As winter began to press in and she began to look for some comfortable spot to "den-up," she decided—perhaps with encouragement—to abandon the Livingston area, which she derided as becoming too civilized. She opined that she was "just about soured on the human race." She made her way toward the rising sun, and settled in Billings by November. She would find, however, that Billings was also becoming civilized and that she became a deserving target of the local law enforcement and a resident of their jail. By mid-December, again with local encouragement, Martha was on the road and sought refuge in the place where she had always found comfort—the Black Hills.

Martha arrived at Madame Dora DuFran's House of Joy in Belle Fourche in early 1903. Dora had been a long-time friend of Martha's and offered her a job as cook and laundress, and a bed at her establishment. Interestingly, Martha arrived at Dora's with Jessie Elizabeth; now 15 years old. This appears to be the first known whereabouts of Jessie since the Summer of 1899, when Martha had re-established custody of her daughter in Livingston. One assumes that Jessie had been living with friends of Martha in central or Eastern Montana and that Martha, perhaps aware her time may be fleeting, once again re-claimed what would be another short-lived custody of her daughter.[25]

Jane at Bill Hickok's grave site

When the winter snow had receded from the roads, Martha said good-by to Dora—and apparently Jessie—and began what must have been a nostalgic tour of the old Black Hills camps which she had once known so well during their glory days. In mid-July, Martha was in Deadwood where, in addition to some saloons, she paid a well-publicized visit to the gravesite of Wild Bill Hickok. A few days later, Martha hitched a ride on an ore train...destination unknown. Martha was once asked by an acquaintance who had encountered her in the '70's as she was staggering down a Deadwood street with a bloody nose: "Where are you going, Jane?" To which Martha had replied, "God knows, I don't." Perhaps that was still the circumstance as she boarded the ore train.

By the time the ore train had reached the camp of Terry (just a few miles from Deadwood), Martha was in significant physical distress and the conductor had the train stopped while he carried her to the Calloway Hotel. After several very painful days, Martha died during the afternoon of August 1, 1903; the cause of death was cited as "inflammation of the bowels and pneumonia."[26]

Bill Hickock's and Martha Canary's gravesite

Martha's remains were returned to Deadwood where, on August 4, her funeral services were held in the First Methodist Church before an overflowing audience of genuine mourners and the simply curious. Perhaps due to the work of the undertakers, several of those in attendance noted that "she looked better in death than she had in the final years of her life." Among her final requests, Martha had asked to be buried near Wild Bill and that her tombstone should identify her as "Mrs. Martha Burk." In a wonderful coincidence, the man who owned the gravesite immediately adjacent to Hickok's learned of Martha's request and, because she had nursed his daughter back to health during Deadwood's Smallpox epidemic in 1878, he donated the site for Martha's grave. Martha would have been thrilled.[27]

"It is easy for a woman to be good who has been brought up with every protection from the evils of the world and good associates. Calamity was a product of the wild and wooly west. She was not immoral; but unmoral. She took more on her shoulders than most women could. She performed many hundreds of deeds of kindness and received very little pay for her work.

With her upbringing, how could she be anything but unmoral?

Dora DuFran, <u>Low Down on Calamity Jane.</u>

"Only the old days could have produced her, Calamity had nearly all the rough virtues of the old West as well as many of the vices...."

William F. Cody (Deadwood Magazine)

Notes:

1. Canary, <u>Life and Adventures of Calamity Jane.</u>
2. Williams, <u>History of Northwest Missouri.</u> Federal Census of 1860.
3. Etulain.
4. Ibid. The genesis of Charlotte's sympathy for the Confederacy posture is puzzling. She, and her parents were natives of Ohio.
5. Appears that Robert never distributed proceeds of his father's estate to his sibling, and likely did not pay debts of the estate.
6. Canary, ibid.
7. *Montana Post*, December 31, 1864.
8. Some sources suggest Lena and Elijah actually accompanied Martha to Ft. Bridger. Martha does appear on the 1869 census report of Piedmont, Wyoming.
9. "an unrepentant...," Etulain. "no high regard...," Deadwood Magazine, "Girls of the Gulch."
10. Etulain.
11. Ibid.
12. Hickok was originally buried in Deadwood's "Boot Hill," but would be reinterred at the Mount Moriah Cemetery. McCall's trial at

Deadwood was held in Langrishe's Theatre, and he was found "Not Guilty" (his falsely claimed defense that Bill had killed his brother obviously swayed some of the jury). Newspaper editor Horatio Maguire would react to the verdict by writing: "Should it ever be our misfortune to kill a man, we would simply ask that our trial may take place in some of the mining camps of these hills." McCall would be later arrested and tried again in Yankton, where he was found guilty of Hickok's murder and hanged.

13. "Prayer" and quote from *Black Hills Daily Times* per Russell.

14. "horse thief…," McLaird.

15. "Her husband is not…," *Sidney Telegraph,* Sidney, NE, August 4, 1877. No evidence she was actually married to Cosgrove.

16. "Calamity Jane has been…," Russell. "…settled down to domestic life," Yellowstone Journal, November 25, 1882. Husband also appears as Bob King in some sources.

17. No further mention of King following death of baby. Speers, 29 years junior to Martha. "one of the most…," Etulain, *Carbon County Journal* (Wyoming), October 30, 1886. Martha would declare in his autobiography she met Burk while traveling in Texas, but most biographers believe that while Burk may have been from Texas, they doubt her claim as living there as another of her "tall tales." Name also appears as "Burke" in some sources.

18. Etulain.

19. Story of benefit per Sollid and Deadwood Magazine. Sollid writes that Jessie did attend St. Martin's Convent at Sturgis, but only briefly.

20. Russell has written that, while visiting the Bozeman area, Martha had dinner at the home of the prominent Lehrkind family and left her boot spurs which she had removed upon entering the house.

21. "broken in…," *Buffalo News,* July 12, 1901. While Ms. Brake seemed to have a genuine interest in helping Martha, it does appear as if she had been employed by Pan-Am organizers to recruit Martha as a Midway attraction; panam1901.org. Horr, which was later known as Electric, was a coal mining location primarily providing coal to the Anaconda Mining Company.

22. Ms. Brake would continue to advocate for Martha, later petitioning for a federal veteran's allowance for—what she believed—was Martha's service in the U.S. Army.

23. Panam1901.org. "reeling…," *Buffalo Evening News,* August 9, 1901.

24. Stop at Pierre, per McLaird, <u>Wild Bill & Calamity Jane</u>. Bucket of Blood story per Pat Hill, "Calamity Jane's Life and Times," Montana Pioneer.

25. Jessie apparently returned to Montana where she would marry twice. Spent later years in California, where she died in 1980 at the age of 92, per McLaird, <u>Deadwood Legends</u>.

26. Brochure, "Calamity Jane," City of Deadwood Historic Preservation.

27. "she looked better…," Russell. Martha would not have been thrilled her tombstone was inaccurately engraved as "Mrs. M. E. Burke." Hickok's brother, Lorenzo, was not thrilled at the location of her gravesite's proximity to his brother's, and sent a letter to the city of Deadwood questioning the situation. Solomon Star, clerk of courts, responded the gravesite was "outside of the lot (fenced) of your Brother's [and that Martha's gravesite] does in no wise conflict or disturb the resting place of J.B."

Sources:
Black Hills Daily Times

Black Hills Pioneer

Buffalo News (Buffalo, NY)

"Calamity Jane" brochure. City of Deadwood Historic Preservation.

Canary, Martha. <u>Life and Adventures of Calamity Jane</u>.

Etulain, Richard. "Calamity Jane A Life and Legends," *Montana Magazine of Western History, Vol. 64, no. 2* (Summer 2014).

Forney, Gary R. "Montana's Pioneer Editor," *Montana Pioneer,*

"Girls of the Gulch: Calamity Jane was part of the overhead." *Deadwood Magazine,* 2001.

Hill, Pat. "Calamity Jane's Life and Times," *Montana Pioneer*, March 2004.

McLaird, James. Calamity Jane: The Woman and the Legend.

_____. Wild Bill Hickok and Calamity Jane: Deadwood Legends.

Montana Post

Panam1901.org

Price, W.C. "Mercer County, Missouri," History of Northwest Missouri, Vol. 1.

Russell, John. "Calamity Jane," In Celebration of Our Past, Papers presented at the Fourteenth Annual History Conference of the Gallatin Historical Society.

Sollid, Roberta. Calamity Jane A Story in Historical Criticism.

United States Census of 1860.

Williams, Robert. A History of NorthWest Missouri, Vol. 1.

Yellowstone Journal (Miles City, MT)

Photo credits

Portrait; Wikipedia

William Hickock; ibid

Jane in kitchen (c1885); ibid

William Cody; Panam1901.org.

Jane at Hickock's grave: panam1901.org

Jane and Hickock's gravesites; author.

WILLIAM ANDREWS CLARK
"The most disgusting character
The republic has produced."

Just as many of the thousands of hopeful immigrants to the gold fields of what would become the Montana Territory, William A. Clark arrived in virtual anonymity. He would leave, however, as one of the most powerful men in Montana and one of the wealthiest men in the world. Along the way he would prove to be the combination of a brilliant opportunist, rascal, rebel, and a ruffian in kid gloves who ruthlessly fought his opponents with piles of cash.

William Andrews Clark was born on January 8, 1839, in Connellsville, Pennsylvania, the second of six children(four girls and two boys) born to John and Mary [Andrews] Clark. John's occupation was as a farmer, and both of William's parents were natives of County Tyrone,

Ireland (present-day Northern Ireland) who had immigrated to the United States. William showed enough promise in his studies at the local elementary school that his parents arranged for him to attend Laurel Hill Academy at age 14. In 1856, the family moved to a farm near Keosauqua, Iowa; adjacent to the Missouri border. The 17-year-old William found employment in the autumn after the family's arrival, as a school teacher in "central Missouri." He remained in this position until his enrollment at Iowa Wesleyan College to study law.[1]

Clark's law studies were interrupted with the outbreak of the Civil War. Although the details appear to be lost, one biographer has written: "[Clark] fought with the Rebels, but he spoke of it to only a few intimates." One may reasonably assume that his service may have been with a unit of the Missouri Militia, and that he may have been inspired by—perhaps even an acquaintance of—Sterling Price. Price, who made his home in Keytesville, Missouri, served as Missouri's Governor (1853-57) and served as General and commanding officer of all Confederate militia forces in the State.[2]

Clark's enthusiasm for military service quickly waned, and although the exact circumstances as to why he left the war will "perhaps never be publicly known." It may be, as with many other young men, the glow of possible riches outshone that of the near-constant terror of a quest to win glory on the battlefields. In any event, by the autumn of 1862, Clark was working as a miner near Central City, Colorado Territory. His time in Colorado was also short-lived, as news of the wondrous new goldfields of the Idaho Territory spread through the Colorado camps. Clark left Central City in early May of 1863, and joined the exodus of miners headed west.[3]

Clark traveled with a small party of other miners and three wagons that arrived in Bannack on July 8th via the present-day Monida Pass. He was very unassuming in regards to both his personal appearance and his lack of possessions upon his arrival at the new camp. One man who was acquainted with him at the time, described Clark as a "little red-headed man...[who] wore a red shirt and an old army coat with one of the tails burned off by too close a proximity to a campfire." Clark would later recall that among his modest possessions at that time was a "library of three books: Poems of Robert Burns, Hitchcok's Elements of Geology, and Parsons On Contracts; one of the text books I had used when studying law at Mount Pleasant...." It has also been observed that Clark brought with him "a keen mind, a hard, ruthless ambition...and inordinate vanity." Although neither the demeanor nor attire of William Andrews Clark would make much of a first impression, he would make a lasting one.[4]

One of Clark's assets which represented the greatest actual value at that particular time, however, was an extremely large set of elk antlers which he had found. He was able to negotiate a deal to sell the antlers for $10 (gold) to Cy Skinner; a notorious character who operated the Elkhorn Saloon in Bannack, and thought the antlers to be the perfect addition to his establishment. Clark used the money for a grubstake and, rather than joining the exodus to the Alder Gulch camps, he went to an area southwest of Bannack known as Horse Prairie, where he staked a claim in Jeff Davis Gulch. His decision to try this area proved to be a good one. Soon after his arrival, Clark was elected as Recorder for the mining district—which provided a modest, but steady income—and he was successful in making good on his own claim. At the end of the mining season, Clark was not only free of all debt, but had "several thousand dollars left in gold dust."[5]

Clark returned to Bannack as his winter base, and where he briefly worked as a woodcutter before traveling to Salt Lake City in November. It isn't recorded whether he made this trip accompanied by others but, to have made this journey in winter, and almost certainly carrying a significant amount of gold, would have represented a very bold—one might say foolish—decision. Such decisions nearly always resulted in either great reward or fatal punishment, and Clark was blessed with reward. He returned from Salt Lake with a wagon load of merchandise which he sold in Bannack "at high winter prices," thus substantially increasing his wealth.[6]

Clark returned to work the Jeff Davis Gulch through the Spring and Summer of 1864, selling his claim at the end of the season. Clark once again made the journey to Salt Lake to purchase a load of merchandise, but this time took his goods to Virginia City. Clark opened a mercantile store in the Alder Gulch camp of Summit, where it is reasonably assumed he made another excellent return on his investment. Clark also spent time in Bannack during the winter of 1864-65, where he sat in on several meetings of the first legislative session of the newly formed Montana Territory. These proceedings must have been a great opportunity for Clark to have met several of the prominent men in the Territory, as well as providing him some valuable lessons in practical politics.[7]

By the Spring of 1865, William Clark had also learned that selling merchandise to miners was generally much more lucrative—and much easier—than being a miner and he extended his mercantile operations with stores in the boom camps at Blackfoot City and Elk Creek. As example of his financial acumen, Clark reported making a 300% profit on one load of goods he brought from Boise to Elk Creek in 1866. Another significant financial coup occurred in 1867, when he was able to obtain the contract to provide mail service between Missoula and Walla Walla. And, in 1868, Clark opened a mercantile operation in Helena in partnership with Robert Donnell.[8]

Although no correspondence is known to have survived, Clark had apparently remained in touch since leaving Pennsylvania with a female friend from Connellsville, Katherine Stauffer. In the early Spring of 1869, perhaps finally feeling some measure of financially security, Clark returned to Pennsylvania and married his childhood sweetheart whom he brought to Helena. The couple would be in Helena for only a year, however, before moving to Deer Lodge, which Clark judged to have "better prospects" than Helena. Clark became a founding partner and President of a bank, and by late 1871, he began to acquire numerous properties and mining claims—particularly in Butte—via methods which present-day bank regulators would find appalling.[9]

Perhaps using his old copy of <u>Elements of Geology</u> as a resource, Clark began to take a special interest in the ore samples produced by some of the mining claims in Butte. Clark made arrangements to enroll in the Columbia School of Mines and traveled to New York in late 1872, taking with him several samples of Butte ore. The samples showed an abundant presence of copper, the presence of which miners generally regarded as a nuisance in their quest to find gold and silver. Clark studied at Columbia for approximately a year before returning to Montana and quietly—but aggressively—acquired yet more property and mining claims in Butte. His education appears to have included not only the knowledge of how to assay ore, but the unique qualities— and bright future—in the value of that meddlesome mineral, copper.

One of the unique arrangements Clark made upon his return to Deer Lodge was to enter into a "management agreement" with Bill Farlin on a mining claim which he owned in Butte. Clark's bank loaned $30,000 to Farlin for the operation of the Travonna Mine, with Clark serving as the manager of operations. After one year, the property did not show a profit in its operations and the bank foreclosed. Clark, as an individual, purchased the property from the bank and within one year was suddenly—amazingly—making "enormous profits." During the next few years, Clark would build Butte's first smelter, stamp mill, water system, electric light companies, and a railroad. He would expand his reach to include dozens of profitable mining claims in Nevada and Arizona, as well as a sugar plantation in California. His holdings also included a large tract of land he used as a service terminal for his rail line. It is now known as Las Vegas, located in what became Clark County, Nevada. Clark also had developed an interest in politics and, by 1876, was serving as Chairman of Montana's Democratic Territorial Central Committee.[10]

Clark's success in Butte, however, did not go unnoticed. In 1876, another Irishman by the name of Marcus Daly came to investigate first-hand the potential of Butte...he decided to stay. Daly was a native of County Cavan, Ireland, who had immigrated to the United States at the age of 15, and had accumulated a wealth of experience in mining which he learned from the ground up. He was adept at scouting assets and had very successfully managed large operations in Arizona, and Utah. After accepting Daly's advice to purchase the Alice Mine in Butte, which proved to be very lucrative, his employers deferred on Daly's recommendation to purchase another mining claim in Butte. Consequently, Daly staked nearly all he owned and formed his own consortium of investors to purchase what had been generally regarded

Marcus Daly
"He spoke with [a] brogue, chewed tobacco,
and loved to have a beer with his fellow miners."

as a mediocre silver claim...the Anaconda Mine. Daly assembled his crew of miners (predominately native Irish and Irish-Americans) and began operations at the Anaconda. At a depth of 400 feet, they discovered a vein approximately 50 feet wide of nearly pure copper. Mr. Clark suddenly had a formidable competitor.[11]

William Clark and Marcus Daly were nearly polar opposites in their personalities. Clark was intense, ruthlessly competitive, and aloof in both his approach to operating his business enterprises and his personal relationships. An associate described Clark as "about as magnetic as last year's bird nest." Daly was described by multiple sources as a popular figure who "was a man of the earth...[whose] unpretentious personality bore evidence of his Irish peasant roots. " Historian Michael Malone also noted that Daly "loved his friends with enduring loyalty, but he hated his enemies implacably and never forgot a grudge." Perhaps the greatest point of implacable difference between the two men, however, was that Clark was an "Orange" Irishman and Daly a very "Green" Irishman. This would have been cause enough for Daly to have regarded Clark as a bitter enemy. Nevertheless, in at least two

Clark with his daughters, Louise (L) and Hugette (R)

respects, the men shared common ground: making money and their political affiliation to the Democratic Party…and both interests would lock them into legendary battles.[12]

In 1888, Clark entered Montana's political arena as a candidate for the coveted position of Territorial Delegate. This position had been held by a Democrat for twenty-two of the twenty-four years Montana had been a Territory, including the previous 16 consecutive years. Most any Montanan would have reasonably considered Clark's election as a fait accompli. Whether based upon commercial interests or simply his Irish-Catholic upbringing, Daly took an interest in engineering Clark's defeat. Daly used his very considerable influence with the employees of the Anaconda Mining Company, the Montana Improvement Company, and the Northern Pacific Railroad to derail Clark. Clark would never forgive nor forget this act of treachery, and later wrote that it was the: "envious and diabolical desire [of Daly] to forever destroy my political influence in the Territory."[13]

On February 22, 1889, Montana was one of the territories offered the opportunity to petition for statehood. One of the requirements for consideration being that it must produce a constitution approved by a majority of eligible Montana voters. Clark was elected to serve as a delegate to the Constitutional Convention, and his fellow delegates elected him to serve as Chairman. Much to their credit, the Convention completed their work by mid-August, the proposed State Constitution was overwhelmingly approved by voters in October, and Montana was formally accepted as the 41st State on November 8, 1889.[14]

"We will send the old man to the Senate or the Poorhouse."

Clark's political aspirations were warmed by the glow of statehood, and he was able to win nomination as one of two Democrats to serve Montana in the United States Senate. Within the new state, however, the balance of political power had begun to even out and the Montana state senate became dead-locked in the attempt to elect their U.S. Senators. The compromise finally crafted was to send both the Democratic and Republican nominees to Washington and let the U.S. Senate sort it out. As historian Clark Spence opined: "To put it frankly, the Montana legislators allowed partisanship to overcome good sense and ended up disgracing themselves." Not surprisingly, the Republican controlled U.S. Senate sent the Montana Democrats home—just in time to take part in another political fight.[15]

In 1892, the war over which Montana city would serve as its capital once again came to the forefront, with William Clark and Marcus Daly squaring off against one another in this high-stakes game. The political war between towns for the mantle of capital was a struggle which had been fought since 1864, and this battle involved the aspiring cities of Anaconda, Boulder, Bozeman, Butte, Deer Lodge, Great Falls, and Helena. Following a run-off election, Anaconda (Daly's preference) and Helena (Clark's choice) emerged as the finalists with the winner to be determined in an election in 1894. In the meantime, Clark was again nominated by the Democrats for the U.S. Senate seat...and Daly once again would take opposition to those ambitions.

Daly masterfully orchestrated a behind the scenes machination in which the Republican front-runner and their long-time standard bearer Wilbur Fisk Sanders, was replaced by Lee Mantle. Another frustrating deadlock in the Montana Senate resulted in an adjournment without selecting either Clark or Mantle. Following adjournment, however, Governor John E. Rickards (a Republican) appointed Mantle to the seat. The U.S. Senate, once again, was not amused by Montana's political antics and refused to admit Mantle into its hallowed halls, leaving Montana with only one U.S. Senator (Thomas Power) for the next year, a very unhappy William A. Clark, and a very happy Marcus Daly.

Still to be decided was the capital issue, and by this time both Clark and Daly had acquired newspapers (Daly, the *Anaconda Standard*, and Clark, the *Butte Miner*) which relentlessly espoused the interest of their respective owner. In addition to the war of words in printer's ink, the battle was also liberally supported with the infusion of cash being passed to influence those men of negotiable ethics. By the time the votes were counted, Daly had reportedly spent no less than $2 million and Clark no less than $400,000 in support of their choice, and the city of Helena had won the honor by less than 2,000 votes. Regrettably, Daly and Clark had set the stage for Montana to join other states in harboring corruption in its elections...only on a much grander scale than most. The victory of Helena may have been one of the brightest moments in what had otherwise been a very difficult previous year for Clark. In addition to the loss of a seat in the U.S. Senate, his wife and mother to his 7 children, Katherine, had died in 1893.[16]

Clark once again stepped into the spotlight in 1899, more determined than ever to win a seat in the U.S. Senate. In a quote attributed to his son, Charles: "We will send the old man to the Senate or the poorhouse." The stage was set. The effort was aided by a recent arrival to Butte, Frederick A. Hienze. Hienze was from a wealthy eastern family, had recently graduated from the Columbia School of Mines, and was an avid Democrat; which checked all the right boxes for Mr. Clark. Heinze acquired some Butte mining properties, began publishing his own newspaper (the *Reveille*), and initiated some innovative processing techniques, as well as some innovative personnel policies. In short order, Heinze was a very popular figure and one which Clark realized could be a valuable ally on two fronts.[17]

By this time, Marcus Daly was in the process of selling the Anaconda Company to the Amalgamated Copper Company (a subsidiary of Standard Oil). Although Daly would remain the titular head of the Anaconda Company, it was now part of an even much larger financial power. Daly was actually in poor health and spending most of his time living in New York City. Clark, while mindful of Daly, realized the enemy (to himself and Heinze) had become an even more formidable corporate challenger. Clark, largely through his surrogates, initiated a no-holds-barred battle to win the U.S. Senate seat by a two-pronged approach: (1) buying as many votes in the Montana Senate as possible, and (2) attacking Amalgamated Copper as a "foreign" invader to the State.

The effort to influence the state Senate on Clark's behalf was led by one of his attorneys, John Wellcome. Wellcome's efforts were publicly revealed by Fred Whiteside, a Senator representing Flathead County, who revealed that Wellcome had given him $30,000 (which he held aloft for all on the floor and in the gallery to see) to buy votes for Clark. A grand jury investigation was initiated and, rather quickly, came to the conclusion there was "inconclusive evidence" of wrong-doing...a judgment which may have been reached with an assist of bribes estimated to be $10,000 per juror. In the meantime, Heinze had unleashed a steady drumbeat of attacks upon Amalgamated in speeches and in the press, with the theme that only W.A. Clark could stand up to the assault of this corporate giant upon the people of Montana. His message was unmistakable in its tenor; as one historian observed, "In a state where invective had long characterized the press, the *Reveille* was egregious."[18]

In the end, Clark was successful—with an "investment" of approximately $300,000—in winning the Senate seat which he had so long coveted. Matters would not end nearly so well for some of the others who played a part in this drama. The Elections Committee of the Montana Senate announced that some "contested votes" were discovered, and recommended that Fred Whiteside be unseated, which he was. In his final address to the legislature, Whiteside chided his former colleagues: "Let us clink glasses and drink to crime...there are forty members seated here who, today, are ready to embrace it...I am not surprised that the gentlemen who have changed their votes to Clark recently, should make speeches of explanation, but I would suggest that their explanations would be much more clear and to the point if they would just get up and tell us the price and sit down." For his part, Mr. Wellcome would be investigated by the Montana Bar and disbarred by action of the Montana Supreme Court. The most interesting chapter of this election, however, was yet to be written.[19]

> *"While I am willing to waive moral rank and associate*
> *with the moderately criminal of the Senators...*
> *I have to draw the line at Clark of Montana."*

Although Clark was initially granted his seat in the Senate, Marcus Daly was so unsettled by his old rival's victory tactics that he encouraged members of the Senate (and the press) to investigate the circumstances of the election. Montana's incumbent Senator, Thomas Carter, filed a petition requesting Clark be removed from his seat due to election improprieties. The Senate Committee on Privileges & Elections subsequently made a thorough investigation, finding several examples of Clark's unscrupulous machinations, and unanimously concluded that Clark should be unseated. Author Mark Twain was so outraged by Clark's exploits that he later vented in an essay published in newspapers nationally: "[Clark] by his example has so excused and so sweetened corruption that in Montana it no longer has an offensive smell... he is as rotten a human being as can be found anywhere under the flag...to my mind he is the most disgusting creature that the republic has produced since Tweed's time." Forewarned of what the committee would recommend, and the near-certain outcome of the Senate's review, Clark and his surrogates developed an outrageously creative response before the Senate took their vote.[20]

On May 15, 1900, Clark was granted the floor to address the Senate. Clark resigned his seat, admitting to questionable practices on his behalf, but not before passionately declaring that his only goal was to save the people of Montana from the Amalgamated Copper Company. Meanwhile, back in Montana, Governor Robert Smith (an avid opponent of Clark) had been contacted by Miles Finlen (an old acquaintance) who asked Smith to meet him in San Francisco to help resolve some legal matters. Meanwhile, Lt. Governor A. E. Spriggs (an avid supporter of Clark) who was at a meeting in South Dakota, received a telegram asking him to return to Helena as soon as possible; which he did. Upon his arrival in Helena, Charles Clark presented him with a copy of Senator Clark's resignation (which Charles had been holding). Spriggs accepted Clark's resignation, and then promptly exercised his power as the acting governor to appoint someone to fill the vacancy... William Andrews Clark! Upon learning of how he had been hoodwinked, Governor Smith immediately returned to Montana to resume his authority, and to rescind the appointment of Clark as Montana's junior Senator.

Never one to back away from a fight, Clark renewed his quest for another appointment as Senator in the general elections of November, 1900. With the continued enthusiastic—and self-serving—support of Frederick Heinze and his newspaper, Clark managed to obfuscate the circumstances of his "resignation" from the Senate and focus attention on the threat of Amalgamated Copper. It was a successful strategy. William A. Clark was again elected to the U.S. Senate by the Montana Senate on November 7th, and this time he was not challenged for his seat. Clark's election may well have represented a final blow to an ailing Marcus Daly, who would die in his New York hotel penthouse on November 11th. Another fatality in the aftermath would be Clark's deceptive relationship with Heinze. Almost immediately following his election, Clark began selling pieces of his mining empire to the Amalgamated Copper Company. And, no longer needing his support, Clark severed his alliance with Heinze. Left alone to fight the war for mining dominance, Heinze would be crushed—financially and emotionally—by Amalgamated in 1903, and would die at the age of 45 in 1914.[21]

Ironically, as tirelessly as he had fought for the U.S. Senate seat, and while Clark seemed to delight in being addressed as "Senator Clark," he had little interest in actually serving as a Senator—and even less interest in serving Montana. Although he would officially serve his term (1901-07), Clark was rarely to be seen in Montana (except for his regular attendance at annual meetings of the Society of Montana Pioneers) preferring to spend his time in California, New York, or Europe. Certainly, another pleasant diversion to the mundane functions of the

Senate was his marriage to Anna LaChapelle in 1901. Alternately described as having previously been the family nanny or Clark's "ward," Anna was the daughter of French-Canadian immigrants and 23 years old at the time of the marriage; Clark was 62. Clark and Anna would have two daughters, Louise Andree (1902-1919) and Hugette (1906-2011).

By 1910, Clark had sold all of his Montana interests and essentially closed that turbulent chapter of his life. And while there is a prominent statue of Marcus Daly in Butte, this author knows of no similar memorial to Mr. Clark in Montana. Perhaps the most notable legacy attributable to Clark's dubious political career was the passage of the 17th Amendment to the U.S. Constitution in 1913, which provides for the direct popular election of U.S. Senators rather than by state senates.[22]

Senator Clark and Anna would primarily spend the next few years at either their 121-room mansion near Santa Barbara, California, or their 42-room apartment on 5th Avenue & 72nd Street in New York City when they weren't traveling. Sadly, their daughter Andree contracted spinal meningitis and died very quickly, just a few days short of her 17th birthday, in 1919. In her memory, Clark purchased 140 acres near Briarcliff Manor, NY, which he donated to the Girl Scouts of American for use as Camp Andree Clark.

William Andrews Clark died on March 2, 1925, at the age of 86 in New York City. Clark's net worth at the time of his death was approximately $2,140,000,000. His assets were primarily designated to Anna and Hugette, but his three surviving sisters, and the children from his first marriage were also beneficiaries. Clark also made the donation of his very substantial art collection to the Corcoran Art Gallery in Washington, D.C. and to the Metropolitan Museum in New York City. He additionally provided $350,000 as a trust for the orphan's home in Butte (honoring his son, Paul), and $25,000 to the Grand Lodge of the Masonic Order of Montana.[23]

William Andrews Clark was interred in a beautiful family mausoleum at the Woodlawn Cemetery in New York. Perhaps a fitting epitaph to his turbulent and controversial life would be Clark's own words in response to a reporter's question regarding the persistent charges of his political bribery: "I never bought a man who wasn't for sale."[24]

Notes:

Epigram: "The most disgusting…," Mark Twain.

1. Magnam, The Clarks of Montana.
2. "fought with…," Ibid. Malone writes that Clark attended Iowa Wesleyan for two years.
3. "will never…," Ibid.
4. "little red-headed…," Gus Graeter in Magnam. "library…," Ibid. "a keen mind…," Malone & Roeder.
5. "several thousand…," Magnam. Malone writes that Clark had $2,000 (+/-) after the first year, and that he sold his claim.
6. "high winter…," Magnam.
7. Session met from December 12, 1864 to February 4, 1865. Contrary to popular lore, Bannack was not the first capital of the Montana Territory, but simply hosted the first legislative session; which selected Virginia City as the capital (Council Bill #2).
8. Magnam.
9. Katherine was 30 years old at the time of marriage. Clark thought Deer Lodge "had better prospects" than Helena; one of his few misjudgments. Bank partners were R. Donnell and S.E. Larabie.
10. Magnam. National Mining Hall of Fame & Museum profile. Railway was the Los Angeles & Salt Lake City line, and the only rail line in the United States totally financed by one man.

Epigram: "He spoke with…," Malone.

11. Daly was born in 1841, the youngest of 11 siblings. Came to the United States at age 14 by himself.
12. "about as magnetic….," "Was a man of…," Malone, Battle for Butte.
13. The Territorial Delegate served as a non-voting member of the House of Representatives. "an envious…," Toole, Uncommon Land.
14. Other territories were North Dakota, South Dakota and Washington. The question of women's suffrage was considered by the delegates, but voted down.

Epigram: "We will send...," Malone & Roeder,
attributed to Clark's son, Charles.

15. At this time the respective state senates elected their U.S. senators. The Montana Democrats nominated Clark and Martin Maginnis, the Republicans nominated Wilbur Fisk Sanders and Thomas C. Power. "to put it frankly...," Spence.

16. Expenditure estimates from Malone & Roeder. Four of the seven children would survive to adulthood: Mary Joaquina, Charles Walker, Katherine Louise, William Andrews, Jr.

17. "poorhouse" quote per Malone & Roeder.

18. "in a state...," Toole. Whiteside gave the bribery money to the State Treasurer.

19. Clark was elected January 28, 1899, with 11 Republican votes. J.K. Howard would testify that Wellcome bought 47 votes for $431,000. Whiteside's speech January 27, 1899.

Epigram: "While I am...," Mark Twain, from Swibold.

20. Twain's essay was written in 1907, he was perhaps influenced by personal friendships with Marcus Daly and Henry Rogers; an executive with the Standard Oil Company.

21. Heinze's cause of death was Cirrhosis of the liver.

22. Memorial to Daly unveiled September 2, 1907. The statue of bronze and granite was created by the famous sculptor Augustus St. Gaudens, and was originally located on North Main Street; near the Post Office, in Butte.

23. Clark's Will was presented for Probate in Butte on April 7, 1925. Anna was designated to receive $2.5 million and, with Hugette, properties including a 42 room New York City apartment. Clark's children, Charles, Katherine and William, Jr. would die within a few months of one another, 1933-34; Mary died in 1939.

24. "Never bought a...," Malone, Battle for Butte. Anna died in April 1963, in New York City.

Sources:

Clark, William A. vertical files at Montana Historical Society.

Emmons, David M. "The Orange and the Green in Montana, A Reconsideration of the Clark-Daly Feud." Montana Heritage: An Anthology of Historical Essays.

Forney, Gary R. Finding El Dorado.

Howard, Joseph Kinsey. Montana: High, Wide, and Handsome.

Lang, William L. "Spoils of Statehood," Montana Magazine of Western History, Vol. 37, no. 4.

Magnam, William D. The Clarks of Montana
_____. The Clarks: An American Phenomenon.

Malone, Michael P. Battle for Butte

Malone, Michael P. and Richard B. Roeder. Montana: A History of Two Centuries.

National Mining Hall of Fame and Museum website

Spence, Clark. Territorial Politics and Government in Montana, 1864-89.

Swibold, Dennis L. Copper Chorus: Mining, Politics, and the Montana Press, 1889-1959.

Toole, K. Ross. Montana: An Uncommon Land.
_____. "The Genesis of the Clark-Daly Feud," Montana Magazine of History, April 1951.

Photo credits:

Portrait; Wikipedia

Marcus Daly; Progressive Men of Montana.

Clark with daughters; Wikipedia

Clark mausoleum; findagrave.com

NEIL HOWIE
Montana's Lawman...And Vigilante

Neil Howie was among the most widely known men in the early Montana Territory. He was the first to be elected Sheriff of Madison County, the second man to serve as United States Marshal for Montana, a founding member of Montana's first Masonic Lodge, a member of the Alder Gulch Vigilante Committee, appointed as a Brigadier General in the territorial militia...and perhaps among the least remembered characters of those early days. Although his discharge certificate from the militia noted that he was only 5'8" tall, any opponent he faced would undoubtedly have said that he played much bigger. Howie would maintain diaries from the Spring of 1864 until the autumn of 1869, during which time he traveled widely throughout the Montana Territory. Upon the pages of little pocket-sized books, Howie carefully recorded financial matters as well as his observations, activities, and encounters with some of the most famous—and infamous—characters and events in the early days of the Montana.[1]

Neil Howie was born at Ayrshire, Scotland in 1835, and immigrated with his family to the United States in 1840; arriving at New York City. His father, Andrew, was born in1807 in Scotland, as was his mother,

Mary, who was born in 1806. It appears that farming was Andrew's principle occupation throughout his life. At the time of their immigration, Andrew and Mary's family included Elizabeth (8), John (7), Neil (5), Margaret (3), William (2), and Duncan (<1). The initial residence of the family was in Passaic Falls, New Jersey, but they soon moved to Albany, New York, where they lived for the next six years, and where two more children would be born; Andrew (1842), and Mary (1844). In the early Spring of 1846, the family move to Hope Township, New York, where another daughter, Jane, was born later that year and the final child, Robert, was born in 1848.[2]

In the Spring of 1855, Andrew moved to Madison, Wisconsin, with his oldest sons, John and Neil. He was able to rent a farm property near the University of Wisconsin, and the rest of the family arrived in Madison soon afterwards. During the time in Madison, Neil enrolled at the "University Commercial School," where he completed a "full course of study" in the winter of 1857. The following spring, Neil left home, alone, for the gold fields of Colorado.[3]

Neil settled in the area near present-day Golden, Colorado, and, unlike most, did well in his initial foray into gold mining. As he prepared to return to Wisconsin in the autumn of 1860, he reportedly sold one of his claims for $4,500. When Neil arrived in Wisconsin, he found that the family was now living on 160 acres which his father had purchased near Vienna—and that his mother was very ill. She died in December, and was buried on the farm property.[4]

Neil returned to Colorado in the Spring of 1861, and his brother, Duncan, traveled with him to the Lake Gulch mining district. It appears as if Neil's initial brush with the "Midas touch" did not return with him, as one source noted: he "had varying degrees of success for the next two years" in Colorado. Many other miners were similarly finding their claims "played-out" by the Spring of 1863 and, as news of big gold strikes in the newly established Idaho Territory began to spread, hundreds of men and women moved westward; including those by the name of Sidney Edgerton, Sarah Bickford, Wilbur Fisk Sanders, Martha Canary, John Bozeman, William A. Clark, Jack Slade...and Neil Howie.[5]

Rascals, Ruffians, and Rebels

"There was little harmony, and good men from those three parties [Colorado, Minnesota, and the western camps] took longer to find each other out, to know who were the roughs and who were their friends."

Howie arrived at Bannack (Idaho Territory), the epicenter of a new gold strike district, in the early summer of 1863. A significant deposit of gold had been discovered along Grasshopper Creek in July 1862, and Bannack had quickly emerged as the principle camp in the district. At its peak, Bannack may have had a population of 3,000 and proved to be a turbulent and deadly collision point between the men who had arrived from all points—and with all manner of enterprise. Although the exact date isn't noted, Howie must have arrived in Bannack shortly after the time of the discovery of gold in Alder Gulch. It is a bit curious that he remained in Bannack, inasmuch as its future prospects were already fading and the vast majority of the population was swarming into the new camps born by the incredibly rich deposits along Alder Creek. Perhaps Neil felt there was greater potential in reworking some of the several abandoned claims along Grasshopper Creek than in trying to establish a new claim site in Alder Gulch.[6]

It isn't certain how he may have attracted any special attention in this colorful mass of humanity, but Neil apparently did so. He was working on a mining claim along Grasshopper Creek when he may have had his first face-to-face encounter with another immigrant to Bannack—one whose reputation as a dangerous man was well-deserved. Henry Plummer had been elected Sheriff of the district just a few months earlier, and was a well-known figure with a dark reputation. Plummer reportedly approached Howie as he was hard at work on his very modestly successful claim, and empathized that such work was "a hard way to get a living," and suggesting that there was an easier way he should consider. "Doubtful as to his meaning, or whether he understood him aright, Howie regarded Plummer with a puzzled expression, making no reply. 'Come with me,' said Plummer, 'and you'll have all you want.' 'You've picked the wrong man,' Howie replied. 'All right,' said Plummer coolly, 'I suppose you know enough to keep your

Bannack (c 1865)

mouth shut." Neil appears to have kept his mouth shut (at least for the short term), but he didn't forget this very memorable exchange… and he could never have likely imagined the circumstances of his next meeting with Mr. Plummer.[7]

As winter closed in on Bannack the mining season was formally closed, and Howie found employment as a freighter transporting goods between Salt Lake City and Bannack. This was dangerous work even in the best of circumstances (both in terms of brutal weather conditions and potential robbery), but it was vital to the well-being—even the very survival—of the hundreds of miners in the territory who relied upon this service to obtain their supplies and to transport gold to Salt Lake in payment. In January 1864, Howie was part of a three wagon train en route to Bannack on the "Salt Lake Road" when they encountered Ben Peabody and another man on horseback riding south. Peabody advised the freighters that John Wagner, commonly known as "Dutch John," had been identified as one of those involved recently in the attempted robbery of another train and was believed to be making his escape from justice along this same road. To abbreviate the follow-

93

ing events, Thomas Dimsdale would later write: "For cool daring and self-reliant courage, the single-handed capture of Dutch John, by Neil Howie, has always appeared to our judgment as the most remarkable action of this campaign against crime.[8]

After taking Wagner into custody, Howie began the journey back to Bannack soliciting those he met along the way to assist him in the task of delivering his prisoner. He was repeatedly rebuffed in his request for help until encountering John Featherstun. Featherstun was unhesitating in his pledge to help, and joined Howie in a grueling trip of three days in bitterly cold conditions to deliver Wagner to Bannack. Upon arriving at Bannack the night of January 5, Featherstun initially sequestered Dutch John at the Sears Hotel while Neil went in search of someone to inform, and the first authority figure Howie encountered was none other than Sheriff Henry Plummer.[9]

Howie advised Plummer that he had John Wagner as his prisoner, and Plummer immediately demanded Howie release him into his custody. As the conversation continued, Howie grew increasingly uneasy about surrendering Wagner into Plummer's care. He concluded their meeting by telling Plummer that after all he had gone through to return Dutch John to Bannack, he wanted to see this through and thought it best that a judicial panel determine the disposition of this matter. Coincidentally, the men who would take the lead in making that disposition—as well as that of Henry Plummer—were riding to Bannack from Virginia City at that very hour.

To summarize the dramatic events which would follow over the next 48-72 hours, a small delegation of men from a newly established Vigilance Committee of Alder Gulch arrived in Bannack around midnight, and sought out others they were confident could be trusted. John Innes would later write that he had been one of the men who had assisted Featherstun in guarding Dutch John, and when the Alder Gulch posse arrived, "They took Howie, and went out and organized the Bannack Vigilantes." These men would advise that they had—what they believed—was reliable information that Henry Plummer was the leader of a large group of road agents, which included at least two of Plummer's deputies and Dutch John. Over the next few hours, this core group recruited others to their cause and, the following evening, executed by hanging Henry Plummer and his deputies Buck Stinson and Ned Ray. Although the exact membership of this hastily formed vigilante group which performed the capture and multiple execution isn't altogether certain, it is a virtual certainty that it included John Lott, Harry King, Wilbur Fisk Sanders, William Roe, and Frank Sears. Following Plummer's execution, the Bannack vigilante group would also determine that Dutch John was deserving of the same fate, and he was hanged approximately 24 hours later.[10]

Howie's diary indicates that he was involved in assisting Madison County Sheriff Robert Knox in collecting local taxes from the miners as early as January 7th in the Bannack mining districts. Howie's reputation as having "grit" was undoubtedly a valuable asset in such employment. By early Spring, however, Neil had moved, as many Bannack residents, to Alder Gulch and appears to have been making his home in the Highland District. He also became involved with the Alder Gulch Vigilance Committee.[11]

The Alder Gulch camps were embroiled in vigilante activity during early 1864, including the multiple execution of five men on January 14th and the controversial execution of Jack Slade in early March of 1864. Howie's role—if any—in either of those events or other vigilante activity at this time is not noted, however, a cryptic entry in the memoranda section of his 1864 diary is the note: "Amount in Jack's purse: Dust 13.00, coin 10.00." Whether this refers to Slade or Jack Gallagher (who was one of the five men hanged in the infamous "Hangman's Building" execution) is an intriguing mystery. Nevertheless, Howie was an active member of the Vigilance Committee and earned a reputation as a reliable, hard-working, and fearless man. And, on April 23, 1864, Neil was appointed as a Deputy Sheriff of Madison County. Two other vigilantes, and friends of Howie, John Featherstun and John X. Beidler, would also become deputies during the next few months.[12]

Howie's diary entries from April through September show him settling in to the role and duties which were probably very typical of a lawman in a bustling mining district. People from all corners of the world and several U.S. states (North & South), many of whom were regularly fueled by "tangle-foot whiskey," enjoyed a wide range of diversions operating on a 24/7 schedule. Howie was regularly traveling throughout the camps of the Alder Gulch serving subpoenas, breaking up fights, making arrests for all manner of offenses, standing guard at the jail, and tracking down fugitives. As it seems is still the case among law officers, the job required using good judgment with regard to handling conflict and having the courage and skills to resolve situations that require protecting oneself or others from harm. An illustration of such a situation is found in Howie's diary entry of July 3, 1864, when he wrote that he was awakened by a tavern owner to help "settle an Irish row" at his establishment. Howie responded and found three men fighting and, as is still often the case, when he attempted to "settle the row," the men collectively turned on him. Howie succinctly noted in his diary that he "arrested two and shot one."[13]

Neil found time to file a few lode claims, enjoyed playing billiards in his free time, and wrote on July 24th that he had attended church services for the first time in three years, and was "very much annoyed with the long prayers." In addition to the Vigilance Committee, Neil would also maintain memberships and attended meetings of at least two other Alder Gulch associations; the Union League and the Masonic Lodge.[14]

Perhaps the most interesting aspect revealed in Howie's diary entries is the evidence of blurred lines between the Vigilante Committee and the duly appointed law officers of the Alder Gulch. Sheriff Robert Knox and at least three of his four deputies (Howie, Featherstun, Beidler) were active members of the vigilante organization, which appears to have served as an adjunct to—and at times superseded—the typical legal process and authority. Three diary entries by Howie serve as example:

On June 26th, it was noted that (____) Maire and William Jarvis had been arrested (charges not indicated) and were held at the jail. Following their trial on the next day, the men were set free on bail. On the 28th, the "Committee ordered Maire and Wm. Jarvis to leave the Territory." The men left the following day.

On August 2, Howie records that "a man named Murphy" was shot by James Brady at a Nevada City saloon. Rather than being held for trial, however, "the Vig [sic] arrested and tried him, was executed about sundown." Jem Kelly, bartender at the saloon, was presumably an accomplice in the incident, and was "whipped and ordered to leave."

Finally, on August 28th, Howie's diary entry ominously notes: "at Williams request I am to start tomorrow for Snake River." James Williams served as the Executive Officer of the Vigilante Committee, and was essentially asking (directing?) Howie to serve on a vigilante posse whose object was to apprehend the aforementioned Jem Kelly. The posse found Kelly near Port Neuf, Idaho Territory, and promptly executed him by hanging.[15]

Rather than serve as an impediment to Howie's law career, his affiliation and active participation with the vigilantes appears to have been a significant asset in terms of his connections to their leadership. Less than a week after the execution of Kelly, Neil received his commission as Sheriff of Madison County, and he appointed his good friends John X. Beidler and John Featherstun as his deputies. Unfortunately, any pleasure he may have felt from his appointment was subdued by the news he received from his brother, Duncan (at Lake Gulch, CO), that their father was very ill. And while his vigilante affiliation may have provided some professional benefit, Neil would soon learn that it could also be a liability in some circles.[16]

In mid-August of 1864, Robert H. Buckner murdered John M. Brown as result of an argument between the men which took place in the Madison Valley. Buckner was arrested and was awaiting trial in the Virginia City jail when, on the night of the 14th, he escaped. Howie unsuccessfully attempted to track down and capture Buckner, and returned to town to learn that rumors had quickly sprung up that Robert Knox and/or Deputy Featherstun had aided in his escape. This was almost certainly a contributing factor in Knox's decision to resign as Sheriff, as well as a source of personal conflict for Howie. By late December, and through means uncertain, Howie learned that Buckner was in Idaho City (Idaho) and he determined to bring the man back to Montana to face the outstanding charges for murder...and perhaps to clear the reputations of Knox and Featherstun.[17]

Howie arrived in Idaho City on February 3, 1865, after an eventful eleven day trip from Montana and a lay-over in Boise to connect with his counterpart, and with those inclined to provide financial or legal assistance. After two weeks in Idaho City, during which time Howie noted that he "[found] it hard work to keep sober," Buckner finally appeared before the District Judge who—after hearing approximately 20 minutes of testimony—ordered Buckner released. The local sheriff, and Howie's new friend, immediately placed Buckner under arrest again as soon as he stepped from the court room on a warrant obtained from the local Justice of the Peace. Three days later, February 20, the second trial of Buckner began ("from 10 a.m. until sundown"). Howie was among the witnesses called to testify, and the Defense Attorney asked Howie "Many questions about the Vigelance [sic] Committee at Virginia City." Howie was recalled to the witness box to provide another two hours of testimony the following day and, on February 23rd, the defense called several witnesses who "state that they have all been in Virginia City, and they knew of no civel [sic] law in that county." Judge Shepherd would rule on February 28, that the charges against Buckner should be discharged and, once again, Sheriff Bowen arrested Buckner as he left the courtroom.[18]

Building used as courthouse, Idaho City, Idaho Territory

On the first day of Buckner's third trial (March 1), now with Justice Burns presiding, the defense attorney threatened to seek a warrant for the arrest of Neil Howie for the execution of Jem Kelly in the Idaho Territory; creating "conciderable excitement" in the packed courtroom. The following afternoon, Justice Burns dismissed the charges against Buckner and ordered his release. The prosecuting attorney advised Howie there was no reason for him to remain, but Howie managed to negotiate a meeting with Buckner and his attorney during which Buckner "gave [me] to understand that neither Knox nor Featherstun had helped him escape [the Virginia City jail]." Howie left for his return to Virginia City the next morning, without Buckner in his custody, but perhaps relived to know his friends were not responsible for Buckner's escape. Any question, however, as to whether Howie may be reconsidering his affiliation with vigilante activity as result of his experience in the Idaho City courtroom was answered during his return to Montana. While stopping at Fort Hall on March 24, he assisted the local vigilante committee in arresting and administering 50 lashes to a man accused of child abuse—which had resulted in the child's death.[19]

Howie's return included a stop in Bannack, where he met with Governor Edgerton for breakfast on the morning of March 31—and perhaps some uncomfortable conversation—before taking the stagecoach to Virginia City, where he received a warm welcome home from his friends and celebrated by going "around with the boys until late." The next day, however, he was back into his routine duties of attempting to bring law and order to Alder Gulch—including attending a meeting of the Vigilance Committee. Howie also likely claimed a letter which had arrived during his absence from his brother, Andrew, confirming the death of his father on January 11th.[20]

Two especially interesting entries to Howie's diary during the next few weeks were on April 14th and April 24th. He noted that on the 14th news had arrived that night of General Robert E. Lee's surrender at Appomattox, and of the riotous behavior which it generated—and which he seemed to have tolerated. On the morning of the 24th, news came of the assassination of President Lincoln, and Howie noted that caused "quite an excitement in town...court adjourned...speeches were made in the afternoon by [Wilbur] Sanders and others…a large meeting at Nevada in the evening where several speeches were made." It appears the mood of the camps was generally somber, however, as Howie further noted an uncharacteristic ambiance that night: "Quiet about town…."[21]

"Helena is not much of a place for observing the Sabbath…."

After initially writing on May 12th that he was "thinking of going to Last Chance," Howie remained in Virginia City attending to routine duties (including appointing Hank Crawford and Joe Riley as deputies and Judge Bissell as Under Sheriff to serve in his absence) before finally leaving for Helena on June 2nd; accompanied by Beidler and Featherstun. His time away included side trips to Fort Benton (where he visited a large Indian encampment) and the camps at Ophir Gulch (where he filed some mining claims). He witnessed the use of a stomach pump on a man who had taken laudanum, and—although not specifically noted—apparently met with George M. Pinney; the United States Marshal for the Montana Territory who had based himself in Helena…and was a man barely one step above criminal in many of his own endeavors. Howie returned to Virginia City on July 9 to resume his duties, although several diary entries indicate a more active participation in his mining interests during July and August; perhaps because he had another career option in his pocket.[22]

On September 26, Howie noted that Marshal Pinney had left [Virginia City] for Helena that morning and that he afterwards "Met [Andy] Snyder, agreed to turn the Sheriff's Office over to him tomorrow." More than two months earlier, Pinney had prepared a formal appointment of Howie as his Deputy United States Marshal. The gap between the date of Howie's appointment and the time when he apparently accepted is curious, but suggests that it required a face-to-face meeting between Pinney and Howie in Virginia City—and perhaps some negotiations— to close the deal. It seems worth noting that in performing the duties of a deputy U.S. Marshall at this time in the Montana Territory was a challenge worthy of a great deal of thought. It often required traveling long distances across a hazardous landscape in brutal weather, to serve warrants or in pursuit of criminals, going into mining camps where there was little respect (often deep-seated animosity) toward law men…and doing so without backup. In short, it was a good way for a man to get killed.[23]

Howie remained in Virginia City for a few more days after resigning his post as Sheriff. He spent the time settling personal affairs and socializing with friends, and also learned of a man offering $1,000 for his murder and that of Beidler; a matter which was peacefully resolved when the repentant braggart sobered up. Howie had a busy final day which included some time in Nevada City, attending a theatre performance and arresting a man for murder before catching the 3 a.m. stage to Helena where he arrived at Midnight; a punishing 21 hour ride.[24]

One of the early—and notable—arrests Howie made as Deputy United States Marshal was that of James Daniels. During the night of November 29-30, 1865, Daniels murdered Andrew Gartley as a result of differences stemming from a card-game. Howie took Daniels into custody and held him in custody until the start of his trial. Following a six-day trial, Daniels was found guilty and sentenced by Associate Territorial Justice Lyman Munson. Munson sentenced Daniels to pay a $1,000 fine and to serve three years at hard labor in a federal prison. Munson further ordered that Daniels be taken from Helena to Virginia City, where he was to be held until his transfer. Daniels' story, however, would subsequently take some interesting turns before its deadly end.[25]

Neil Howie transferred Daniels to Virginia City, where he was confined to the Madison County jail on January 1, 1866. Not long afterwards, a contingent of Helena residents paid a visit to Acting Governor Thomas Francis Meagher in Virginia City. The men presented Meagher with a petition signed by "thirty-two respectable citizens of Helena"; including some who had served on the jury during Daniels' trial. The essence of the petition was that Andrew Gartley had been the aggressor in the dispute and that Daniels had acted in self-defense, therefore the sentence by Judge Munson was unduly punitive.[26]

After listening to the Helena men—and, no doubt, cross-examining them (Meagher had been a practicing attorney)—Meagher also spent time reviewing the Territorial Organic Act. Meagher concluded that there was justification to reconsider the case and that he had the authority to grant a reprieve of Daniels' sentence until the matter was reviewed by President Johnson. Daniels was subsequently released from custody and, after a few days of celebration in Virginia City, he inexplicably decided to return to Helena...where different versions of the subsequent events all arrive at the same fatal conclusion.

The consensus of these alternative stories indicates that Daniels, shortly after arriving in Helena, met with his attorney who advised him to submit himself into the custody of Deputy U.S. Marshal, John Featherstun. On the night following, Featherstun left Daniels in a store

John X. Beidler

while he went on rounds. When Featherstun returned, Daniels was gone. The store clerk stated that three men (whom he claimed to not know) had entered the store. After a brief conversation, Daniels left the store with the men. The following morning, March 2, James Daniels (with the pardon signed by Gov. Meagher in his pocket) was found, hanging from a tree commonly used by the local Vigilantes to dispatch justice. Neil Howie is known to have been in Virginia City at the time of Daniels' execution, but the whereabouts of Deputy X. Beidler remains a tantalizing mystery.

Although now based in Helena, Howie traveled throughout much of the Montana Territory, regularly meeting with a diverse collection of residents; including some of the foremost figures of the territory as well as the most malicious. He also continued to regularly visit Virginia City, commonly for extended stays. One of the prominent figures Howie met—and obviously befriended—was Thomas Francis Meagher, a legendary Irish patriot (and convicted traitor to Great Britain) who had also served as a Brigadier General with the Union Army. Meagher had arrived in Montana in late September as the appointed Territorial Secretary, only to learn that Governor Edgerton was leaving—which thereby thrust Meagher into the dual role of Acting Governor and Territorial Secretary. Howie would accompany Meagher to a treaty session with the Blackfoot and Gros Ventres tribes held near Fort Benton (during which time they "had a good deal of fun"), and would be on hand as the controversial Second Legislative Session was opened in Virginia City. Howie afterwards attended the celebration party hosted by Meagher where he helped the legislators to "make the brandy & wine fly…." It would seem to be a friendship which was genuinely based upon mutual respect, and would last until Meagher's untimely death.[26]

Howie's time in Virginia City also frequently included attending theatre performances and sessions of the territorial legislature, playing billiards, and oftentimes in the company of "Mrs. R." Neil also cultivated a relationship with the prominent newspaper men and authors, Horatio Nelson Maguire and Thomas Dimsdale. Howie was a partner in some Helena property, was in collaboration with Maguire on a book, and was a devoted friend to Dimsdale. In late July, during the final weeks of Dimsdale's life, Howie spent long hours by the bedside of his friend, and noted in his diary that he: "waited on Prof. Dimsdale nearly all night. He had a hard night of it."[27]

Two other examples of Howie's character are reflected in entries made during 1866:

In early May, a disagreement arose in the matter of some mules which needed to be repossessed. Howie wrote: "At noon met Joe Gray, talked very foolish about us replevening the mules. Feel very unkindly towards Joe Gray, he has wronged me & must not do so again."

On the night of October 6, Howie learned that there was some public outrage about a prisoner being held: "some excitement about town concerning Foster, reported they were going to take him out and hang him. Went to the jail with shot gun to defend it." Howie's only further mention of the incident was the next day: "Did not go to bed last night."[28]

Although Howie once confided in his diary that he had "been thinking a good deal about going into the merchant business," and that Judge Lyman Munson had offered to pay his fare back to "the States," he remained in his position as Deputy and often served in the role of Marshal during the increasingly frequent absences of Marshal Pinney. When Pinney finally—formally—moved on to more lucrative pursuits, Neil was appointed to the position of United States Marshal for the Montana Territory on April 1, 1867. Once again, aided by his faithful deputies, X. Beidler, John Featherstun, and William Birkin, he continued his service as a conscientious and fearless lawman in what must have been oftentimes nearly overwhelming circumstances.[29]

Since the summer of 1866, the significant immigration of White settlers and miners into the Montana Territory had greatly encroached upon the traditional lands of the Native Americans. Reported incidents—both real and imagined—of Indian attacks upon wagon trains and isolated settlers and miners were becoming more frequent, and news of the "Fetterman Massacre" along the Bozeman Trail in late December had increased the anxiety of many Whites.

News of further White/Indian conflict continued into the Spring of 1867, and perhaps reached a tipping point in mid-April with the reports that the trailblazer, John Bozeman, had been killed by a small

John Featherstun (L) and Neil Howie (c1867)

party of Indians. Although there may not have been much genuine grief over Bozeman's death (and whose murder was almost certainly not committed by Indians), it did create genuine panic and a petition was presented to Acting Governor Thomas Francis Meagher request-ing protection. Meagher responded by initiating a call for men to serve in the territorial militia and appointed officers and a general staff; in-cluding Neil Howie as a Brigader General in command of units from Edgerton, Jefferson, Deer Lodge, and Meagher counties. X. Beidler and John Featherstun were appointed to serve as as recruitment officers in those counties, each with the rank of Captain.[30]

Howie seems to have eagerly accepted his assignment with the mi-litia and led the men under his command from what was considered one strategic site to another, creating posts known as Fort Howie and Camp Thomas Francis Meagher. As may have been expected, how-ever, generally inexperienced officers charged with leading generally inexperienced soldiers against much more skillful opponents was a futile gesture. No direct contact was made by the militia troops with the Indians (who probably knew every movement of the militia) and the troops soon became discouraged; not only from boredom, but also from a nominal pay allowance of forty cents a day. Following the death of Meagher in July, Governor Green Clay Smith "reorganized" the militia and offered Howie a commission as "First Major." Howie refused this dramatic adjustment to his rank, but subsequently agreed to continue to serve when offered the rank of Colonel. By August, Howie noted in his diary that "a great many of the men asking for furlow [sic]," and a great many others were simply drifting away without asking. Neil, along with the remnants of the militia, were formally discharged by Governor Smith on January 9, 1868. Smith would later ruefully acknowledge that, upon dispersing, "a large number" of the men stole most of the militia's remaining supplies and equipment, including at least 250 horses and mules. It would subsequently become the task of "professional" soldiers to battle the Indians of the territory...and commit terrible atrocities in doing so.[31]

"General Neil Howie...has returned [to Virginia City]. His duties as U.S. Marshal having ended...."

Although there is not a diary known to exist, we can track some of Howie's whereabouts and activities during 1868 via accounts in the *Montana Post* and *Helena Herald*. By these accounts, it appears he resumed his normal routine of splitting time between Helena and Virginia City and continued to be a popular and respected figure. His term as U.S. Marshall expired, and, although he did not seek re-appointment, he agreed to remain as a deputy to the new Marshal, William Wheeler. Howie's diary entries were much less frequent during 1869, although he did mention the massive Helena fire in April, and in his memoranda notes, we learn he made some significant—and ill-advised—loans to his old boss, George Pinney. Neil also received a letter from his brother, Andrew, in which he wrote that he was in Golden City, Colorado, and was attempting to "engage to go north [with] a train," and that he had "ordered my mail to be forwarded [to Neil]." Andrew would close his letter by stating that it was "remarkably dull here but there is a prospect of times getting better soon." Andrew would later manage to make his way north, however, things would not go better for the young man.[32]

In the early Spring of 1870, Neil received notice that his brother,

Andrew, had been arrested on the charge of murder at Laramie, Wyoming. Neil appears to have quickly settled accounts and left Helena to support his brother. The events leading to the murder charge began as Andrew was reportedly asleep in his room at the Sherman Hotel. "Sometime after midnight" a local rowdy (apparently under the influence of too much whiskey) began a boisterous rampage, and Andrew went downstairs to determine what the commotion was all about. As he entered the bar, the drunken man—who was brandishing a revolver—spun around to face Andrew and declared "I'm gonna' shoot you!" Those were apparently the last words the man spoke, as Andrew drew his gun and killed him.[33]

Andrew Howie's trial was particularly noteworthy inasmuch as it was the first trial in the United States to have women seated as part of a jury. The *Cheyenne Daily Leader* lamented upon this scandalous situation and opined: "It will be a miracle if some of the delicate women who are going through this painful ordeal do not sink...and return home with shattered nerves and ruined health." Miraculously, it seems that each of six female jurors bravely made it through the ordeal in good order; Andrew was not so fortunate. He was found guilty of manslaughter after two days of jury deliberations, and Judge John Howe sentenced Andrew to ten years at hard labor to be served in the federal prison in Detroit.[34]

Regrettably, Neil's time following his brother's trial is not well documented. He reportedly spent the next two years traveling in Wyoming and Colorado (and possibly some time in St. Louis) before arriving in Utah in 1872. Apparently, the spirit of wanderlust was deeply embedded into his soul, and it seems as if Neil never settled in one place for any significant time—and it also appears that he never went into the merchant business. It is certain that early in 1874, he heard of gold strikes in South America and, perhaps recalling the exhilarating days of early Montana's gold rush days, headed in that direction.[35]

By the Spring of 1878, Howie was working as the Assistant Superintendent of the Remington Company's Quartz Works on the island of Trinidad...where it seems his experience with rough and lawless situations was very valuable. One story which emerged from this time was of an attempt by detail of "soldiers" to confiscate some of the horses and payload of the pack train which he was accompanying. Howie killed two of the soldiers/would-be robbers, and the remaining soldiers fled the scene. Later, as Howie was standing in the local saloon, he was joined by an officer of the deceased men's unit. The man, a Captain, had heard of the incident and acknowledged to Howie his men were wrong to attempt the robbery, but that had he been on the site, he "would have had [Howie's horse]." The Captain then stepped back from the bar and made a motion to draw his pistol, but "Howie got there first, and shot the captain dead in his tracks." As may have once been the case in Montana under similar circumstances, Howie "was not held for trial, and became the hero of the camp."[36]

Just a few months later, however, Neil Howie—a man who had endured the physical hardships of Montana winters, single-handedly arrested known murderers and countless drunken, armed miners—died "of fever" on the island of Trinidad on July 12, 1878. Upon learning of Howie's death, the editor of the *New North-West* (Deer Lodge, MT) wrote: "Thus ends the history of one of the bravest and best known men of the early days of Montana, the incidents of whose life would eclipse the story of the novelist...."[37]

Notes:

1. "Final Statement" of discharge from the Montana Militia, January 1, 1868. Discharged at the rank of Colonel after an adjustment in rank by Governor Green Clay Smith.

2. Biographical Review of Dane County, Wisconsin.

3. Ibid.

4. MHS SC#302: had claims on the Calhoun and Caledonian lodes, both in the Lake Gulch Mining District. Andrew purchased Vienna property in 1859 for $2,000. Census of 1860 declares his land value at $3,000, personal property at $500.

5. Idaho Territory established March 3, 1863. "varying degrees...," Dane Co. Review. "List of Early Settlers," Edward Purple, Contributions I (1876).

Epigram: **"There was little…,"** Diary of James Fergus, Contributions, Vol. II.

6. Although a part of the Idaho Territory at the time of Howie's arrival, Bannack would be included in the Montana Territory, 5/20/64. Population estimate per Bannack State Park website. The Alder Gulch discovery men returned to Bannack on May 29, 1863.

7. "Doubtful of…," Langford, Vigilante Days and Ways. Plummer was elected Sheriff of the Bannack Mining District on May 24, 1863.

8. See Langford or Dimsdale for complete version of events. "Salt Lake Road, " "for cool daring…," per Dimsdale. Wagner reportedly involved in robbery of Moody Train with Steve Marshland. Howie's capture of Wagner no doubt aided by frostbite conditions of Wagner's hands.

9. Featherstun's name appears variously in other sources, as used here is what appears in Howie's diaries and most commonly.

10. Plummer and deputies hanged January 10th per Langford. John Innes wrote that he was one of the men in charge of guarding Wagner, and that Wagner was moved to Sayer's Corral by the time posse arrived at Bannack. No mention in Howie's diary of his participation, if any, in Plummer's hanging.

11. Knox appointed as Sheriff by the Madison County Commissioners, Commissioner's Journals Book A. Howie had a claim in partnership with Henry Grinnell on the General Grant Lode, filed April 30, 1864 (Record Book A). Diary entries begin with Saturday, April 23, 1864: "rec'd appointment of Deputy Sheriff from Mr. Knox & was sworn in."

12. Multiple hanging and Slade's hanging occurred in Virginia City.

13. Howie diary, July 3, 1864.

14. Mining claims included: General Grant, Star, Constitutional, Caledonia, and El Dorado (Fairweather District Record Book A). Union League clubs came into existence during early years of Civil War as men's clubs promoting loyalty to the Union, the Republican Party, and Abraham Lincoln. Dues receipts show Howie to be member of AF & AM Montana Lodge #1 (SC 302).

15. Despite original prognosis Murphy survived his wound. In July, a stagecoach en route to Salt Lake City to Virginia City was robbed and Kelly was thought to have been among the road agents. Port Neuf near present-day Pocatello, Idaho.

16. Commission dated September 4, 1864, sworn in by Sidney Edgerton on September 13. Letter from Duncan dated August 23, 1864, from Lake Gulch, CO (SC 302).

17. Per Spray: Dispute over cattle grazing in Buckner's hayfield which led to Brown calling Buckner "a coward." He wasn't. Bucker commonly known by his middle name, Henry.

18. All quotes from Howie diary.

19. Quotes per Howie diary. Charge of Howie's role in execution of Jem Kelly, Idaho World, February 18 & 25, 1865. Entry in Howie diary of 3/24/65 re lashes to a "Mr. Tweed."

20. Howie submitted bill for expenses of Idaho trip in amount of $3,000. Letter from Andrew (SC 302, fldr 7)

21. Quotes per diary.

Epigram: "Helena is not…," Howie diary, June 18, 1865

22. "Last Chance Gulch" in what would become Helena; site of a gold discovery on July 14, 1864.

23. Quotes per diary. Letter of appointment dated July 10, 1865 () SC 302)

24. Arrested John Peoples for death threat.

25. Arrested Daniels November 30th; sentenced by Munson December 26. Howie was in Virginia City at the time Daniels was executed by vigilantes (March 1, 1966).

26. Diary of Neil Howie. "thirty-two…" Boyer mss. Forney, Thomas Francis Meagher.

27. Quotes per Howie diary, 11/12/65, 3/5/66. Tribes specifically mentioned at the treaty session were the Blood and Piegan (Blackfoot) and the Gros Ventres.

28. "Mrs. R" appears to be same woman at other times he referred to as "Mrs. Rogers." Several other women noted in Howie's diary, most commonly residents of Bozeman or Helena. Helena property in the

Green Clay Smith addition and partners included J. Featherstun. Maguire mss, SC 445: Working title of book was History of the Settlement of the Rocky Mountains, but manuscript was destroyed in the "Great Fire" of Helena (1869) per *Avant Courier* September 15, 1900. Only surviving portion of manuscript was an excerpt, "Lewiston, The Capital of the Idaho Territory," published in *Helena Herald*, March 21, 1867. Dimsdale suffered from tuberculosis, and died September 22, 1866.

29. Quotes per diary; "went to jail…," October 6, 1866.

30. Quotes per diary. Howie appointed U.S. Marshal by Judge Lorenzo Williston, April 1, 1867.

31. Bozeman killed April 18, 1867. Howie appointed May 10.

32. Only approximately 250 men (25% of whom were appointed officers) in total enlistment of militia. Meagher referred to force as "not invincible, but invisible." Howie discharged with rank of Colonel.

Epigram: "General Neil Howie…," *Montana Post*, November 27, 1868.

33. Pinney became manager of *Montana Post* in August 1868, when it was moved to Helena. Letter of Andrew to Neil, July 9, 1869 (SC 302).

34. Sodaro & Adams, <u>Frontier Spirit</u>.

35. *Cheyenne Daily Leader*, April 17, 1870. Andrew paroled after 2 years at Wayne (Detroit) Michigan, and appears to have lived remainder of his life near Chippewa Falls, WI, with brother John.

36. Howie's whereabouts during the period from May of 1870 until May of 1872 is very uncertain.

37. *Fort Benton Weekly*, October 6, 1881, story per Tom Conner.

38. Ibid. "Fever" assumed to be Malaria.

<u>Sources:</u>

Avant Courier

Biographical Review of Dane County, Wisconsin.

Boyer, William mss (SC 1545) Montana Historical Society.

Contributions to the Montana Historical Society, Vols. I, II.

Diaries of Neil Howie, 1864-1867 and 1869. (SC 302; Montana Historical Society).

Dimsdale, Thomas J. Vigilantes of Montana.

Graves, F. Lee. Bannack: Cradle of Montana.

Helena Weekly Herald

Howie mss, SC #302, Montana Historical Society.

Howie vertical file, M.H.S.

"Reminiscences of John C. Innes," University of Montana-Western.

Langford, Nathaniel. Vigilante Days and Ways.

Martinez, Randy A. "Biography of Neil Howie."

Maguire, Horatio N. mss SC #445, MHS.

Montana Post

Montana Territorial records (LR-Terr 1, box 1, fld 1; MHS)

New North-West (Deer Lodge, MT)

Pace Archives (Thompson-Hickman Madison County Library).

Purple, Edwin. "List of Early Settlers," Contributions to the Montana Historical Society, Vol. I.

Sanders, Helen F. and William H. Bertsche, Jr., editors. X. Beidler, Vigilante.

Rodriguez, Cristina M. "Clearing the Smoke-Filled Room: Women Juries and the Disruption of an Old Boys' Network in 19th Century America." Yale Law School, Faculty Scholarship Series, paper #4329.

Sodaro, Craig and Randy Adams. Frontier Spirit-The Story of Wyoming.

Spray, James S. Early Days in the Madison Valley.

Photo credits:

Portrait; usmarshal.gov.

Bannack, c1865.

Building used as courthouse, Idaho Territory: author

John X. Beidler: Pinterest

Howie and Fetherstun; Pace Archives.

SARAH FANNIE FORBIS
MISSOURI REBEL—MONTANA PIONEER

"My father owned 30 slaves and 640 acres of rich farm land in Platte County, Missouri." Thus begins the recollections of Sarah Forbis of her life before the Civil War, and the incredible adventure which would be the first year of her life in the Montana Territory.[1]

Sarah (most commonly known by her middle name, Fannie) was born in November of 1846 at the family home which—certainly by standards of the time—would have been regarded as a Missouri plantation. Sarah was the second child of her parents, John Franklin ("Frank") and America [nee Perinn] Forbis, who were natives of Madison County, Kentucky. Frank and his younger brother and his wife, America's sister, had immigrated to northwestern Missouri with their father, John W., in 1846 from Stanford, KY. Although educated as an attorney, John W. would primarily focus upon mercantile operations while his sons, Frank and his brother, became successful farmers in the fertile bottom-lands of the Platte River.[2]

Since 1840, Platte County (including Greene Township) had seen a dramatic growth in its population and corresponding expansion of agricultural, business, and cultural concerns. Among the institutions

113

noted at this time were the Pleasant Grove Missionary Baptist Church (organized in the Spring of 1839), the Platte City Presbyterian Church (organized in April of 1843), and the Camden Point Female Academy (founded in 1848). Although not confirmed that the Forbis girls attended the Camden Point Academy, both John F. and John W. were two of the twelve founding Board of Managers who each contributed $200 to establish the school. The area was also served by *The Eagle*, a newspaper established by Eziekel S. Wilkinson; who would later establish another paper the Forbis family would have the opportunity to read far from Platte County.[3]

John F. Forbis (first on left); William Forbis (third from left)

Typical of such families at the time, the Forbis family had grown accustomed to a lifestyle which relied heavily upon their slaves to sustain. As Sarah would later acknowledge, she had very little house-keeping or cooking skills prior to leaving Missouri. Consequently, when the Emancipation Proclamation was issued (January 1, 1863) its impact sent waves of dramatic change that swept over an already divided and deeply troubled Missouri. The pain and feelings of betrayal were still near the surface many years later as Sarah shared her recollections: "I can still recall [my father] as...[he met with the slaves]...and told them that the president said that they were all free." Moreover, her father acknowledged he could not operate the plantation without their help, and offered to pay wages to all who remained and to give each man a plot of land on which he could build his own home. From Sarah's perspective, however, the former slaves lacked any understanding of the responsibilities of freedom—or appreciation for what her father had provided them—and they "were like little children." Soon afterwards, the family awoke to that find all but one of the former slaves had left in the night.[4]

To compound the misery of the Forbis family, they were being regularly visited and harassed by troops of the Union army. As Sarah wrote, "It was well-known that our sympathies were with the Rebels...," a fact which her parents made no effort to disguise. In addition to being former slave-holders, Frank had openly offered his services to the political congress espousing the Confederate States of America and, not so openly, had made efforts to join the secessionist army led by General Sterling Price. Sarah recalled that "Our cattle was driven off, our crops were destroyed, our house was searched again and again and robbed." Finally resigned to the necessity to leave the area, Mr. Forbis made plans to take his family west. He agreed to join a wagon train of other similarly-minded families and to make a new start in the Oregon Territory.[5]

Sarah noted that the family's wagon train assembled at Camden Point, Missouri, and left there on May 16, 1864. As evidence of her father's precarious situation, Sarah would recall that he had not slept in their home for three months prior to their departure for fear of assassination...a fear which was obviously justified. Shortly after the Forbis family left their home, the man who had purchased the property was shot and killed by "Border Ruffians" when he answered the door one night; the men mistakenly believed he was John Forbis. Further evidence of the tensions in the area was also evidenced when, on July 13, a cavalry unit of the Missouri Militia was attacked by Union troops near Camden Point. In addition to the militia men killed in battle, the Union soldiers executed four men who had been taken prisoner, and also burned the town. Sarah also recorded that it was "Shortly before we left Missouri, I married David Leroy Irvine of Buchanan County, Missouri. I was seventeen then."[6]

David Leroy Irvine was born near Richmond, Kentucky on September 11, 1835. He was educated at Bethany College in Bethany, Virginia (present-day West Virginia), and—like his father—had become an attorney. The family had deep roots in the area which was a settlement originally known as Irvine's Station, founded by William & Christopher Irvine in 1778. One of the few records found regarding David's time in Kentucky is that of a petition introduced to Kentucky's House of Representatives, in May of 1861, requesting that he "and others" be allowed to "deliver certain guns of the State to the trustees of the town of Richmond." The petition was referred to both the Committee on Federal Relations and the Committee on Military Affairs, but was not passed out of either committee. One assumes that the request of David "and others" must have been a reaction to the outbreak of the Civil War, and their possible interest in establishing and arming a local militia force in sympathy to the Confederacy.[7]

David's uncle, William Leroy Irvine, had moved his family to Missouri from Kentucky in 1849, and settled in Buchanan County, Missouri. In 1864, David's family, including brothers Edward, Thomas, and David C., accompanied their parents to Buchanan County, Missouri, adjacent to Platte County. Although no direct evidence has been found of their initial association, the Irvine and Forbis families resided in adjoining counties in Kentucky, and made their homes near one another in Missouri. David's brother, Edward married Sarah's sister, Agnes, and they had a daughter, Ella, born in Platte County. Moreover, the families must have shared concern as to their future in the area, inasmuch as the Irvine family was also among those who joined the wagon train to Montana.[8]

David's brother, Thomas, would remember that the initial wagon train, which formed at Camden Point joined with another train soon after crossing the Missouri River at a site known as "Mormon Grove." Thomas recalled that the combined parties formed a large group, but that "Maj. John Forbis owned the greater portion of the train." Sarah noted that her "father equipped 30 Studebaker ox-wagons…with our cargo of ham, bacon, whiskey, sugar, corn-meal, raisins, coffee, tea,and flour." Initially each wagon was pulled by a pair of oxen, but the rigors of the trail resulted in the death of several oxen, resulting in the abandonment of some wagons and the discarding of many items--including flour. Sarah remembered that "we unloaded the flour from time to time, leaving it stacked log-cabin style as high as the men could reach…."[9]

En route to Oregon, news reached the wagon train of a major gold strike which had occurred in the Idaho Territory, and the party agreed to change their destination to this site. After a journey of more than four months, via the South Pass, the train reached Virginia City—the epicenter of the Alder Gulch—on September 25, 1864. One of the first observations made by Sarah was that "flour was selling for one hundred dollars a sack," in Virginia City—obviously a sad reflection upon how many thousands of dollars worth of flour the party had left stacked beside the trail. Sarah and David remained only briefly in Virginia City, however, "for it had fallen my husband's lot to take the cattle to Deer Lodge Valley where they could spend the winter on good grazing land." It must have been a very difficult experience for Sarah to not only leave her family, but to face the prospects of her future in this raw, new place for which neither she nor David were truly prepared. It was on October 4th when they arrived in the Deer Lodge valley, and the new immigrants "pitched our tents on Demsey Creek [sic]."[10]

There were seven other family groups (approximately 34 people) who made the journey to the area which became known as Race Track, including three of David's younger brothers and—most significantly—the family of George Lucas and his wife. Mr. Lucas had been the Captain of the emigrant train from Missouri, and was also a capable man who possessed some practical skills that would prove vital to the survival of the "pilgrims."

"I know not whence I came,
I know not whither I go,
But the fact stands clear
That I am here
In this world of pleasure and woe.
And out of the mist and the murk
Another truth shines plain,
It is in my power
Each day and hour
To add to its joy or its pain."

The first order of business for the new arrivals was to prepare hous-ing. Sarah acknowledged the genesis of the challenge they faced: "All of us had grown up in an environment in which the labor had been done by the colored folks, but we set to work the best we knew...." She described the process by which they built their new homes, including how approximately six inches of dirt was laid atop a mud plaster which was spread across poles laid for the roof. Sarah observed that, "this made a warm roof that was sometimes water-proof. Often it was not." Captain Lucas built the fireplaces for the cabins and would also whip-saw lumber for furniture. Sarah recalled that "until about Thanksgiving time we had no door nor window glass. In the window frame the men nailed small split poles so we could look out between the cracks. To close the door opening we used the tent propped with a tent pole."[11]

The new settlers—and their livestock—faced nearly daily chal-lenges in adjusting to this unfamiliar territory. And as one reads Sar-ah's account of this time, it is obvious this young woman was quickly growing in maturity and self-reliance. From treating the frozen feet of a brother-in-law and self-administered dental work, to facing a party of Indians who appeared at the cabin while she was alone, Sarah grew increasingly more confident and self-reliant...with the notable excep-tion of her kitchen skills. The Lucas family, however, would again come to the rescue.

In early December, David had to make a trip to Virginia City, and Margaret Lucas (an unmarried sister of Captain Lucas) came to stay with Sarah. Sarah wrote that "Miss Margaret" was "one of the lovliest [sic] characters that I have ever known…it was she that taught me to keep house." "Miss Lucas showed me how to wash and rinse dishes, how to scour the pot and pans with wood ashes…she taught me how to wash [clothes, and] how to make delicious food from our meager supplies. My husband and my brother-in-law were probably very grateful to Miss Lucas for that visit, too."[12]

Sarah and David were among those invited to the Lucas home for Christmas dinner; an invitation which they eagerly accepted. Dressed in their wedding clothes and, as requested, carrying their set of silver dining utensils, they arrived to find a table set for 15 people, covered with a freshly laundered white linen cloth, and a welcoming fire in the large fire-place. Sarah remembered the setting included "in the center of the table was a cake of butter about four inches square. This was the first butter that we had seen in Montana and since we had learned to live without it, no one touched it. After dinner it was put carefully away." No doubt buoyed by the good food and fellowship, Sarah announced she wanted to host New Year's Day dinner, and invited all to attend. All accepted her invitation—although one suspects that some must have done so with gracious hesitation.[13]

Sarah didn't record whether she later regretted her spur of the moment invitation, but it would have been understandable. Sarah and David had only a small table, one chair, and two stools, so the dining table and seating was extended by finding some long boards, which they set atop some wooden boxes. Sarah had unused table linens she had brought from Missouri, but "had to borrow dishes from the whole settlement." And, once again, "Miss Margaret" came to the rescue. Sarah wrote: "Miss Margaret came early in the day to help me. I think she knew that if she did not come to oversee the dinner, there might not be any."[14]

The New Year's dinner included "a large venison roast, stewed beans, hominy and some of Miss Lucas's famous light rolls. For dessert there was ice-cream, eggless, butterless cake, and Poor Man's Pudding and sauce." An ice cream failure—and perhaps others—was averted by Margaret's intervention when she discovered that the reason Sarah could not get the mix to solidify was that David and Sarah had put ice around the freezer but not salt. At the center of the dinner table was the treasure of the settlement. Sarah remembered that "Mrs. Lucas brought the pat of butter that had ornamented her Christmas table. It was an ornament again; it was much too precious to be eaten. No one touched it. Mrs. Lucas wrapped it carefully and took it home with her. I never did know its fate."[15]

In March, a "false Spring" break in the weather prompted Sarah and David to make a trip to Virginia City for a long-awaited reunion with her parents and siblings. The couple was accompanied by Mrs. Lucas and another woman identified as "Miss Vivian," presumably another resident of the Race Track settlement. Sarah's parents and five of her siblings were living in a one-room log cabin, which the family had converted into two rooms (a sleeping room and parlor) that "provided privacy from sight but not from sound" and built a lean-to addition which served as the kitchen. Sarah was very impressed by the creative touches her mother had added with fabric and lace curtains to make the space "cozy" and which "made me realize that we could have beautiful homes, even in Montana." It appears to have been a relatively short visit, but during the time they were there, the cabin must have been indeed very cozy with the regular occupancy of seven increased by the four visitors from Race Track. As an interesting addendum to her account of the trip, Sarah noted that Mrs. Lucas was: "a strong, bright Yankee woman. More than the rest of us, perhaps, she saw the possibilities in Montana...."[16]

"When spring really came...," apparently during the second or third week of April in 1865, Sarah and David again left Race Track, this time for an extended stay in the Alder Gulch area. With some difficulty, they found a home in Nevada City, and were soon afterwards greeted by some startling news. Sarah vividly recalled that it was "On April 25, when we entered the store of R.W. Donnell, he came up to us with a grave face and said, 'We have just heard that Lincoln has been assassinated.' We were Southerners but we were shocked and sorrowful at his death." Paris Pfouts, the mayor of Virginia City, an ardent Southern sympathizer and also once a resident of Platte County, Missouri, expressed similar emotions. "Having learned with deep regret" of Lincoln's death, Pfouts issued a proclamation requesting that all city businesses close from 1:00 p.m. until sundown and ordered that flags be lowered to half-mast. At midnight there was a solemn procession with a band playing "The Dead March," and speeches were made appropriate to the sad occasion. Thomas Dimsdale reported in the *Montana Post* that "the demeanor of the city's population well became American citizens...."[17]

David and his brother, Edward, decided to join the many men making good money by gold mining and bought a claim in Alder Gulch. The men worked hard at the claim through the summer and into the early autumn, but it appears the only one to have made money on the claim was the man who had sold it to the brothers. As Sarah dejectedly recounted, "They didn't find anything but mud. We had paid out our money on a mud mine…we had lost every cent we had in the world." In early October, David's brother, Thomas, arrived from Race Track with an oxen-pulled wagon to collect his brothers, their wives, and their modest collection of belongings and return to the Deer Lodge valley.[18]

The first night of their return trip was cold and brought a light snow. The next day, however was filled with sunshine, which quickly melted the snow and revealed their route was passing through vast fields of wildflowers and snow-capped mountains all around. Sarah became pensive as the wagon slowly made its way, and reflected that this was "a splendid, splendid land! And yet, in Missouri every thicket would offer its bounty. The hazel nuts and the black walnuts would be ready to eat, the fox grapes and haws and papaws would be ours for the gathering. In the fields would be hogs and corn and pumpkins. They would be making sorgum soon, and cider."[19]

"Suddenly Montana looked barren. We had been here a year. We had left our homes with the cut glass pendants on the chandeliers and with stone porticos to come and live in a one room log cabin made by men not trained in manual labor. We had sold our fertile fields, where water-melons and nuts and corn grew, to buy a mine that yielded only mud. We had come to hundreds of miles of prairie that grew bunch grass and sage-brush—these we could have for the taking. We had left

121

schools, churches, homes, we had left doctors, dentists, and friends. We had left behind us reconstruction in a war-ravaged land, we had left hatred and strife. I wonder how many of us would have willingly returned to it?"[20]

After returning to their home at Race Track, David became increasingly involved with establishing his law practice and was elected Probate Judge for Deer Lodge County. He would also serve the county as Superintendent of Public Instruction in 1869, and was the Secretary and Superintendent of the Rock Creek Ditch Company (a privately-operated irrigation collective). David and Sarah would have a son and a daughter during those busy and happy years together, and move from the little cabin at Race Track into the town of Deer Lodge.[21]

In the late Spring of 1872, David contracted pulmonary disease and died on August 21, 1872, as result of what was identified as "a hemorrhage of the lungs." The high regard in which he was held by the community was reflected on the day of his funeral services when all business was suspended, stores closed, flags placed at half mast, and his funeral procession was reportedly "the largest that ever wended its way through the streets of [Deer Lodge]." The newspaper editor wrote: "A good man has gone from among us—an upright, exemplary Christian gentleman...his death brought deep sorrow...the entire community felt sincerely there had been taken from it one of the noblest, purest and best of men." David was only 37 years old at the time of his death.[22]

Sarah would remain in Deer Lodge and, in 1875, would marry Rev. James R. Russel. James was a native of Danville, Kentucky, and the youngest of nine siblings. James attended Centre College (which his father was involved in founding) and graduated from Princeton University. He was ordained as a minister of the Presbyterian Church at the age of 23, and eagerly volunteered to serve the missionary efforts in the West. After a brief posting in the Denver area in 1872, James was assigned to help establish congregations in the Montana Territory, and arrived in Deer Lodge in 1872. He immediately became significantly instrumental in the organizing efforts of the Presbyterian Church, including the pastorate at Deer Lodge.

Sarah and James moved to Butte in 1875, where he would serve as pastor until his retirement as an active minister in 1884. In addition to occasionally performing weddings, funeral services, and counseling those in need, James was also appointed to serve on the Board of Trustees of the relatively short-lived Presbyterian college (the College of Montana); established in Deer Lodge as the first college in Montana. He would selflessly serve Butte in several capacities: as the City Treasurer, as a contributing writer for the *Butte Miner*, as Superintendent of Butte schools from 1886-1892, as Butte city librarian, and he served as the Vice-Counsel to Greece during his "retirement."[23]

While James was busy serving the Butte community in his many roles, Sarah was primarily spending her time caring for a growing family. Sarah and James would have six children, five daughters and one son, James, who died at age 6. Four of her daughters would remain in the Butte area as adults, as well as two of Sarah's brothers (John and James) who followed a Forbis family tradition and entered into the legal profession in Butte. All of this family was no doubt a great support to her when James died in March of 1928, at the age of 80.[24]

Sarah lived the remainder of her life in Butte, remaining active in the Presbyterian Church, the Butte Woman's Club, and the Homer Club. Surrounded by her daughters, Sarah died on July 16, 1934, at the age of 87, and was buried beside James at the Mount Moriah Cemetery. The *Montana Standard* eulogized Sarah as a woman "of kind and generous disposition…by her many acts of kindness endeared herself to hundreds of Butte people." At the time of Sarah's death, her only surviving sibling was her youngest sister, Mira.[25]

It is a bit staggering for one to reflect upon the lifespan and quiet strength of Sarah. A woman raised in a "Southern" family's plantation home in the time of America's Civil War, who journeyed to a raw, unknown land as a 17 year-old bride to make her home a single-room log cabin, to see her adopted land become a State, and to see people travel the route she did in a covered wagon now speed along in trains, automobiles and airplanes. She was a Rebel who courageously left the past behind to help build a better future for a new land.

Notes:

1. "My father...," Russel, "My First Year in Montana." (SC 165, Montana Historical Society).

2. Each of John and America's six children (3 boys, 3 girls) were born in Missouri. John W. served in the 1852 Missouri House of Representatives during the term Sterling Price served as Governor. A prominent resident of Madison County, KY, was Green Clay; who owned a "vast economic empire," was a slave-holder and the maternal grandfather of Green Clay Smith, who would become the second governor of the Montana Territory.

3. Williams, History of NW Missouri. Between 1840-1850 the population of Platte County increased from 8, 912 to 16,923. Church located ½ mile North of Camden Point. The Wilkinson family emigrated to Montana and established the *Rocky Mountain Gazette* in Helena during August of 1866.

4. Quotes from "First Year."

5. Ibid. John would later recall the Willamette Valley as their intended destination. (Forbis mss SC 54, MHS).

6. Quotes, Op sit. "not slept...man killed...," Fannie's presentation of 11/19/1920.

7. Collins, History of Kentucky, Vol. 1. House Journal of 1861.

8. Irvine family from Lincoln County, which was originally formed from Madison County. William Leroy Irvine (referred to as "Colonel") would move family to Montana in 1865. Ella would marry Wiley Mountjoy in Montana. In 1875, Ella's parents would gift to her a Steinway piano which is now in the care of the Elling House Arts & Humanities Center of Virginia City.

9. T.F. Irvine. F. Russel. John Forbis would later recall the train would be joined by others and "at times, consisted of more than a hundred wagons," J. Forbis mss.

10. "First Year." "South Pass" per T. Irvine.

Epigram: "I know not...," Unidentified author, from "My First Year."

11. "First Year."
12. Ibid.

13. Ibid.

14. Ibid.

15. Ibid.

16. Ibid.

17. Ibid. "having learned…the demeanor…," *Montana Post*, April 29, 1865. Pfouts had been publisher of the *St. Joseph Gazette*, which "warmly espoused the Southern cause," and—as the Forbis family—had left Missouri with the strong encouragement of Federal troops.

18. "First Year."

19. Ibid.

20. Ibid.

21. Only find children identified as "Mrs. J.B. Wellcome and "P.W. Irvine."

22. "a hemorrhage…a good man…," *New North-West* (Deer Lodge, MT), August 24, 1872.

23. Edwards: College of Montana founded March 3, 1883, closed June 8, 1900.

24. Appears her son, P.W. Irvine, preceded her in death. Daughter, Charlotte, was law librarian at the University of Montana; brothers John F. and James became attorneys in Butte. John practiced with Hiram Knowles (Montana Supreme Court Justice) and served in Montana House of Representatives.

25. "of kind…," *Montana Standard* (Butte), July 17, 1934.

Sources:

Bancroft, Hubert Howe. History of Washington, Idaho and Montana, 1845-1889. (1890)

Butte Miner (Butte, MT)

civilwartalk.com

Collins, Lewis. The History of Kentucky, Vol. 2. (1882)

Forbis, John mss (SC 54, Montana Historical Society).

Edwards, Rev. George. The Pioneer Work of the Presbyterian Church in Montana.

Journal of the House of the General Assembly of the Common wealth of Kentucky (1861).

Irvine, Thomas F. "A Pioneer's Experience," *Madisonian*,
    September 1, 1899.
Kerr, Charles. History of Kentucky, Vol. 1. (1922).
Leeson, Michael A. A History of Montana 1739-1885.
Missouri Secretary of State website.
Montana Standard (Butte, MT)
New North-West (Deer Lodge, MT)
Paxton, William M. Annals of Platte County, Missouri. (1897)
Progressive Men of Montana
Russel, Fannie Forbis Irvine. "My First Year in Montana, 1864-
    1865," Remininences of Fannie Forbis
 Irvine Russel. (SC 165, Montana Historical Society)
_____. Presentation to the Junior Historical Society, November 19,
    1920. Op cit.
Stout, Tom. History of Montana.
United States Census of 1860.
Williams, Walter. The History of Northwest Missouri, Vol. 1 (1915).

Photo Credits:

Portrait photo; *Montana Standard*, July 17, 1934.
Forbis brothers; Pace archives.

Thomas Francis Meagher
Irish rebel

Of the many notable personalities who have played a significant role in the history of early Montana, few, if any, led a life with more fervor, more audacity, and more steeped in controversy as Thomas Francis Meagher. And yet despite his oftentimes cheeky audaciousness, cutting wit, and uncompromising outspokenness, a magnificent memorial to Meagher graces the entrance to Montana's capitol.

Meagher was born in Waterford, Ireland, in 1823. As the son of a very prosperous shipping merchant, he lived in a magnificent family home, was educated in boarding schools, and was generally sheltered from the economic and ethnic struggles which the majority of Irish-Catholics were facing under British rule. After completing his

Bronze statue of Thomas Francis Meagher sculpted by Charles J. Mulligan, 1905 on the lawn of the Montana capitol in Helena

college-level education in England, Meagher returned to Ireland in 1843 to find that political dissent was nearing a boiling point, fueled not only by the deep resentment of British rule, but also the fact that much of the country was on the cusp of a horrible famine. Meagher was deeply touched by these calamities and, rather than take his place in managing the family business, he soon became active in the Repeal Association.

Founded by Daniel O'Connell in 1823, the Catholic Association had successfully convinced the English Parliament to eliminate, or modify several of the terribly repressive Penal Laws; originally enacted in 1695. Consequently, O'Connell had become a widely revered figure among the Irish Catholics; the predominate population of Ireland. O'Connell's success led him to subsequently establish the Repeal Association in 1830. The mission of this organization was to work toward a repeal of the Acts of Union, thereby restoring a measure of political independence for Ireland. O'Connell made it clear from the start, however, that neither complete independence from Great Britain nor the use of armed force to achieve independence were among the intended objectives of the Association. Earning O'Connell's favor, Meagher quickly became his trusted confidant and a frequent orator on behalf of the association. Typical of Meagher's passionate nature, however, he was soon drawn into a circle of the Repeal Association members who chafed at what they perceived as O'Connell's humbly cautious approach in pursuing Ireland's over-arching necessity—total and complete political independence from Great Britain.[1]

Rallying around William Smith O'Brien (a native-born Irishman, an active member of the Repeal Association, a Protestant, and a member of England's Parliament), a group of predominately young, well-educated men began to meet and share thoughts on the best course of action to lead towards the political independence of Ireland. The group initially called themselves the "'82 Club," but soon embraced the moniker "Young Ireland" after O'Connell used the phase in a dismissive remark directed toward the young radicals.

At a general meeting of the Repeal Association held in Dublin in July 1846, Meagher rose to address the delegates on behalf of the Young Ireland faction in what amounted to a last-ditch attempt to direct and energize the Repeal Association into a more aggressive posture. Afterwards known as the "Sword Speech," Meagher, with forceful eloquence, created pandemonium among the delegates as he set forth the proposition that the time had come for Ireland to reclaim its independence and that armed revolution should not be removed as a possibility. Not too surprisingly, John O'Connell—who was acting as Chair of the meeting in the absence of his father—declared that: "The sentiments Mr. Meagher avowed are opposed to those of the founder…and therefore the Association must cease to exist, or Mr. Meagher must cease to be a member." As a result of this declaration Meagher and the men of Young Ireland, followed by many new converts, left the hall—and the Repeal Association.[2]

Although some futile attempts were made in the aftermath of the July meeting to seek resolution between the Young Ireland faction and the Repeal Association (including an appeal by Daniel O'Connell), the philosophical rift had grown too wide. Consequently, the adherents of Young Ireland split away and formally organized as the Irish Confederation; their name reflecting their optimistic intention of uniting Protestants and Catholics in the cause of Ireland's political independence.[3]

Meagher would become a leading member and the principal orator for the Irish Confederation, attracting world-wide attention for his stirring (some would judge as inflammatory) speeches critical of Great Britain's callous treatment of the people of Ireland. Strongly affected by the suffering and wretched conditions he was witnessing during his travels, he prophetically reproached an audience in Belfast for the reluctance of the people to rise up with tragic prescience: "And you—you who are eight million strong—you who boast that this island is the finest that the sun looks down upon…you will be beggared by the millions—you will perish by the thousands—and the finest island that the sun looks down upon, amid the jeers and hootings of the world, will blacken into a plague spot, a wilderness, a sepulcher." Sadly, Meagher underestimated how many of the Irish would be beggared, forced to emigrate, or perish in what became widely known as the "Potato Famine" or, in Ireland, as "An Gorta Mor" (The Great Hunger).[4]

In addition to his tireless travel and speaking engagements, Meagher also made another significant contribution to their cause by designing the flag which was a physical representation of the Irish Confederation's identity and which became—and remains—a symbol of Ireland. Almost certainly influenced by the flag of the French Republic, Meagher's flag is also a tri-color, with equal parts Green (representing Irish Catholics) and Orange (representing Irish Protestants) separated by White (representing a lasting alliance between the two groups). This perfectly symbolized the goal of the I.C.: a united and independent Ireland. By the Spring of 1848, Young Ireland had established dozens of affiliate clubs throughout Ireland and their rallies were attracting thousands of participants…and attracted the ominous attention of British authorities.

On July 22, 1848, the British House of Commons suspended the right of habeas corpus in Ireland, and there followed a tumultuous course of events which led to the arrest of Meagher and four other leading revolutionaries of Young Ireland. The men were tried and found guilty on the charge of treason against Great Britain, which carried an automatic sentence of death by hanging, beheading and dismemberment. After waiting approximately ten days in Dublin's Kilmainham Gaol (prison), where executions were commonly carried out, the men learned that Queen Victoria had commuted the death sentences of the Young Ireland rebels. Their punishment was changed to life banishment from Ireland, and it was directed they be sent to the penal colony of Van Dieman's Land (present-day Tasmania). The decision was almost certainly motivated not from any compassion for the rebels, but the realization of the Queen (or perhaps her advisors) that to execute these popular men would have made them martyrs to the Irish people and probably further agitated an already unsettled situation.

After serving a bit more than two years of a comparatively idyllic exile (during which time he married the daughter of another Irish exile), Meagher was assisted in making his escape to America. His subsequent appearance in New York City was greeted by a massive outpouring of support and adulation. Newspapers from coast to coast gushed at the arrival of the new Irish immigrant…which was certainly not characteristic of the welcome most Irish immigrants received. Meagher received scores of invitations to meet with prominent statesmen and to address organizations and several governmental assemblies and, within a few weeks of his arrival, Meagher submitted his formal Declaration of Intention to become a citizen of the United States.

During the next nine years, Meagher traveled across much of the United States on various lecture tours, he was admitted to the New York Bar and took part in two high-profile legal trials, founded a newspaper (*The Irish News*), made an extended tour of Central America, served as legal counsel to negotiate a railway right-of-way between the Atlantic and Pacific oceans across Costa Rica, became personally acquainted with numerous congressmen, may—or may not—have become a member of the Fenian Brotherhood, and he was widowed and remarried. As many others, however, the course of Meagher's life would take one of its most dramatic turns with the outbreak of the American Civil War. Despite the hopeful anticipation of many Southerners who expected him to support their bid for "independence," Meagher unhesitatingly gave his voice and his service to the Union. He would later answer this criticism by stating: "When they ask me how it is possible that while I contended for the independence of Ireland, I am opposed to the independence of the South, I answer this, had Ireland been under the enjoyment of such privileges and such rights, and such guaranteed independence as South Carolina enjoyed, I would not have been here tonight."[5]

After completing his initial period of enlistment with the 69th New York State Militia, and earning recognition for his bravery at the First Battle of Bull Run, Meagher re-enlisted and zealously worked to recruit and organize a new brigade for the Union Army. Principally consisting of Irish and Irish-American recruits from New York City and Boston, the unit became widely known as the "Irish Brigade," and Meagher was appointed by President Lincoln to serve as its Brigadier General. The example set by Meagher inspired many other Irishmen to enlist for service in hundreds of units throughout the Northern states; units which would determine the course of several battles. In all likelihood, Meagher's motivation was two-fold: (1) he believed the Irish who had immigrated to the United States owed a debt which could be repaid through their service (and their place in their adopted country well-earned); and (2) he was still mindful of a greater purpose, as he declared in a speech to potential recruits: "…if only one in ten of us come back when this war is over, the military experience gained by that one will be of more service in a fight for Ireland's freedom than would that of the entire ten as they are now." Regardless of his motivations, Meagher's decisive role in drawing thousands of Irish men into the Union Army is truly worthy of lasting recognition.[6]

The men of the Irish Brigade would distinguish themselves in virtually every major battle of the eastern campaign, and Meagher would prove to be a courageous and popular officer among the men in his brigade. The brigade paid a fearsome toll for their bravery, however, due to the questionable decisions of various commanding officers. Following the debacle of the Battle of Chancellorsville in May 1863, Meagher lost the spirit to continue leading his men toward what he may have reasonably believed would be the total decimation of his brigade. In his letter of resignation, Meagher wrote: "I feel it my first duty to do nothing that will wantonly imperil the lives of others, or, what would be still more grievous and irreparable, inflict sorrow and humiliation upon a race, who, having lost almost everything else, find in their character for courage and loyalty an invaluable gift, which, I for one, will not be so vain and selfish as to endanger."[7]

Meagher returned to New York, but would be called back into active service in September of 1864, and served until late February of 1865, although he had no further combat command in the closing months of the War. As many other veterans at the end of the war in April 1865, Meagher found himself adrift. No longer interested in reviving any of his pre-war professions, he anxiously sought out new possibilities (including federal appointments as a territorial governor or a military command) and—through a remarkable series of coincidence—he found Montana.

Meagher may have been initially enticed by the opportunities promised by the relatively new Territory of Montana, at a presentation made by James Fisk at the Cooper Institute in New York City. Fisk's presentation captured Meagher's imagination and opened a new world of possibilities in his mind. He traveled to St. Paul in the summer of 1865, with the intention of joining Fisk's emigrant train to Montana. Meagher was warmly greeted by the residents of the area, especially including its large community of Irish Catholics. Invited to make a presentation to the Irish Immigration Society of Minnesota, Meagher announced that it was his hope to colonize Montana with a strong Irish Catholic population, and he also proposed the radical concept that "the Black heroes of the Union Army have not only entitled themselves to liberty, but to citizenship...." While in St. Paul, on August 2, 1865, Meagher learned that President Johnson had appointed him as Territorial Secretary for Montana. Meagher subsequently made plans to travel by stage coach as a faster means of reaching the territory than Fisk's train, and arrived at Bannack on September 28, eager to assume his duties.[8]

As surprising as receiving the appointment of Secretary may have been to Meagher, it must have been positively stunning when—within a few hours of his arrival at Bannack—he assumed the additional responsibility of acting governor. Sidney Edgerton, the territory's first governor, took the next stage heading out of Montana—and never returned. Apparently Edgerton provided little more consultation to Meagher other than to advise him that the session of the territorial legislature had selected Virginia City as the first territorial capital, and that he should probably establish an office at that site; a task which Edgerton had avoided.[9]

Executive Office, Montana Territory, Virginia City (adjacent to bank)

After a couple of days rest in Bannack, Meagher rode to Virginia City with—as local lore maintains—all of the official records of the territory in one of his coat pockets. Although his baggage was indeed probably very modest, his arrival was greeted with enthusiastic fanfare and serenades. Meagher soon thereafter established the Territorial Executive Office, near the busy intersection of Wallace and Van Buren streets, and immersed himself in the turbulent waters of Montana politics and the wildly eclectic mass of humanity which called the Territory their home.

At the time of Meagher's arrival, the territory's most heated point of political controversy stemmed from Edgerton's veto of a bill at the end of the First Session to expand the number of legislators, and his subsequent refusal to call for a Second Session. Meagher initially supported the argument of the Republican Party representatives who claimed there was no legal authority to either hold new elections or to call the legislature back into session. By early February of 1866, however, Meagher made a dramatic about-face. Citing Section 11 of the Organic Act and Section II of the Territorial Act, Meagher claimed the authority to call the legislature into session. It was a decision which would have dramatic consequences for the territory, and elevated Meagher to being regarded as public enemy number one in the hearts of the Radical Republicans...some of whom began making bitter and spurious accusations against him which they liberally shared with any and all contacts they had in Washington, D.C and other eastern cities.

Without going into a detailed review of all the colorful political and personal machinations in which Meagher would become embroiled during his time in Montana, let it be summarized by stating that Meagher was generally admired by the "common man," and generally loathed by the common Radical Republican; one of the notable exceptions being United States Marshal Neil Howie. Certainly, some of the more memorable events of Meagher's life during that period would have to include: challenging another man to a duel (which never transpired), granting a temporary pardon to a man convicted of manslaughter, his critical leadership in establishing the Catholic Church in Montana, and serving as the acting governor for two very controversial sessions of the territorial legislature. It was his boldness in calling the legislature back into session—essentially restoring the democratic process—which perhaps earned Meagher the greatest outpouring of slanderous venom and which, unfortunately, was accepted as fact by those unaware of the true nature of circumstances and of those making the accusations.

Early territorial Montana was a collision point of miners and merchants from the mining camps of California, Washington and Idaho, with those from Colorado, combined with fresh "pilgrims" from not only the Northern and Southern states, but many others who were recent immigrants from several countries. All of whom brought their own ambitions, language/dialect, tradition, prejudices, and religion, and moral code—or lack thereof. And although the number of "Southerners" has been often greatly exaggerated, certainly one of the most contentious matters embedded in the milieu of that time—and particularly espoused by the Radical Republicans—was the prejudice toward those who had emigrated from the Southern states; and most especially those men who had served with Confederate forces.[10]

Considering that he, more so than probably most anyone in the territory, had witnessed the deaths and brutal maiming of friends and comrades before the Confederate Army, Meagher spoke remarkable words of healing and reconciliation. In a speech presented at Helena on February 21, 1866, Meagher said: "On the battlefields which they held for four tempestuous years, the soldiers of the South had lowered their colors and sheathed their swords. The spirit in which they had surrendered, as well as the spirit with which they fought, entitled them to respect…But the war is over, and I would not plant thorns where the olive has taken root. Here at all events, among the great mountains of the new world, no echoes should be awakened save those that proclaimed true and glorious peace, the everlasting brotherhood of those who had been foes upon the battlefield."[11]

Although he had formally resigned as Territorial Secretary, Meagher was continuing to serve in that capacity when he rode to Fort Benton in late June of 1867. He expected to accept a shipment of arms which was being sent from St. Louis for use by the Montana Territorial Militia in combating a wildly exaggerated Indian conflict. However, in circumstances which will forever remain shrouded in mystery and Montana legend, Thomas Francis Meagher disappeared during the night of July 1. And although it is a near certainty that Meagher's death was simply a tragic accident, it is understandable that many continue believe that one who lived such a grand life deserves a much grander story of death.[12]

Just as many of us, not all of his traits or decisions were laudable but, on balance, there is much to be admired about the life of Thomas Francis Meagher. He made difficult decisions (often with significant

Ancient Order of Hibernians memorial to Thomas Francis Meagher (Fort Benton, Montana)

personal sacrifice); he was intensely loyal to his friends and those who served with him in war; he was faithful to his Church; he remained fiercely devoted to the great cause of his life—the political independence of Ireland—and he stood boldly against those who would deny Montanans their political rights.

With the opportunity to live a life of privilege, Thomas Francis Meagher instead chose to literally stand on the front lines of conflict and face death, both in Ireland and the United States. And while he certainly enjoyed being in the spotlight as he eloquently spoke from hundreds of stages before many thousands of admiring spectators, Meagher may have discovered some of his happiest moments among the quiet peacefulness of Montana's mountains. Whatever else may be said of him, it must be admitted he lived his life true to himself and true to the Meagher family motto: "Boldness in dangers and trust in heaven."

Notes:

1. O'Connell proposed that Ireland be permitted to establish its own legislative functions, but would declare a "pledge of loyalty" to Great Britain.
2. Cavanagh
3. Irish Confederation formally organized January 13, 1847.
4. "And you...," Bowers.
5. Fenians established in both the United States and Ireland (1857 +/-) as a militant organization devoted to Irish independence. "When they ask...," Lyons.
6. Meagher initially served with the rank of Captain, was later promoted to Major. "...if only one in ten of us come back...," Conyngham.
7. "I feel it...," Cavanagh.
8. "the Black heroes...," *St. Paul Press*, August 3, 1865. James Fisk had served as Captain with the Emigrant Overland Escort Service, established by the War Department, and went into private enterprise when the EOES was decommissioned.
9. The Montana Organic Act provided that the Territorial Secretary would serve as Acting Governor in the absence of the Governor. A common misconception is that Bannack served as the capital of Montana. Actually, Bannack served as the site for the First Session of the Legislature which—in accordance with the Organic Act—selected Virginia City as the first capital. (Council Bill #2). Some Virginia City residents had attempted to raise funds to build a "Governor's Home," but were unsuccessful, almost certainly due to Edgerton's wide-spread unpopularity.
10. The Federal Census of 1870 enumerated less than 5% of residents to have been born in "a Southern state." The majority of residents cited their birthplace outside of the United States, including approximately 10% who were natives of China.
11. "On the battlefields...," Maginnis.
12. Meagher disappeared from the steamboat, *G. A. Thompson*.

Sources:

Bowers, Claude G. The Irish Orators.

Cavanagh, Michael. Memoirs of Gen. Thomas Francis Meagher.

Chittenden, Hiram. History of Early Steamboat Navigation.

Conyngham, David P. The Irish Brigade and its Campaigns.

Council Journal of the First Legislative Assembly of the Territory of Montana.

Federal Census of 1870.

Forney, Gary R. Thomas Francis Meagher: Irish Rebel, American Yankee, Montana Pioneer.

_____. Dawn in El Dorado.

Lyons, W. F. Brigadier-General Thomas Francis Meagher: His Political and Military Career.

Maginnis, Martin. "Thomas Francis Meagher," Contributions to the Montana Historical Society, Vol. 6.

Montana Post

St. Paul Press

United States Statutes of the 39th Congress, Second Session, Section 6, Chapter 150.

Wylie, Paul. The Irish General.

Photo Credits:

Portrait; Pace archives

Executive office in Virginia City; ibid.

TFM memorial at Ft. Benton, MT; author.

TFM Statue: Pinterest

George M. Pinney
"The most Accomplished and unmitigated Villain that ever cursed this Territory."

There's an old adage which suggests that one can "fool some of the people some of the time, but not all the people all of the time." George Pinney may have been an exception.

George Miller Pinney was born in Crawford County, Pennsylvania, on January 15, 1832. In 1846, his parents—with 14-year-old George in tow—moved to Ripon, Wisconsin. Ripon proved to be a relatively short-lived stop for the young man. By the age of 17, George had developed a case of gold fever. He traveled to California, where he—as many others—quickly found gold mining to be very difficult and usually disappointing work. Unlike most others who typically returned to the East to farms and factories, however, George signed on as a crew member for a ship headed to the Pacific islands; presumably Hawaii.

This author has not been able to find details of George's life as a sailor, but one cruise was apparently enough to convince him it was—as mining—another career he did not want to pursue. Approximately two years after leaving Wisconsin, George had made his way back to the family home for an extended visit. By 1853, George was ready to venture forth once again and this time, he did so after hearing another calling...one other than the lure of gold. He traveled east to enroll at the University of Rochester (NY) and study for a career in the ministry.

Pinney apparently learned all he needed to know about religious studies rather quickly, and began practice as a Baptist minister. This career path, however, was also very short and he turned his attention to the practice of law, presumably under the tutelage of an attorney rather than a law school. By 1856, Pinney had established himself in Windsor, Wisconsin, as a practicing attorney and now with a wife, Harriet Maria Whitney.

Pinney became involved in land speculation while in Wisconsin with a group of others who organized as Pinney, Barnard & Company on August 26, 1856. The organization filed a townsite claim on land in present-day Dodge County, Nebraska, and platted out the town of Fremont. The men also created another company known as the Platte Valley Claim Club to secure additional claims. During this time, Pinney dropped his political affiliation with the Union Party to become an active and outspoken member of the nascent Republican Party, and a devoted supporter of Abraham Lincoln—a decision which would soon pay dividends.

In early 1861, George and Harriet moved to Bon Homme County, Dakota Territory, and he quickly established himself as an enterprising young man. Among his initial efforts was to enter the political arena. Pinney declared as a candidate for Representative and, in November, he was elected to serve in the first Session of the Territorial House of

Yankton, Dakota Territory (c1861)

141

Representatives. Incidentally, Pinney was one of the three members of the Bon Homme Election Board and a subsequent investigation revealed the polling place in Bon Homme was changed at the last minute to Pinney's home…a fortuitous convenience to Mr. Pinney in several respects. Historian Howard Lamar characterized Pinney at this time as "a young lawyer of tremendous ambitions and few scruples," an opinion soon to be illustrated by Pinney's negotiable loyalties.[1]

One of the principal issues facing the First Session of the Dakota legislature, which opened on March 17, 1862, at Yankton, was to select a town to serve as the territorial capital—certain to be an economic plum to the chosen site. Before the Session formally opened, Pinney had hosted a series of "back-room" meetings in which he pledged support to the town of Yankton as capital in exchanges for their representatives' support of him to serve as Speaker of the House. Pinney was elected to serve as Speaker, but when the capital bill naming Yankton was presented for a vote, Pinney's double-dealings were exposed. Pinney, in front of the House, crossed out the name of Yankton, entered Bon Homme and called for a vote. As soon as this "amendment" was defeated, Pinney crossed out Bon Homme entered Vermillion and again called for a vote. This time, the vote resulted in a tie, which Pinney—as Speaker—broke by voting in favor of Vermillion. Several of Pinney's colleagues were outraged at his duplicitous machinations and resolved to take matters into their own hands.[2]

A faction of the Dakota legislators, including the Sergeant-of-Arms for the House, James Somers, plotted to throw Pinney out of a second-floor window of the House chambers and (apparently assuming he would survive) elect a new Speaker during Pinney's recuperative absence. Pinney learned of the plot, however, and persuaded Governor William Jayne to provide a bodyguard of militia volunteers. When Governor Jayne was later advised as to the true nature of the conflict between Pinney and his colleagues, he not only recalled the bodyguard but also forced Pinney to resign his post. In a case of adding injury to insult, the aforementioned Sergeant-of-Arms was a man who not only held a grudge, but also held firm to what he regarded as a good idea. Encountering the ex-Speaker in a popular Yankton watering hole, Somers proceeded to throw Pinney through one of the saloon's windows and into the street. Pinney interpreted this assault as a good time to resign, and the House would subsequently reintroduce—and pass—a bill naming Yankton as territorial capital.[3]

Despite the injury to his reputation—and body—Pinney's well-placed political connections allowed him to land on his feet. In July of 1862, he received the appointment as United States Marshal for the Dakota Territory. In March of 1864, Pinney was nominated by Governor Jayne (and others) to President Lincoln for the appointment of Pinney as Provost Marshal and Captain of the calvary of the Territory. Lincoln responded to Governor Jayne that he disliked "to make changes in office so long as they can be avoided...Send me the name of some man, not the present marshal, and I will nominate him to be the Provost-Marshal for Dakota." Although there was, perhaps, frustration, there was evidently no animus directed at Pinney in Lincoln's response.[4]

By the summer of 1864, many Dakota residents were joining a general immigration to the gold fields of the new Territory of Montana. Eager to ride this wave of potential opportunity, Pinney sought federal positions in the new territory, one of which was as superintendent of the proposed Virginia City-Lewiston Road project. While the appointment for that post was under consideration, Pinney also sought—and received—the appointment as U.S. Marshal for the Montana Territory in February of 1865, which he eagerly accepted. Before heading west, however, Pinney made arrangements for his pregnant wife, Harriet, to return to her family home in Rockford, Iowa. Tragically, Harriet would die during childbirth on September 25, 1865. The child, a boy, survived and was named George M. Pinney, Jr. and would be raised by Harriet's family.[5]

Meanwhile, Pinney had arrived in the Montana Territory in the Spring, and, despite Virginia City being the territorial capital and the largest city at this time, he established his office in Helena. One may assume he had the prescience to recognize Helena would become the dominant city, or perhaps, more likely, George wanted to have some distance between him and the executive officers of the territory. In any event, he quickly became a popular figure in the bustling new community, and was given the honor of presenting the keynote address at the 1865 Fourth of July celebration held at Owyhee Park. As he had done in the Dakota Territory, Pinney also made important friendships with the some of the leading Republicans in Montana.[6]

Among the first official tasks Pinney attended to was building a staff of deputies to assist in carrying out the responsibilities of the United States Marshal for the impossibly large Montana Territory. Coincidentally, Neil Howie, the Marshal of Madison County (wherein Virginia City is located), made a trip to Helena in early June to serve a warrant. Howie made a few side-trips, but generally remained in the Helena area for approximately two weeks. Although he did not document such in his journal, Howie obviously met with Pinney at some time during this visit and obviously made a good impression. Neil Howie was commonly known to be a member of the Alder Gulch vigilantes yet, despite this seemingly conflicting association (or perhaps because of it?) Pinney extended an offer to Howie to serve as Deputy U.S. Marshal.[7]

Howie did not accept Pinney's appointment until late September, following a visit by Pinney to Virginia City. While in Virginia City, Pinney signed a lease agreement for "one large room in the rear portion of the upper story of the stone building on the NW corner of Jackson and Wallace streets" for use as a courtroom. Pinney also met, and apparently negotiated with Neil Howie an agreement regarding his service as a Deputy U.S. Marshal and perhaps additional staffing. In any event, soon after Howie's acceptance, John X. Beidler and John Featherstun (both active vigilantes and deputies to Howie in Madison County) were also appointed as Deputy U.S. Marshals. Judging by the entries which Howie would subsequently make in his journal, it would seem as if he assumed a major role in directing the actual "field" work and supervision of his fellow deputies while Pinney was frequently an absentee Marshal. For example, Pinney appears to have left Helena (and probably the Territory) in early 1866, not returning until late May, and left again in early October for an extended trip to Washington, D.C.[8]

Pinney's trip east in late 1866 would prove to be memorable—and very profitable. His primary interest in visiting Washington appears to have been to lobby government officials, on his own behalf, for payment which he claimed due to him for "government services" in the staggering amount of $28,000! Even more remarkable, however, is that he received payment in full. It is possible that he helped his cause and gained favor among Republican legislators when newspapers reported, during his stay in Washington, of his beating of "a Secessionist" with his cane in the lobby of the Willard Hotel. Nevertheless, by the time Pinney began his return trip to Montana, he had a substantial bankroll, some influential new friends, and a bit of national notoriety.[9]

During his return to Montana, Pinney made an extended stop in Iowa, where he presumably spent time visiting his young son and made a significant change in his life. Flora Matilda Crawford was an actress and a native of Australia. Pinney met Flora in Council Bluffs, Iowa, which would have been a logical stopover point for the Overland Stage route. In what must have been a whirlwind romance, George and Flora were married and the couple spent their honeymoon en route to the Montana Territory. It isn't clear as to the exact sequence of events, but it was also during this time when Pinney sent notice of his resignation as U.S. Marshall. On April 1, Federal Associate Justice Lorenzo Williston formally appointed Neil Howie as successor to Pinney.[10]

Upon returning to Helena, Pinney resumed his professional life as an attorney, was elected as Chairman of the Central Committee of Montana's Union Party, and established a private bank. He also renewed his personal association with Neil Howie; which would seem to be—as with many of Pinney's associations—a rather one-sided relationship.

In the late Spring of 1867, there developed a wildly exaggerated "Indian War" in the territory, which resulted in little more than an op-portunity for some merchants to feed at the government's trough and for several men to receive officer appointments in the territorial mi-litia. Among those commissioned as officers was George Pinney. In July, Pinney was appointed by Governor Green Clay Smith as Aide-de-Camp with the rank of Captain; a position which gave a bit of polish to his resume` yet kept him safely removed from any danger of actually encountering a hostile. By the end of the year, however, Pinney would have the opportunity to become more closely engaged in combat.[11]

Among the services provided by Pinney's bank, was to hold secure such documents as deeds, contracts, etc. One of his clients for such service was William Albert Charles Ryan (most commonly known as "Whack"). Ryan was the son of Irish immigrants, a Civil War veteran of the Union, considered a "brave, but reckless man." He was also "a man of strong Republican principles," and he had an admiration of Thomas Francis Meagher, the former Acting Governor of Montana and legendary Irish patriot, "which knew no bounds." By all accounts, Ryan was not a man to be trifled with—but Pinney did.[12]

Ryan entrusted a sealed packet of documents into Pinney's care in the autumn of 1867. When Ryan went to retrieve the packet in late December, he discovered that the seal had been broken. Understandably upset, Ryan confronted Pinney in a heated exchange in which Pinney referred to Ryan as "a damned liar." Pinney further escalated the situation by indicating he would fight Ryan "in any way you please." If the challenge was intended as an attempted bluff by Pinney, it was a strategy badly misjudged. In keeping with the protocol code of a duel, Ryan subsequently sent a formal message to Pinney stating that he accepted Pinney's challenge, and will "fight you when and where you please,… or on sight." Ryan further advised that H.P.A. Smith would be serving as his agent in arranging the "preliminaries." This little drama ended with a whimper rather than a bang, as Pinney "would 'crawfish' in a very humble manner."[13]

Within a few months of the incident with Mr. Ryan, Pinney retired from the business of banking and found an opportunity to extend his capacity to insult and defame by joining the Fourth Estate. After having given assurances to the subscribers of the *Montana Post* that the paper would remain based in Virginia City, Benjamin Dittes bought the interest of his partner, Daniel Tilton, and promptly moved the paper to Helena in April of 1868. Dittes, who had been living in Helena, offered Pinney a position as both editor and general manager—which he eagerly accepted.[14]

Although Pinney may have admitted to any lack of experience with the task of managing a newspaper, he would certainly do his part to help stimulate circulation with biting editorials which attacked his rivals of all stripes. A frequent target was Robert Fisk, a Republican opponent and founder of a competing newspaper, the *Helena Herald.* In one editorial Pinney wrote: "Should John Potter, through the proximity of the *Herald* outfit, become so contaminated as to merit transportation to the Dry Tortugas, he should take with him the romantic Bob Fisk for a bedfellow; thereby securing himself against attacks of centipedes, tarantulas, scorpions, gallnippers, and all such reptiles as congregate in the *Herald* office."[15]

Pinney took leave from his mud-slinging at the *Post* to serve as a delegate to the Republican National Convention. Held in Chicago, the convention of 1868 was a dramatic departure from present-day extravagances. The convention was in session for only two days (May 20-21) and elected a ticket of U. S. Grant as their nominee for President, and Schulyer Colfax as Vice-President. It doesn't appear to have been documented as to whether Pinney had the opportunity to meet with General Grant, but one can easily imagine it would not have been for lack of effort.[16]

On July 10th, the *Montana Post* noted that George Pinney had left "to New Haven, Conn. to attend the Collegiate & Commercial Institute of Gen. William H. Russell." Perhaps this was a genuine effort on the part of Pinney to gain a better understanding of business management, but the evidence suggests it may have been no more than an expenses-paid trip to the East—not necessarily Connecticut. The *Post* would succinctly note that Pinney returned to Helena on August 21, an incredibly brief term of study when one factors in the necessary travel time between Helena and New Haven. In any event, during Pinney's absence a reorganization of the *Post* had occurred. On August 1 a new entity was established known as the Montana Post Publishing Company with Pinney named as the business manager. Noticeably absent from the list of Directors was Benjamin Dittes, who had sold his interest in the paper to the new consortium.[17]

While he may have been formally positioned as the business manager of the publishing company, Pinney's actual role with the *Post* appears to have been something more closely akin to that of a publisher. Alexander Beattie was recognized as the business manager who administered the day-to-day financial matters. And although James Mills was the paper's editor, Pinney continued to occasionally contribute inflammatory editorials—with deadly consequences.

*"Going inside I found Gov. Beall
lying on the floor against the wall, his face
toward the floor. There was a pool of Blood on the floor
and the blood was oozing from his head..."*

The September 25, 1868, morning issue of the *Post* included a column written by Pinney, which accused Samuel W. Beall (the former governor of Wisconsin) of stealing a watch. While this accusation would have been enough in itself to provoke Mr. Beall, Pinney heaped further insult: "...the old fossilized liar S.W. Beall, he whose beastial nauseous carcass...is about to drag his slimy length out of Montana. To the old worn out pest—the rotten hearted animal that signs himself 'Public Functionary,' every decent man in Montana can feelingly say 'Fare thee well most foul.' Go back to your dirty den, your drunken haunts, your vices and your crimes, and rot, as one who has sunk far below contempt itself." The article drew a quick response.

Mr. Beall confronted Pinney soon after the release of the morning edition of the paper and, in very strong terms, expressed his outrage at the slanderous/libelous articles with such force that Marshal Neil Howie was called to separate the men. Later that day, at approximately 2:00 p.m., two gunshots exploded from within the offices of the *Post*. Marshal Howie was near the *Post*, and heard the shots. Howie ran to the newspaper office to find Samuel Beall lying on the floor with blood oozing from his head and holding a derringer in his right hand. Howie was advised that George Pinney was responsible for the shooting, and that he was in the paper's composing room at the back of the office. Howie took Pinney into custody along with his pistol and Beall's derringer. Mr. Beall was removed to the home of Solomon Meredith where he died the next day, never regaining consciousness.

Court proceedings against Pinney convened the morning of September 28. Testimony from Marshal Howie focused upon a statement of events which Pinney had made to Howie at the time of his arrest, indicating that Mr. Beall was the aggressor in the fatal encounter. Pinney's statement (as given by Howie) was subsequently supported by William Winet, printer of the *Post*, who had witnessed a portion of the exchange between Pinney and Beall. The only other witnesses were two doctors who had examined Beall's wounds. The prosecution did not call any other witnesses, despite several men being in the *Post's* office during the attack, and instead briefly huddled together following Winet's testimony. They then announced that they wanted to withdraw charges against Mr. Pinney, which Judge Cornelius Hedges accepted and ordered Pinney released from custody.[18]

Other than editorials extolling the virtues of General Ulysses Grant and expressing the fervent hope that he would be elected President, Pinney was relatively subdued during the remainder of the autumn and early winter. It would seem, however, that he may have been distracted by his efforts to accumulate financial resources. At least one of the individuals who loaned money to Pinney during this time was Neil Howie; who gave Pinney $3,000. Another source of funds appears to have been the *Montana Post*.[19]

Undoubtedly thrilled at the election of Grant, Pinney made plans to go to Washington. Ostensibly to attend the inauguration ceremonies, it was far more likely in the hope of feeding at the federal trough in some manner. He was joined in this quest by Wilbur Fisk Sanders, "Warhorse" of the Montana Republicans, who almost certainly shared Pinney's goals. Neil Howie noted in his journal that it was January 21, 1869, when "G.M. Pinney & Sanders left for States."

In late February, Howie received a cryptic telegram from Pinney with the message: "Answer no letter from Department about rents until you hear from me." No further comment was noted by Howie, but it seems reasonable to assume that Mr. Pinney may have been asked some thorny questions by the U.S. Marshal's service regarding his expense reports. Nevertheless, Pinney remained in Washington for the next several months and, other than his wife experiencing some financial hardship, Montana continued to march along without much notice of his absence...until early June.[20]

On June 10th, the Sheriff of Lewis & Clarke County appeared at the *Montana Post* office and served a lien upon the paper for debts incurred by Mr. Pinney. As editor James Mills would write in the June 11 edition of the *Post*: "[due] to an obligation unknown to us [Mills and business manager A.H. Beattie], the material of [the *Post*] was attached." Apparently Mills or Beattie immediately contacted Pinney via telegraph, and Mills would optimistically share in the next issue of the paper that "Mr. Pinney, who has entire control of the matter, writes he will be home in a few days." Regrettably, Mr. Pinney neither had control of the matter nor returned home to resolve the *Post*'s financial dilemma. Mills would write in the final issue of the *Post* that "The confidence which I had expressed was misplaced...and the *Montana Post* like the traditional time-piece had stopped—never to go again." And, thus ended the Montana Post Publishing Company and the life of Montana's first newspaper.[21]

Perhaps understandably, this author could not find any evidence to indicate that George Pinney returned to Montana following the demise of the *Post*. Flora Pinney, however, not only remained in Helena, but made a celebrated return to her acting career. After a few singing engagements at Jack Langrishe's Opera House, "Jack invited her to become the feature member of his company for a while. The public had been delighted with her songs and were anxious to hear her again in a more 'historionic' capacity." The *Rocky Mountain Gazette* reported that "The Opera House was crowded [for Flora's debut] ...and the audience were more than pleased and gratified." "Mrs. Pinney stayed on with Langrishe for many weeks, and appeared in several performances including "Pride of the Market," "The Maid of Munster," and "Lady of Lyons." Flora also accompanied a traveling troupe of Langrishe's company that played a brief engagement in "The Maid of Milan" at the Opera House in Deer Lodge, in which she was lauded as "an unequivocal success." In a decision which Flora may have later deeply regretted, she once again left the stage and rejoined her husband who was already weaving new webs of financial intrigues in a promising new venue.[22]

At approximately the same time as Flora was appearing on stage in Helena and Deer Lodge, George Pinney arrived in California and established himself in Oakland where Flora joined him. He purchased a home in Alameda, and placed the deed in Flora's name; which would become a contentious issue. And, as testament to his consummate skills as a scoundrel, he soon found a lucrative position.[23]

Later characterized as "a mere formality," Pinney enlisted in the Navy and was immediately assigned to the Naval Pay Office. In a scheme which was obviously predetermined, Pinney became the facilitator of some equally corrupt politicians who were interested in helping—for a price—specific contractors for naval projects and services and for which Pinney received a share of the kick-backs. Pinney also acquired a seat on the San Francisco Board of Trade, apparently as a means to further enrich himself and "launder" his ill-gotten gains. One source indicates that "at one time [Pinney] was worth over a million dollars...." In what must have seemed a bit of déjà vu, Pinney was held in such high regard in the area that he was invited to present the keynote address at the Fourth of July celebration at Placerville, California. As those who invest in the stock market, or participate in other forms of gambling often soon learn, however, the tides of good fortune can quickly recede.[24]

By early 1875, Pinney's time of high life had begun to unravel at virtually every seam. What appears to have been a long-term philandering and the physical abuse of Flora resulted in her filing for divorce in what became a public spectacle. Upon news of this situation reaching Montana, the *Helena Herald* reported in a front-page article entitled "Pinney in the Role of a Wife Beater," stated that: "It is a well-known fact that when George M. Pinney lived in Helena he frequently whipped his wife and in many other ways abused her in the most brutal manner." The *Sacramento Record* reported that "near the close of his career," Pinney insisted that Flora sell their house and give him the proceeds. When she refused, he "knocked her down and dragged her about the house by her hair." Flora would get her divorce—and keep the house.[25]

In addition to his domestic problems, charges of embezzlement, fraud and forgery were filed against Pinney for his performance in the Naval office. The *Sacramento Union*, in an article headed "The Case of George M. Pinney, Outline of His Rascalities," opined that: "There are degrees of rascality, and while a thief is a thief without regard to the amount he steals, there are speculators whose deeds are so rascally superior as to inspire a sort of criminal admiration for very boldness or grandeur. Of this class of thieves was George M. Pinney...." The *Helena Herald* shared a similar opinion, noting that "[Pinney] was the most accomplished and unmitigated villain that ever cursed this Territory." J.P. Young perhaps best summarized the situation by writing that: "unfortunate ventures put [Pinney] on the toboggan and political and other complications suggested flight." Indeed, Pinney escaped these incriminating complications by taking flight from the area—and the United States—in September of 1875, with "an artificially auburned haired female." If there is anything to be admired in the character of George Pinney, perhaps it would be his uncanny ability to rise from the ashes.[26]

In early May of 1877, Pinney resurfaced in Washington, D.C., following "a foreign tour," and surrendered himself as a deserter to U.S.Navy authorities "with no other object than to unload his story and get even [with his co-conspirators]." Pinney was returned to San Francisco to stand trial on the charges previously cited and was apparently allowed to remain free on bond. Remarkably, after a three-year court battle, he was acquitted of all charges. Soon after his acquittal, Pinney once again boarded a ship out of the San Francisco harbor...this time without an escort.[27]

Pinney made his way to London, England, where he engaged as a broker, selling and trading mining interests in western United States properties. Perhaps one would be justified, based upon his background, to question whether Pinney actually had authority to sell such interests...or whether some properties even existed. During approximately the next six years he split his time between England and the U.S., including a brief visit to Helena in August of 1892. It was during the period of approximately 1881-1883, that Pinney achieved one of his grandest schemes.

Pinney held mining claims on three properties which he had acquired in early 1875, before his financial bubble burst. The properties, generally known as the Panamint Mines, were located in Death Valley and had never produced anything of value prior to Pinney's ownership. He formally established these properties in the Spring of 1882 as the Inyo Consolidated Mines, prepared an enticing prospectus, and issued $500,000 in stock. Pinney wasn't the first to ever conceive of a plan to fraudulently misrepresent a worthless enterprise, and "Although he seems to have improvised the script as he went along, the basic plot was to simply put on an appearance of running a steady, dividend-paying venture, which he then hoped to unload on even the most conservative of investors." Pinney proved himself to be a Grand Master of the game. In fact, he was so successful, he formed another venture he called the Richmond Mining & Milling Company in the autumn of 1882, and sold another $500,000 in stock. Shortly afterwards, however, his web of machinations began to unravel and—following a fire of mysterious origin which destroyed the company's stamp mill in December—the stockholders were left poorer for their trust in George Pinney.[28]

In early 1889, Pinney passed through Montana in what appears to have been a very brief—and his final—tour of the soon-to-be new state. John ("X") Beidler noted in his diary that he had encountered Pinney in Helena, and that "he is on his way to New York." By 1904, Pinney had worn out his welcome in England and returned to the United States—deeply in debt. A report in the *New York Times* echoed an article from San Francisco which announced that: "George M. Pinney, well known in the United States and Europe as a mining broker and stock speculator, filed a petition for bankruptcy...with liabilities of $92,000, [and] nominal assets of $1,100. The principal creditors are English brokers...." Shortly after this report, Pinney was known to be living with his son, George M. Pinney, Jr. George, Jr. had become a well-educated and respected attorney in the metropolitan New York City area. Although the disparity between father and son would seem to have been substantial, George, Jr. provided a home and care for his father until his death on May 13, 1906. He also honored the wish of his father to be buried beside his first wife, Harriet, in Charles City, Iowa.[29]

Notes:

Epigram: "The most accomplished...," *Helena Herald*, October 14, 1875.

1. Dakota Territory established March 2, 1861. "a young lawyer...," Lamar, Dakota Territory 1861-1889.

2. Dakota Territorial History 1861-1875, Vol. VI.

3. Pinney resigned April 9, 1862.

4. Basler, Letter of Abraham Lincoln to William Jayne, February 26, 1864.

5. Nomination for Virginia City-Lewiston Project made by J.B.S. Todd, Dakota Delegate to Congress and first cousin to Mary Todd Lincoln. Appointment went to Wellington Bird of Springfield, IL. Work abandoned after one year and expenditure of $50,000. Cornelius F. Buck initially appointed as U.S. Marshall for Montana (6/22/64), but he declined to serve.

6. Fourth of July per Leeson.

7. Howie's letter of appointment dated July 10, 1865.

8. "one large...," Pinney mss (SC 643). One-year lease in amount of $600 paid in Territorial script. Pinney's absences per 1866 Howie diary (Howie mss, SC 302).

9. "a Secessionist," *Helena Weekly Independent*, October 21, 1875.

10. U.S. Marshals website. Pinney resigned March 17, 1867.

11. Appointment per "General Order #1," July 14, 1867.

12. "brave...," *Helena Herald*, November 8, 1873. "an admiration...," Ryan.

13. Quotes per letter of Ryan to Pinney, December 23, 1867. "would crawfish...," Ryan vertical file.

14. Dittes had previously attempted to establish the *Tri-Weekly Republican* in Helena. First issue of the *Montana Post* in Helena on April 25, 1868.

15. "Should John Potter...," *Montana Post*, September 25, 1868.

16. Colfax was a native of Indiana and served as Speaker of the House of Representatives.

17. Leeson: Montana Publishing Co. Directors included James Whitlatch, John Potter, and William Thompson.

Epigram: "Going inside...," Howie's testimony, *Montana Post*, October 2, 1868.

18. *Montana Post*, October 2, 1868.

19. Howie diary of 1869, Memoranda section: "Hold one Note against G.M. Pinney in the amount of $3,000 dated about twelve months ago."

20. Ibid, undated entry: "loaned to G. M. Pinney cash on a note given to me by his wife, $600.00." Pinney based at the National Hotel in Washington.

21. *Montana Post*, June 11, 1869. "Reminisces" of James Mills.

22. Porter, Esther. *Rocky Mountain Gazette,* January 22-29, 1870. *New North-West*, February 4, 1870.

23. *Sacramento Record*. U.S. Marshals website.

24. "a mere...over a million...," *San Francisco Chronicle*, April 30, 1921.

25. "well known fact...," *Helena Daily Herald*, October 22, 1875. "knocked her down...," *Sacramento Record* from *Helena Daily Herald,* October 22, 1875.

26. *Sacramento Union*, October 5, 1875. *Helena Weekly Independent*, October 21, 1875. *San Francisco Chronicle*, April 30, 1921.

27. "for tour...," *San Francisco Daily Union*, May 5, 1877. Lingenfelter writes that Pinney, at least initially, fled to South America. "with no other...," *San Francisco Chronicle*, April 30, 1921.

28. Lingenfelter.

29. "he is on...," Beidler diary entry of March 16, 1889 (SC 300, MHS). "well known...," *New York Times*, March 4, 1904. George, Jr. was a graduate of Harvard Law School, and served as District Attorney for Richmond County (Staten Island), New York.

Sources:

Bancroft, H.H. and Francis F. Victor, <u>History of Washington, Idaho, and Montana 1845-1889</u>. (1890)

Basler, Roy P., editor. <u>Collected Works of Abraham Lincoln, vol. VI.</u>

Blake, Henry N. "The First Newspaper of Montana," Contribtions to the Montana Historical Society,
Vol. V, (1904).
Elliott, Karen, editor. Andreas' History of the State of Nebraska, "Dodge County."
Forney, Gary R. Dawn in El Dorado: The Mining Camps of Montana and Early Settlement of the Montana Territory.
Goodspeed, Weston, editor. Dakota Territorial History 1861-1875, Vol. 6.
Helena Daily Herald
Helena Weekly Herald
Helena Weekly Independent
Howie, Neil mss, Montana Historical Society (SC #302).
Leeson, Michael. The History of Montana 1739-1885.
Lingenfelter, Richard. Death Valley and the Amargosa: A Land of Illusion. (1986)
Mills, James H. "Reminisces of an Editor," Contributions, Vol. V. New North-West (Deer Lodge).
Pinney, George M. mss, MHS (SC #643).
Porter, Esther, The Early Theatres of Montana (186401880), Master's Thesis, University of Montana.
Russell, Steve F., editor. Virginia City and Lewiston Wagon Road.
Ryan, John. The Life and Adventures of General W.A.C. Ryan, The Cuban Martyr.
Ryan, W.A.C., Vertical file, MHS.
Sacramento Daily Union
San Francisco Chronicle
United States Federal Census of 1850
United States Marshals website biography of George M. Pinney

Photo credits:
Portrait; usmarshal.gov.
Yankton, Dakota Territory; Wikipedia.com.

Wilbur Fisk Sanders
"He was a master of eloquence and wit and sarcasm...."
"The most unscrupulous man that ever disgraced
the legal profession...."

One quickly forms the opinion that Wilbur Sanders was a man who evoked strong feelings by others...and that he didn't much care what those feelings may have been. Many respected his tenacity and feared him as a legal opponent. There were those who admired as well as those who derided his fierce devotion to his political beliefs. And there were many who would never forgive him for his leading role in such notable events as the establishment of the Alder Gulch Vigilante Committee, the nullification of the Second and Third Legislative Sessions of Montana and—as some suspect—his role in the death of Thomas Francis Meagher. Nevertheless, whether one loved him or hated him, and there were plenty in each camp, one has to admit that Wilbur Fisk Sanders was one of the most influential forces to be reckoned with in the very colorful early history of Montana.

Wilbur Fisk Sanders was born May 2, 1834, at Leon, New York. His parents, Ira and Freedom (Edgerton), were both natives of the New England area and devout Methodists. Wilbur attended the public schools of Leon, followed by two terms at the Phelps Academy. By August of 1856, Wilbur had moved to Akron, Ohio, where he taught school while reading law under the tutelage of his maternal uncle, Sidney Edgerton. Edgerton was not only a respected attorney in the Akron area, but would serve in the U.S. House of Representatives (1859-1863) on behalf of the northern Ohio district. Sanders proved to be an eager and talented student of the law and soon became a very capable junior partner to Edgerton. In 1858, Sanders married Harriet Peck Fenn, a well-educated and talented young woman, at Tallmadge, Ohio.[1]

Upon the outbreak of the Civil War, Sanders quickly responded by helping to organize a battery of artillery and a company of infantry to serve the Union Army. Certainly, this accomplishment is testament to the effectiveness of Sanders as a public speaker and his powers of persuasion. Sanders was elected to serve as a Lieutenant with the artillery battery, but was soon appointed as Assistant Adjutant General of the 64th Ohio Infantry in October 1861. This post was also relatively short-lived, as Sanders resigned his commission in early August of 1862. Several accounts attribute his resignation "on account of physical disability," although the exact nature of this disability appears to never have been fully explained. One source, however, indicates Sanders actually resigned in opposition to an order to arrest fugitive slaves.[2]

Sanders returned to Akron where he resumed his law practice with his uncle until March of 1863, when Sidney Edgerton was appointed as a Federal Justice for the newly created Idaho Territory. Sanders determined to remain with his partner and patron, and made plans to accompany Edgerton to the territorial capital at Lewiston, Idaho. The Edgerton and Sanders families left Akron on June 1, 1863, for the Idaho Territory—and what would prove to be an adventure none of them could have possibly imagined.

The Edgerton/Sanders families secured four wagons and several oxen to carry them and their household goods to the Idaho Territory. En route to Lewiston, near the Snake River ferry, Edgerton and Sanders decided to detour through Bannack. Although they would later attribute this deviation to a concern that winter weather may close in on them before reaching Lewiston, one may also reasonably speculate that perhaps learning of the gold discoveries at Bannack and Virginia City may have been an even greater influence. The first resident of Bannack whom the party would meet (at the Snake River crossing) was the Sheriff of the Bannack mining district, Henry Plummer. Plummer was accompanying his wife, Electa, who was leaving the territory to return to her family home in Iowa—another matter of continuing speculation. The Edgerton and Sanders families finally arrived at Bannack on September 18, 1863, after a wagon train journey of three months and 18 days. Harriet Sanders would later write: "Bannack looked to us most unattractive and disappointing…though we were happy in feeling that we had reached the end of our journey."[3]

Both Sanders and Edgerton found cabins in an area across the creek from Bannack proper, known as "Yankee Flat." Their homes were neighboring James and Martha Vail—sister and brother-in-law of Electa Bryan Plummer. Sidney Edgerton purchased a cabin at auction for

Sidney Edgerton

$400. Sanders rented a two-room, dirt floor, log cabin for his family at the rate of $15 per week—in gold (approximately $1,400 in present-day value). Harriet optimistically opined that, "we consoled ourselves with the idea that a log cabin would be a great improvement over the wagons and tents." Both the Sanders and Edgerton families were invited to Thanksgiving dinner at the Vail home, an event Harriet Sanders would later recall as "one of the most memorable dinners I have ever attended." Harriet remembered that the "repast was one of the most sumptuous dinners I ever attended," including "turkey [which] cost forty dollars in gold."[4]

Harriet also recalled the appearance and mannerisms of Henry Plummer at the dinner: "He was slender, gracefull [sic] and mild of speech. He had pleasing manners and fine address, a fair complexion, sandy hair and blue eyes,—the last person whom one would select as a daring highwayman and murderer." As events would play out, there were those who believe Mr. Plummer was, indeed, capable of robbery and murder.[5]

Although Bannack was within the boundary of the Idaho Territory, Edgerton would not assume his position as Justice; which would have required him to take an oath of office in Lewiston, Idaho. Sanders, on the other hand, wasted little time in hanging out his shingle—made of paper. As he later reminisced, "I got an office at Bannack, [a corner in a mercantile store] which was occupied by a friend of mine…[and] I got a piece of brown paper out of a grocery store and took it down to a wagon and with axle grease made a law sign out of it—put my name on it and added the words 'Law Office' and tacked it up on the front of the store, and went to practicing law."[6]

The population and business enterprises in the camps along the Alder Gulch, especially Virginia City, had been dramatically increasing since June. Wilbur Sanders was soon a frequent traveler between Bannack and Virginia City, making numerous contacts and building a reputation as an indomitable litigator. On the morning of December 19, Sanders had concluded some business in Virginia City and was prepared to board the A.J. Oliver stage back to Bannack when he was approached by a messenger on behalf of John & Mortimer Lott; prominent merchants in Nevada City. Sanders subsequently met with the Lott brothers and agreed to serve as the prosecuting attorney against George Ives, John Franck, and George Hilderman who were charged for the murder of young Nicholas Tbalt; commonly known as "the Dutchman." With the strong encouragement of Judge Byam, one of the two judges elected to administer the proceedings, Charles Bagg was added as co-prosecutor. In the opinion of at least one observer of the trial, Sanders would have found it "hard to compete" without Bagg's assistance.[7]

As documented in many books and articles, Ives was convicted (in spite of very questionable evidence) and—at the urging of Sanders—his execution by hanging was promptly carried out when, as some sources indicate, Sanders shouted the fatal command, "Men do your duty." Sanders would later write that he heard Ives speak his last words: "I am not guilty of this murder." Sanders made no further declaration on the matter other than to note that he was escorted back to his lodgings in Virginia City by "a large number of men." Others would confirm Ives' words but, unlike Sanders, would state that Ives also added: "Alex Carter killed the 'Dutchman.'"[8]

The arrest and execution of Ives galvanized the men who had a growing desire to punish those thought to be responsible for various robberies and assaults which had taken place in the Bannack/Alder Gulch region. In the week following the Ives hanging, Sanders remained in Virginia City and, as he noted, was accompanied by an ever-present bodyguard. During this time, Sanders and Paris Pfouts became principals in establishing a vigilance committee—a development which soon became an open secret and was not warmly greeted by all residents. As Sanders would later acknowledge: "Several parties in Virginia City proposed to organize a counter society [led by] two lawyers in town. Insisting…upon the sacred right of trial by jury and upon the sanctity of judicial administration…The Vigilance Committee decided the most effectual way to suppress this movement was to signify to these lawyers that their presence in [Virginia City] was undesirable and they should retire."[9]

Three days prior to the Virginia City vigilante organizational meeting, a vigilante group led by John Lott, William Clark, and James Williams was established just a mile away in Nevada City. The Nevada City and Virginia City Committees were soon merged and Wilbur Sanders, in absentia, was elected as "Official Prosecutor" of the Alder Gulch Vigilance Committee. It was also during this period Sanders wrote to his sister an immodest account of his recent exploits, noting that he expected to be paid "between $200 and $300" for his services as prosecutor at the Ives trial. Sanders also blustered that "there was talk of buying me a watch and chain," and grandiosely noted that, among the several attorneys in the area, "I am...the only lawyer of the Union persuasion in the territory...and, of course, I think the best."[10]

A few days following Sanders' return to Bannack, a small posse of the Alder Gulch Vigilantes paid him a late night visit with some rather astonishing news...Sheriff Henry Plummer and his deputies, Ned Ray and Buck Stinson, had been identified as part of an elaborately organized gang of road agents. With some difficulty, a group of Bannack men were recruited to supplement the Virginia City contingent, and the accused road agents—without benefit of a trial—were hanged on gallows which had been built at the direction of Plummer. This appears to have been the only vigilante execution in which Sanders participated, although he would proudly acknowledge his membership in the vigilante organization throughout his remaining years. Some sources also indicate that Sidney Edgerton observed this extra-legal execution and did nothing to intervene.[11]

The Sanders family moved to Virginia City in early February of 1864, and Wilbur formed a law partnership with Jerry Cook. Harriet noted the comparative elegance of the family's new home, a log cabin of three rooms "a sleeping room, a kitchen and a dining room..." [and that Wilbur] had been so extravagant as to purchase a cast iron cook stove." The house was located "about ¾ mile from town...[near] a spring of fine clean water." And, unlike their home in Bannack, this cabin had lathed, plastered and painted walls and "smooth" floors. Harriet would write that: "...I shall never forget the laugh we had when a friend called one day and said that she had heard the neighbors say that Mrs. Sanders was very aristocratic, living as she did in a house of three rooms, and possessing a [rocking] chair and cast-iron stove and a carpet." A few years later, however, Wilbur would provide even more elegant accommodations for his family.[12]

Soon after the Sanders' move to Virginia City, the Territory of Montana was created thanks in large part to the efforts of Sidney Edgerton—and perhaps a bit of subterfuge. In late January of 1864, and with the support of several influential men in the Bannack and Virginia City area, Edgerton returned to Washington, D.C., to lobby his former Congressional colleagues to create a new territory from the existing Idaho Territory. In addition to the gold dust and nuggets which he carried from Bannack (sewn into his overcoat), Edgerton received an imposing supplement in early February. Francis M. Thompson, en route from Bannack to visit his family in Massachusetts, stopped in Washington to apprise himself of the progress toward gaining territorial status. Thompson carried a misshapen retort (bar) of gold which Edgerton persuaded him to entrust to his care. Edgerton subsequently made it a custom to carry the retort, and to prominently display it upon the desk which he had been graciously provided on the floor of the House of Representatives. Edgerton later acknowledged that he did nothing to dissuade the many admiring Congressmen and visitors of their impression that the imposing lump of pure gold was a nugget, rather than a malformed bar.[13]

Edgerton's lobbying efforts to establish a new territory were successful, in large part attributable to the support of William H. Wallace (Idaho's Territorial Delegate) and Ohio Representative James Ashley, Chairman of the House Committee on Territories. While there was some concern expressed regarding the proposed name of "Montana" for the new territory, perhaps the most difficult hurdle was a proposed amendment which would extend voting privileges in the territory to any male citizen above the age of twenty-one. After a good deal of wrangling, it was determined to substitute a compromise which provided that—for the initial territorial election—only White, male citizens above the age of 21 would be eligible to vote, but that the territory's residents could subsequently change the terms of suffrage. Thus resolved, the Montana Organic Act was approved on May 26, 1864, exactly one year to the day following the original discovery of gold at Alder Gulch.

Not too surprisingly, Edgerton was appointed by President Lincoln to serve as the Territorial Governor, and as one of Edgerton's first order of business upon his return to Bannack was to make arrangements for the first election of legislators; which became a mud-slinging free-for-all. Wilbur Fisk Sanders was often—quite literally—center stage in the election proceedings as a candidate for the post of Territorial Delegate, and flag-bearer for the Radical Republicans. Sanders and Sidney Edgerton were outspoken critics of the Democrats, labeling them as "traitors" and "uncultivated savages." Sanders warned that "if the so-called Democrats get into office, not even a breath of air would go untaxed… and [one] would not be able to go [from Virginia City] to Nevada [City] without encountering a toll gate." Despite the effusive—and very biased—support of the *Montana Post*, the Democrats earned an equal number of seats in the legislature and, despite some ballot chicanery by Edgerton, Sanders failed in his bid for the position of Territorial Delegate. It would prove to be the first of several humbling elections for the Republican Party in early Montana, and the first of several unsuccessful runs for various political offices for Wilbur Sanders.[14]

Just prior to the seating of the first legislative session, an edict was issued by General Irvin McDowell, U.S. Army commander for the region, that all Indians associated with attacks against Whites and their property were to be arrested and handed over to civil authorities. Although this directive was a prime example of how generally ignorant non-resident authorities were of the reality of the Western frontier, Governor Edgerton made an effort to comply. Edgerton issued a proclamation calling for the establishment of a territorial militia, and appointed his nephew to the rank of Colonel; an honorific which Sanders proudly utilized for the remainder of his life. The request for volunteers was, however, widely ignored, and the militia never materialized as a viable force.

Although he was not an elected legislator, Colonel Sanders was certainly not forgotten by the Legislature in its first session. Held in bitterly cold weather at Bannack, the legislature appointed Sanders to serve on the committee to select—and acquire—a site for the capitol building in Virginia City; which the legislature had selected as the first capital of the territory. Sanders was also one of the leading proponents of the legislature establishing the Montana Historical Society; signed into law on February 2, 1865. The first meeting of the Society would convene in Virginia City on March 25, 1865, and Sanders was elected President; a position he held until 1891.[15]

Meanwhile, Edgerton was struggling in his tenuous relationship with the legislators who stubbornly held their own opinions regarding how the new territory should be shaped. Edgerton refused to temper his pre-election rhetoric and delivered a tirade at the opening of the First Session against any and all who would oppose the Union, followed by a demand that all legislators take the "Iron Clad" oath. Near the end of the Session, he similarly drew criticism from both sides of the political aisle, with his veto of the legislators' bill to revise apportionment; a duty specifically prescribed to them by the terms of the Montana Organic Act. The failure to pass this bill prior to adjournment left the legislature in a state of limbo and management of the territory in the hands of the federally appointed (Republican) officers…which may well have been Edgerton's intention.[16]

By September of 1865, Edgerton had clearly tired of the role as Governor, and the majority of Montana's residents had tired of him. Relief—for both parties—arrived via stagecoach on September 23rd. Thomas Francis Meagher had been appointed to serve as Territorial Secretary by President Johnson, and Meagher (who was already en route to Montana) had eagerly accepted the assignment. Meagher, a native of Ireland, was a devoted Catholic, a strident Irish nationalist, a Civil War general of the Union Army, and, quite literally, a well-known figure throughout the world. Oh, and he was a celebrated escaped convict from the British penal colony at Tasmania.[17]

As he stepped down from the stagecoach, many of Bannack's residents must have been struck by the dramatic difference between their new Secretary and Governor Edgerton. Although only five years younger, one can assume that his dark hair, bright blue eyes and ebullient manner would have presented a startling contrast to Edgerton. It would be Meagher, however, who received the greatest surprise. Within hours of his arrival, Edgerton announced that he and his family were leaving "for a few months" to return to Ohio, thereby leaving Meagher (the second-ranking federal appointee) in the dual role as the Territorial Secretary and acting governor. It is certainly very questionable what sort of working relationship Edgerton and Meagher may have been able to forge, but it soon became obvious that Meagher would never have Wilbur Fisk Sanders as a close, personal friend.[18]

In the meantime, Sanders had continued to build his reputation—for better and worse—as a skillful and aggressive attorney, and the tirelessly devoted advocate of the Republican Party. During the course of one particularly bitter campaign, Sanders had so offended and enraged Samuel Word, a Democratic opponent and native Southerner, that Word challenged Sanders to a duel. Sanders must have quickly calculated that to refuse the challenge would have meant an embarrassing loss of respect, so he accepted. As customary, the recipient of a challenge was entitled to the choice of weapons, and Sanders cleverly avoided bloodshed and dialed down the temperature on the situation by his choice of weapons: "the war whoop of a Nez Perce Indian." Despite his wit and best efforts, however, Sanders was painfully aware by the end of the territory's Third Legislative Session, that the Republicans—largely as result of Meagher's leadership—were near the point of totally losing political control of the Montana Territory. In response, Sanders decided to make a bold assault.[19]

Accompanied by Lyman Munson (a Federal Associate Justice for Montana), Sanders traveled to Washington in early January of 1867. Against the backdrop of the unprecedented drama of the impeachment proceedings against President Andrew Johnson, Sanders and Munson lobbied the predominately Republican Congressional legislators to reconsider the Organic Act by which the Montana Territory was established. Sanders and Munson argued that the Act did not provide Acting Governor Meagher the authority to call the Second and Third legislatures into session. The House would subsequently pass a bill which called for minor adjustments to the Organic Act, but retained the validity of the Second and Third Sessions. The bill was not agreeable to the Senate and, after several back-room meetings, an extraordinary bill was approved by Congress on March 2nd. The bill provided that: "all acts passed at the two sessions of the so-called legislative assembly of the Territory of Montana…are hereby disapproved and declared null and void.…" Furthermore, in an obvious personal victory for Judge Munson, the bill also amended the original Organic Acts of Idaho, Utah, and Montana to provide that the federally appointed judges would now determine the boundaries of their judicial districts rather than being assigned by the territorial legislatures.[20]

When Sanders returned to Montana in early May, he agreed to address a public meeting in Virginia City to explain his actions. Standing before a crowd of hundreds of angry residents assembled at Content's Corner, Sanders attempted to vindicate his role by stating he was motivated on behalf of "the poor orphan" (Montana) and that because of his efforts that it was possible to procure new laws "which should be a reproof to the apostles of disorder." If Sanders entertained any thoughts that he would be embraced by an appreciative host, however, he was sadly mistaken. To most Montanans—as expressed by even the normally partisan *Montana Post*—it was a stinging disappointment that a group of politicians back East had erased the good-faith efforts of their duly elected territorial representatives. Sanders' role in this landmark event earned him the everlasting enmity of many Montanans, and the next territorial legislative session not only passed a joint resolution protesting the action of Congress, but also changed the name of Edgerton County to Lewis & Clarke County, and re-approved virtually all the laws enacted by the Second and Third Sessions. And, as fate would have it, it would only be a few weeks before Wilbur Sanders would—this time inadvertently—make another trip which would again place him in the center of a lasting controversy in Montana history.[21]

In the Spring of 1866, Harriet Sanders (with her 3 children) had also traveled East for an extended visit with her family. After Wilbur was finished working his magic in Washington, he met the family in Ohio, and made arrangements to return to Montana. The family boarded the steamboat *Abeona*, leaving St. Joseph, Missouri, the morning of April 24, 1867. En route, Wilbur disembarked at Omaha, and later re-boarded the boat on June 16, as it made its laboriously slow journey against a strong current and high water. Wilbur remained on board for twelve days before again leaving to travel overland to await the *Abeona's* arrival at Fort Benton.

Also arriving in Fort Benton, on July 1, was Thomas Francis Meagher. Governor Green Clay Smith had asked Meagher to meet a shipment of arms from St. Louis which were intended for use by the Montana militia. En route, Meagher had become very ill, remaining for six days at Sun River before feeling well enough to complete the ride to Ft. Benton, where he arrived "perspiring and unsteady" and "didn't seem to be in the best of health." Among those who came to greet Meagher as he rested during the day in the store of Isaac Baker was Wilbur Fisk Sanders and Johnny Doran. Doran was the captain/pilot of the riverboat *G.A. Thompson*, which had arrived only a few hours earlier and was now docked near Baker's store. Doran had met Meagher the previous year, when his wife, Elizabeth, had been one of Doran's passengers and had also arrived at Ft. Benton. From this point of commonly accepted circumstances, contradictory accounts—and many rumors— diverge regarding the remaining hours of Meagher's life.[22]

The most detailed, albeit disparate, accounts of Meagher's final day were later provided by Sanders and Doran. Although it is possible that the truth of events lie somewhere between the versions of Sanders and Doran, the unmistakable consequence of the night of July 1-2 is that Meagher disappeared and was presumed drowned. Rumors began to swirl throughout the territory as news of the tragedy quickly spread, many of which linked Sander's presence in Ft. Benton to Meagher's disappearance. Some have opined that Sanders' primary motivation in presenting his account of events was an effort to respond to those rumors and to cast himself in the role of Meagher's good friend. And, in doing so, his detractors may forgive and forget his previous disparaging comments toward Meagher, and Sanders' role in the nullification of the Second and Third legislative sessions. While there are certainly details of Sanders' account which suggest they were based upon second—or third party information, any direct involvement with Meagher's death by Sanders doesn't seem reasonable; although the rumors still persist.[23]

After 73 days en route, the *Abeona* finally arrived at Fort Benton on July 4th, and the Sanders family left "at once" for Virginia City and their newly completed home. After two days of rest in Helena from the rigors of steamboat and stage travel with three young boys (ages 7, 5, 3), one can almost feel the excitement and relief from the exhausting trip in Harriet's diary entry of July 14th: "Slept in new house last night first time." As had previously been the case, however, Wilbur increasingly found that his client base was moving, and he was spending less of his professional time in Virginia City.[24]

In the fall of 1868, Sanders and his family joined the slow, but steady exodus from Virginia City to Helena. Sanders quickly became a prominent figure in not only the political milieu of Helena, but also cultivated his territory-wide contacts as an active member and officer of cultural and fraternal organizations; including the Montana Historical Society, the Society of Montana Pioneers, the Masonic Lodge of Montana, the Montana Bar Association and the Grand Army of the Republic. Sanders also served as the founding president of Montana Wesleyan College.

One of the other endeavors in which Sanders became embroiled would be the location of the territorial capital. As noted previously, while the Organic Act authorized the First Session of the territorial legislature to select the site of the capital, subsequent legislatures could submit the question to the general population. And, the legislatures of 1866, 1867 and 1868 had passed resolutions proposing to move the capital from Virginia City. None of those resolutions had succeeded, however, and with each failure the animus of Helena's residents had justifiably grown increasingly bitter.[25]

In February of 1874, the Eighth Session of the legislature passed yet another resolution which would move the capital—specifically, to the city of Helena—to a vote of the people in August. Prominent among those who had been eagerly supporting the cause of relocating the capital was none other than former Virginia City resident, Wilbur Fisk Sanders. The *Madisonian* made no effort to hide its contempt for the man it felt had betrayed the interests of the town where he got his start. The newspaper noted that Sanders "has in preparation a lecture to be entitled 'The Acquisition of the Capital,' [which] Mr. Sanders is peculiarly fitted to explain...." The paper further noted that "Mr. S. has the reputation of being a wicked man—and if the *Herald's* readers find many crooked truths in that sheet, due allowance must be made therefore."[26]

The 1874 referendum was a bitterly contested issue and the voting process in August was brimming with irregularities. Almost immediately after the polls closed, the people of Helena began celebrating their victory based upon unofficial returns. A large celebration convened at the St. Louis Hotel where Sanders gave "an eloquent address;" which one presumes may have been well re-hearsed. The celebratory joy of Helena, however, was short-lived. When the official canvass of the votes was made on September 2, there were several issues regarding the balloting, but the end result was that Virginia City was declared to have been retained as the site of Montana's capital. The *Madisonian* crowed that "Helena...[is] agitated beyond endurance...[and that] Helena people are as fond of making resolutions as little ducks are of paddling in water."[27]

Within a few days following the announcement of the election results, Sanders led a small delegation representing Helena to Virginia City for a meeting with Governor Potts, at which they demanded a re-canvass of the ballots. Their request was denied, which led to an appeal before the Montana Territorial Court followed by another appeal before the U.S. Supreme Court which directed the question back to Montana. The Territorial Court ruled the ballots should be re-canvassed, which resulted in Helena being declared the capital. Although it may not have been wise for Sanders to visit Virginia City in the aftermath of this decision, the exercise certainly enhanced his stature in Helena. Meanwhile, the *Madisonian* bitterly chronicled the painful transition: "to the jingle of a string of bells on a mule team, the last remains and remnants of the moving Capital of [the] Montana Territory passed down Wallace Street on a couple of Murphy freight wagons. It was an indifferent lot of old second-hand chairs, tables and three-legged stools...[but] when it gets to Helena the Herald will call the truck a large invoice of valuable furniture...So be it."[28]

Sanders home in Helena (built 1875)

Of course, aside from his legal practice (which included a lucrative post as attorney for the Northern Pacific Railroad) Sanders' focus was always fixed upon the affairs of Montana's Republican Party—sometimes to its chagrin. Over the years, the strident rhetoric and political machinations of Sanders would offend many Montanans, including Governor Benjamin Potts (himself a Republican) who opined that Sanders was "the most unscrupulous man who ever disgraced the legal profession...no satellite of W.F. Sanders shall hold office in Montana if I can prevent it." And although Sanders was consistently defeated in his bids for election as Territorial Delegate, he was elected to serve in the Territorial House of Representatives from 1872-80. His political endurance was ultimately rewarded in 1890...predictably amidst great controversy.[29]

After admission to statehood in 1889, Montana held its first election for the U.S. Senate which—true to course in early Montana elections—

171

ended in dispute. Unable to resolve the deadlock, the State Senate sent two Republicans (Sanders and Thomas Power) and two Democrats to Washington. The impasse was resolved by a vote of the Republican-controlled U.S. Senate, which seated both Republicans. Lots were drawn between Power and Sanders in order to stagger the terms of the newly appointed Senators and Sanders, literally, drew the short straw; which gave him only three years in office. Sanders returned to Montana following his brief stint in the Senate and was never re-elected to public office. One thing Sanders apparently never lost was his acerbic wit. Following one of his frequent and convincing political defeats, he offered Helena's citizens one of his classic retorts: "When I was nominated by the Republican convention…it was said around town that 'you could beat Sanders with a yellow dog,' and you did."[30]

In what would be one of his final political battles, Sanders found himself fighting fellow Republicans rather than Democrats. When Charles Hartman was elected to his second term as Montana's U.S. Representative in 1894, the battle over "Free Silver" was already brewing and Hartman—a Republican—expressed his opposition to the Party's stance. When the Montana Republican Party Convention convened at Helena in early September of 1896, the Party was already badly fractured between those led by Wilbur Fisk Sanders (who supported the repeal of the Sherman Silver Purchase Act), and those who opposed repeal; including Hartman. Consequently, the convention split into two tickets: the traditional Republicans and the new "Silver Republicans" Party.

Bozeman's *Avant Courier* was generous in its praise of a speech Sanders made in Bozeman on October 31, 1896. The paper reported that the hour and half speech by Sanders was "a masterpiece of sound logic and eloquence." The damage, however, may have already been done to Sanders' credibility by an earlier editorial in the *Courier* which called into question Sanders' political financing: "It is hardly to be supposed that Colonel Sanders spoke unadvisedly…when he said that the Northern Pacific railroad contributed $10,000 towards Montana's senatorial campaign last winter. For several years…the talented Colonel occupied quite a prominent seat at the Northern Pacific's financial pie counter, himself…It is barely possible, however, that the Colonel may have the happy faculty of forgetting…the same corporation nursed in its generous bosom about $55,000 worth of anxiety to see its own attorney returned to the U.S. Senate."[31]

Similar to the current political landscape, there were also reports at that time that outside interests were sending contributions to help the Republican cause, to which Hartman famously replied: "Montana needs some extra circulation…let them send it up; it will do me no harm, and it may do Montana some good." And, less than a week after Sanders' stirring speech in Bozeman, the *Courier* would have to sheepishly acknowledge that "the Republicans in this county and state were manifestedly beaten." When the final election tally was reported, Hartman had received 33,942 votes compared with his opponent's 9,492. In all probability, Sanders' role in this election cost him an appointment to the Montana Supreme Court, a possible outcome which he must have acknowledged. Nevertheless, he still showed the courage to fight the good fight—even when it wasn't a battle supported by most Montanans. Perhaps his years of accumulated political baggage was becoming too much an encumbrance for the old War Horse of the Republican Party. The *Dillon Tribune* would later opine that "[Sanders] was loud, always to his own worldly detriment, in his condemnation of political dishonesty or fraud, and within his own party, he oftentimes stood alone upon a separate platform."[32]

For several years it appears that Sanders had been a benefactor to the old Alder Gulch Vigilante, John X. Beidler. "X" had made his home in Helena after serving as a Deputy U.S. Marshall, Federal Collector, and—most probably—an organizer of some of the vigilante activity in early Helena. Beidler's diary indicates that he subsided on the goodwill of those who provided small gifts of money, rail passes from Sanders, and saloon patrons who would buy drinks in exchange for his colorful stories. X died, alone, in his bed at the Pacific Hotel on January 22, 1890. His funeral expenses ($185.50) were paid by the Society of Montana Pioneers, no doubt at the urging of Sanders, and Sanders delivered a touching eulogy at the Benton St. Cemetery in which he poignantly observed: "The new life did not come to him happily and [X] could not adapt himself to the changed conditions..."[33]

In his last appearances in Virginia City, Sanders served as a co-counsel to the Madison County Attorney in 1898, and again at the appeal trial in 1900, prosecuting Martin Peel for the murder of William Ennis. Sanders' participation in this role would seem to have been compromised by the fact Peel had contacted him for advice regarding his difficulties with Ennis prior to the murder. This point led to what was "the most dramatic scene" in the appeal trial. Peel, in response to a question by Sanders, shook "a trembling hand" at Sanders and asked the judge, "Must I answer this man...this man who sold me out? He did not even condescend to let me know that he had sold my life. If he had not sold me out I would not have brought this disgrace upon myself and my children." At Peel's appeal trial, Sanders would again cross swords with Charles S. Hartman, who was now serving as one Peel's defense attorneys and, once again, Hartman would prevail. After a closing argument by Hartman which the *Madisonian* described as "concise, eloquent and exhaustive," the jury reduced the previous verdict to second degree murder; thereby avoiding the death penalty for Peel.[34]

It seems to have been a widely known secret that, for quite some time, Sanders had been in poor health. As was subsequently reported in the *Helena Herald,* "For about 28 years Col. Sanders had suffered from a cancerous growth of the eye. In December, 1901, he went to Chicago, where an operation for the trouble was performed. It was a dangerous and delicate one, but after months in the hospital he came out, apparently in better health than he had enjoyed for years, and returned to his home in Helena. For some time, it appeared as though he was going to be once more his strenuous self, but after a few months his friends noticed he lacked the activity of former years, and, save on rare occasions, he was not the aggressive man of other days. For several weeks it was believed he could not recover, but all the time there was hope that a change would come for the better...but from the time he was last confined to his home...each day he grew weaker."[35]

In one of his last interviews, Sanders was asked why he had decided to remain in the West when life could have been easier—and more financially rewarding—back East. After a thoughtful pause, Sanders responded: "I went to school with half a dozen boys of my own age who are now captains in Wall Street. They have traveled the 'primrose path' there…while I have stumbled across placer diggings, prospect holes and prickly pears and knocked at the door of Dame Fortune where I was always compelled to leave my card…and yet, these men have told me each time I have gone East that life was nothing but vanity—vanity and vexation of spirit; and so I have come to think that, after all, I have got just about as much out of life as they have."[36]

No doubt it was very gratifying to Sanders when, on February 7, 1905, the Montana legislature voted to establish Sanders County in his honor, and—unlike that of his uncle—it has been an enduring honor. Wilbur Fisk Sanders, a pioneer of Montana and of many of its seminal organizations, died at his home in Helena on July 7, 1905. His death came just three days after a memorial statue in front of the capitol was dedicated to Thomas Francis Meagher, one of his former rivals. Just a few blocks from the Sanders home, it's likely he may have heard the band and cheers of the crowd on the capitol lawn as he lay in his bed. In 1913, Sanders would also receive a spot at the capitol, as he was honored with a memorial statue; largely financed by William A. Clark. Currently located within the capitol building, the statue is inscribed with perhaps one of the briefest, but most memorable statements attributed to Sanders: "Men, Do Your Duty."[37]

Wilbur F. Sanders statue, Montana Capitol

Notes:

**Epigrams: "He was a master…," A.C. McClure;
"The most…," Benjamin F. Potts**

1. Ira a native of Rhode Island; Freedom a native of Connecticut. Harriet attended Lake Erie College, and would later become active in the Women's Suffrage movement.

2. Opposition to arrest orders per Rev. W.W. Alderson, *Avant Courier,* October 28, 1886.

3. "Bannack looked…," Harriet Sanders, Reminiscences.

4. Quotes per H. Sanders, ibid.

5. Ibid.

6. "I got an office…" *Anaconda Standard,* July 28, 1905.

7. "hard to compete," George Bruffey, Eighty-one Years in the West, pg 36.

8. "I am not…," W. Sanders, "History of Early Montana." At least one source, A.B. Davis, would state in interview with *Alder Gulch Times*, September 15, 1899, that it was James Williams who gave command. Frank (who had testified against Ives) and Hilderman were banished from the area.

9. "Several parties…," Ibid. Sanders wrote that the vigilance committee was established December 26th at "a small cabin on Jackson Street, opposite where the Clasby House afterwards stood." He also claimed to have administered an oath of secrecy to 7+ men who were in attendance. H.P.A. Smith & James Thurmond were the attorneys "expelled" by the Vigilantes. Smith would return to Montana, resuming law practice in Helena until his death. Thurmond settled in Texas, serving as mayor of Dallas, and was killed in courtroom during a trial.

10. The William Clark referred to is not William Andrews Clark. "between $200…there was talk…I am…," WFS to sister, December 26, 1863, Sanders & Taylor. Sanders was elected in absentia.

11. The *New York Sun* reported, August 10, 1892, that Plummer was executed for "high treason against the Territory of Montana."

12. Quotes per H. Sanders "Reminisces."

13. Montana Territory establish May 26, 1864. Edgerton in "Edgerton & Lincoln."

14. "traitors" "uncultivated savages," Burlingame & Toole. "if so-called...," *Montana Post*, October 22, 1864. Forney, Dawn in El Dorado. The term "Radical Republicans" refers to those who espoused a particularly punitive attitude toward the States which had seceded and the individuals who had fought with Confederate forces.

15. Legislature in session December 12, 1865-February 9, 1866. Site committee was allotted $200 to purchase a site for the capitol. They purchased a 3 acres plot on the hill directly North of the present-day county courthouse site committee also included George Christman and R.B. Parrot. The Montana Historical Society is the second oldest historical society West of the Mississippi River.

16. The Iron Clad Oath required a pledge that one had never borne arms against the Union, nor offered any form of encouragement or support to those who had. Although this created a good deal of rancor among the legislators, only one (John H. Rogers of Madison County) refused to sign.

17. The post of Territorial Secretary, which Samuel Hauser had sought, had been previously offered to—and refused by—Rev. Henry Torsey of Maine and John Coburn of Indiana.

18. "for a few months," *Montana Post*, September 30, 1865.

19. "the war whoop...," *Anaconda Standard*, October 16, 1905.

20. "all acts...," U.S. Statutes, 39th Congress, 2nd Session.

21. "poor orphan, "reproof," *Montana Post*, May 11, 1867. Spence, "Clarke" was changed to "Clark" in 1905.

22. "perspiring...didn't seem...," I.G. Baker interview in *Montana Standard*, September 9, 1901. Green Clay Smmith was appointed Governor on July 13, 1866.

23. Sources of accounts per H.F. Sanders, A History of Montana.

24. "Slept in new...," H. Sanders, "Reminiscences."

25. Although the 1866 election overwhelmingly and legitimately favored Virginia City, the 1869 election results are questionable. The resolution of 1867 was vetoed by Governor Green Clay Smith.

26. "has in preparation...," *Madisonian,* February 28, 1874.

27. "an eloquent...," Campbell. "Helena agitated...," *Madisonian,* September 12, 1875.

28. "to the jingle...," *Madisonian,* October 9, 1875.

29. "most unscrupulous...," Potts to R.R. Hayes, December 28, 1878 (D.S. Wade file, Department of Justice, National Archives).

30. "When I was...," Sanders and Taylor, Biscuits & Badmen,

31. "a masterpiece...," *Avant Courier,* November 7, 1896. "It is hardly...," Avant Courier October 12, 1895.

32. "Montana needs some...," *Anaconda Standard,* September 19, 1896. Senator (OH) Mark Hanna, the "boss" of the Republican Party was the presumed source of campaign funds. "the Republicans in...," *Avant Courier,* November 7, 1896. "was loud...," *Dillon Tribune,* July 17, 1905.

33. "the new life...," unidentified news clipping in Beidler mss (SC 300). Beidler's remains were later re-interred to Forestvale Cemetery by the Society of Montana Pioneers.

34. "the most dramatic...must I answer...?" The *Madisonian,* June

35. "For about 28...," *Helena Herald,* July 8, 1905.

36. "I went to school...," Sanders mss, (MC 53).

37. The resolution to create Sanders County was introduced by Amos Buck, a Republican Senator of Ravalli County. Marcus Daly led the effort to create the statue of Meagher, and it was widely advertised that all contributions to the memorial fund would be accepted —except from Wilbur Fisk Sanders. The bronze statue of Sanders was created by Sigvald Asbjornsen of Chicago, and paid for by William A. Clark. It was originally placed in the capitol building on June 23, 1913. Harriet would die on April 25, 1909, and was buried beside Wilbur at Forestvale Cemetery.

Sources:
Beidler, John X. mss (SC 300), Montana Historical Society.

Blake, Henry N. "Wilbur Fisk Sanders," in History of Montana, Vol. 2, by Harriet F. Sanders.

Burlingame, Merrill and K. Ross Toole. <u>A History of Montana, Vol. 1.</u>

Campbell, William. <u>From the Quarries of the Last Chance Gulch, Vol. 1.</u>

Edgerton, Sidney. "Edgerton and Lincoln," edited by Anne McDonnell. Montana Magazine of Western History, Vol. 1, no. 4.

Forney, Gary R. <u>Dawn in El Dorado: The Early Mining Camps and Settlement of the Montana Territory.</u>

_____. <u>Thomas Francis Meagher, Irish Rebel, American Yankee, Montana Pioneer.</u>

_____. "Bozeman's Charles Hartman," *Montana Pioneer*, March 2012.

_____ . "The Trials of Martin Peel," Papers of the Fifteenth Annual History Conference of The Gallatin Historical Society. (2003).

Lane, Samuel. <u>Fifty Years and Over of Akron and Summit County, Ohio.</u> (1892).

Madisonian

McClure, Col. A.C. "Wilbur Fisk Sanders," <u>Contributions to the Montana Historical Society, Vol. 8.</u> (1917)

Montana Historical Society, "Pioneers' Reminiscences 1884-1943." (MC #64, MHS)

Montana Post

Potts, Benjamin. Letter to Rutherford B. Hayes, National Archives, Department of the Interior.

Sanders, Harriet P. "Reminisces of My Trip Across the Plains and of My Early Life in Montana." (SC #1254), Montana Historical Society.

Sanders, Helen F. <u>History of Montana, Vol. 1.</u>

Sanders, Wilbur Fisk mss. "History of Early Montana," (MC 53, bx 4, file 8) MHS

Special Collections of Montana State University.

Spence, Clark <u>Territorial Politics and Government in Montana 1864-89.</u>

Sanders, II, W.F. and Robert Taylor. <u>Biscuits and Badmen.</u>

Thane, Jr. James L. <u>A Governor's Wife on the Montana Frontier.</u>

Photo credits:

Portrait; rootsweb.ancestry.com
Sidney Edgerton; Wikipedia.com
Sanders home in Helena; author.
Wilbur Fisk Sanders statue; author

Joseph and Maria Slade

"He was a fearless man, the bravest I think I ever saw...
very intelligent, and, when sober, one of the most
pleasant men to talk to you could find."

"She was a large, fine-looking woman,
raised in Carthage, Missouri."

Freight wagon (c1864)

By the Spring of 1864, farmers, ministers, and schoolteachers had begun to appear with increasing frequency in the newly created Territory
of Montana. This was, however, first and foremost, a land of mining
camps and the population was still dominated by many men—and a
few women—who preferred to live life on the edge of civilization and
on their own terms. Perhaps none are better examples of those legendary "free spirits" than Jack Slade and his wife, Maria. Jack and Maria
arrived in Virginia City in the early autumn of 1863. Jack's fearsome
reputation, however, had preceded him.

Joseph Albert Slade was a native of Carlyle, Illinois a settlement
which his father, Charles, was instrumental in establishing. A native

of England, Charles lived in Alexandria, Virginia, before settling in southern Illinois. Charles became a prosperous and well-respected community member who operated a ferry, built a mill dam, opened a mercantile store, was the area Postmaster, and served as a school trustee. He also employed "19 Free Negroes and 5 slaves." Charles married Mary D. Kain, and built a home that was considered "a mansion" for her and his family. Joseph, who would be known as "Jack," was born in 1829, the youngest of four children, to Charles and Mary. His older siblings were Charles, Jr., William, and Virginia. Jack distinguished himself at an early age as the most "spirited" member of the family.[1]

After serving two terms in the Illinois legislature, Charles Slade was elected to the U.S. House of Representatives in 1830. Tragically, however, he became ill during his return to Carlyle from Washington in 1832, and died en route at Vincennes, Indiana. The cause of his death was reported as Cholera. Perhaps this loss of a strong father at such an early age contributed to Jack's streak of unruliness.[2]

Jack left home in May of 1847, to serve with a company of volunteers in the United States' war against Mexico. It is possible, as some have written, that his enlistment was motivated (perhaps encouraged by authorities) as a result of a dreadful incident in which Jack—along with some other boys—threw rocks at passing townspeople from a hidden site. Tragically, one of their targets was struck in the head and died, and Jack was held to blame for throwing the deadly stone. What is certain, however, and possibly what would have served as stimulus for Jack's enlistment in Co. A of the First Illinois Volunteers, is that his older brother, Charles, had previously enlisted for service in that unit. Jack was assigned to work as a teamster for the Company, which served as the training ground for his later career. It appears that neither Charles nor Jack made it any closer to Mexico than Santa Fe; where Charles became ill and died. Jack was given an honorable discharge from service on October 16, 1848, and returned to Carlyle. Interestingly, in light of his later reputation, Jack's discharge certificate notes his height at 5'6". Perhaps more ominously, the certificate cites the color of his eyes as "black."[3]

Upon his return to Carlyle, Jack found that his mother had re-married during his absence to Elias Deming; a respected figure in the area. Typical of many young men who have had the experience of going off to a war, however, Jack was not content to return to the tedium of his former life and began to dream of life in the West. In February of 1849, his step-father wrote to the War Department on behalf of Jack, requesting a warrant of 160 acres in recognition of his war service. Elias mentioned in his request that Jack—no doubt inspired by news of recent gold discoveries—was "disposed to go to California." The warrant was granted on March 14…and perhaps not a moment too soon.[4]

There are several accounts which relate that Jack got into a fight at a Carlyle watering hole which ended with him killing a man. These accounts indicate, as previously, that no charges were filed against Jack. It isn't unreasonable, however, to imagine that this high-spirited young man was strongly encouraged by many to proceed with his plans to seek his fortune in California—or anywhere other than Carlyle. Jack's route to California (if that was his intended destination) took him through Carthage, Missouri where, in the Spring of 1849, he met a young woman by the name of Maria Virginia Dale. Jack became enamored with Maria, whom many would remember as an attractive young woman with a "commanding presence." Maria would prove herself to be a strong woman with fortitude more than equal to the task of coping with Jack's reckless ways. With an obvious admiration, Nathaniel Langford later described Maria: "She possessed many personal attractions. Her figure was queenly, and her movements the perfection of grace. Her countenance was lit up by a pair of burning black eyes, and her hair, black as the raven's wing, fell in rich curls over her shoulders. She was of powerful organization, and having passed her life upon the borders, knew how to use the rifle and revolver, and could perform as many dexterous feats in the saddle as the boldest hunter that roamed the plains."[5]

Jack's relationship with Maria was complicated, however, by the presence of another suitor. Simply described as "a railroad man," this fellow contested Slade's romantic interest in Maria to the point it led to a physical confrontation. Alex Davis would relate that the matter was settled when Jack "either killed him outright or beat him so seriously that he died…." In any event, Jack and Maria would subsequently elope (and perhaps escape prosecution) to Texas, where they were married.[6]

It isn't certain how long the couple remained in Texas, but by the Spring of 1858 Jack was working as a freighter between Kearney, Nebraska, and Salt Lake City. One can reasonably assume he had earned a reputation as a very competent employee inasmuch as he was the "boss" of a wagon train when Granville Stuart was introduced to Jack. Stuart would recall that several trains, including the one of 16 wagons led by Slade, were camped one evening at Henry's Fork (present-day Wyoming). Stuart wrote that: "the wagon boss [Slade] had gotten drunk at Green River, about 15 miles back, [and] was cussing one of the drivers about some trifle, the driver had talked back and the 'boss' drew his revolver and shot the man dead." This is the first evidence of what would become a dangerous pattern for Jack.[7]

By late 1858, or early 1859, Slade was employed by Russell, Majors & Waddell as one of five men hired to establish 190 stations and recruit riders for the Pony Express. Slade named one of the stations which he established "Virginia Dale Station," and it became the residence of Maria and Jack when he wasn't patrolling his route. It is widely accepted that Jack was soon recognized as a dependable, fearless, and fiercely devoted employee. William ("Buffalo Bill") Cody—whom Jack would hire as a Pony Express rider—would later write: "[Slade] was easily the best superintendent on the line." Perhaps as evidence of Cody's statement, Slade would be soon offered another significant appointment.[8]

When Russell, Majors & Waddell collapsed in 1861 (largely due to the economic failure of the Pony Express), the company's assets were purchased by Ben Holladay, president of the Overland Stage Company. Some reports indicate that it was none other than Mr. Holladay who hired Jack Slade to re-purpose the Pony Express stations to function as stagecoach stations. Slade was given increasingly important responsibilities— which he capably handled—and he was rewarded with an appointment to the position of Division Agent with the Overland Stage Company. Slade was assigned to an especially perilous stretch of the Overland route known as the Sweetwater Division, which stretched between Kearney and Salt Lake City…very familiar territory to Jack.[9]

Overland Stage Company, Sweetwater Division

Robberies and "lost" equipment and livestock had plagued the Sweetwater Division since its inception as a Pony Express route. Jack, with a few handpicked assistants, quickly, decisively and ruthlessly established order along his assigned division. Although probably exaggerated, Slade's reputation for dispensing justice became a very effective deterrent to would-be robbers and horse thieves. Thomas Dimsdale was among those who would provide testament to Slade's fearsome celebrity. Dimsdale would succinctly capture this formidable reputation by writing that: "[Slade] was feared a great deal more, generally, than the Almighty, from Kearney, west." Slade appears to have also extended his own authority to include administering punishment to those who committed crimes other than those related to the Overland. In one such instance, Jack not only tracked down and killed three men who were involved in the murder of a doctor, but provided financial aid to the doctor's widow and children.[10]

The one incident which perhaps most firmly established Slade's fearsome reputation—and is well documented—involved Jules Beni; commonly known as "old Jules." Beni was the manager of an Overland Company stage station that he had originally established as a trading post village, and which bore the name, Julesburg. Long before they arrived at this site, wagon train immigrants were commonly forewarned that Julesburg was a place where they needed to carefully watch their belongings, including livestock, and where they could find the "vilest of liquor at two bits a glass." In short, Julesburg's sobriquet as the

"Wickedest City in the West" appears to have been fairly earned and well deserved.[11]

Since the opening of the Overland route, there had been numerous losses of Overland Company equipment and stock reported from the Julesburg station. Mr. Beni always attributed these crimes to Indian raids or to some unknown thieves. Apparently with good cause, however, Slade suspected that it was actually Beni who was responsible for stealing the property and dismissed Beni from his lucrative post as station manager. Angered by his dismissal, and perhaps fearful of an even more permanent termination, Beni decided that his best course of action was to take the initiative.[12]

In the Spring of 1860, Jules Beni made a deadly early morning ambush upon an unarmed Jack Slade, shooting him six times with a revolver and then emptying both barrels of a shotgun into him before leaving Slade for dead. Slade's friends recovered his body and, after extensive medical care (including time in a St. Louis hospital), Jack remarkably recovered...and returned to Julesburg with eight slugs remaining in his body and a deep desire for revenge. Without going into greater detail, Slade made it a point to inflict a lingering, painful death upon Jules Beni, followed by cutting off Jules' ears—one of which Jack thereafter carried in his vest pocket as a watch fob.[13]

It was soon after Slade's execution of Jules Beni that a young man on his way West—and his way to a career as a noted author and humorist—had the opportunity to meet Mr. Slade. Mark Twain (Samuel Clemens) accompanied his brother on a journey to the Nevada Territory in the Summer of 1861. En route, as Twain recounted, they "... rattled up to a stage station and sat down to breakfast. The most gentlemanly appearing, quiet and affable officer we had yet found along the road in the Overland Company's service was the person who sat at the head of the table. [Slade] was so friendly and so gentle-spoken that I warmed to him in spite of his awful history. We left him with only 26 dead people to account for, and I felt a tranquil satisfaction in the thought that, in so judiciously taking care of No. 1 at that breakfast table, I had pleasantly escaped being No. 27."[14]

Twain's observation of Slade was very consistent with most all who met him, with the obvious exception of those who attempted to prey upon the Overland Stage Company. And although commonly described as personable—even charming—by his many friends and business acquaintances, everyone also acknowledged that Slade had a "Dr. Jekyll and Mr. Hyde" personality. The potion that released Slade's dark side was whiskey. After lubricating his system with a generous portion of rot-gut whiskey, Slade would frequently create a path of destruction upon saloons and other properties and, occasionally, innocent by-standers. These episodes appear to have increased in both frequency and violence following his near-death experience at the hands of Jules Beni. To his credit, however, once he sobered up, Slade would apologetically return to the scene of his crimes and make restitution for the damages. One particularly outrageous spree at the military post of Fort Halleck, in which he caused considerable damage to the sutler's building appears to have been the proverbial "last straw." Although he did not physically harm anyone during this incident, the Overland Stage Company determined that it no longer required the services of Joseph Slade.[15]

Slade resumed his career as a freighter, and in the early Spring of 1863 encountered James Williams. Williams was serving as "Captain" of a train of miner bound for the Idaho mines, and was a man who would become a significant figure in the Slade story. Later that year, Slade secured a contract to transport a supply of goods for Henry Gilbert to the new gold camp of Virginia City. Jack, accompanied by Maria, arrived at the bustling new town in late September—and quickly decided this was an area where they wanted to settle.[16]

Slade established a successful freighting business based in Virginia City. Jack also filed claim on 320 acres, primarily as a hay ranch, "on the banks of the Madison [River] a little southerly from the mouth of Meadow Creek, to which he gave the name 'Ravenswood.'" He also acquired 160 acres and had a stone house and corral built approximately 4½ miles East of Virginia City on Trail Creek, in what Langford described as "one of the wildest dells of the mountains overlooking [the Madison Valley]." Jack named this property the Spring Dale

Ranche, and intended it to serve as the principal residence for him and Maria. Jack also intended this site to serve as the tollhouse for a road that he planned to develop between the Madison Valley and the Alder Gulch mining camps. Jack was generally regarded as a good business-man and, coupled with his charming personality, he soon acquired a large entourage of new friends; "one of his chief cronies was William H. Fairweather, leader of the 'Discovery Party'...a man whom everybody liked."[17]

Slade's Stone House at Spring Dale Ranche (c1959)

Slade also became something of a local hero (and a wealthy man) when, in late summer of 1863, he agreed, "on behalf of merchants in Bannack and Virginia City," to deliver a shipment of badly needed sup-plies which had been off-loaded from a steam boat at a supply post on the Milk River. The merchants advanced Slade a retainer of $3,460; a present-day value of $250,000.00 (+/-). Slade assembled his train and made the journey of approximately 350 miles across rough coun-try, through bad weather, and under the near constant threat of Indian raids. When Jack safely returned with the shipment, it seems many Al-der Gulch residents absolved Jack of his previous sins, and celebrated him as a hero upon his return. Jack's newly found respectability—and

189

perhaps in recognition of his old skills—would earn him membership in a newly established organization.[18]

During Jack's absence, in mid-December of 1863, the brutal murder of a young man (Nicholas Tbalt) occurred in the Ruby Valley; approximately 15 miles from Virginia City. The victim had been employed in mining near Nevada City and was described as having "the engaging friendliness of a bull-terrier puppy [and] Everybody knew him and liked him." This murder set into motion a furious chain of retaliatory events which led not only to the hanging of the man accused of Tbalt's murder (George Ives), but to the establishment of a vigilance committee in Alder Gulch. Several men banded together in an effort to bring an end to the epidemic of "major" crimes taking place in the area, and to punish—with extreme prejudice—the perpetrators of those crimes.[19]

Whether Jack volunteered for service with the Vigilantes, or whether he was sought out by its organizers isn't certain, though his reputation for boldness and experience in handling a firearm would have made him an obvious asset to a group dedicated to arresting and executing those accused of being thieves and murderers. Similarly, it isn't certain how active a member Slade may have been with the Vigilantes. At least one account, however, relates that he was not only a participant, but perhaps a significant force in what must be regarded as the most noteworthy posse of the Alder Gulch Vigilantes.[20]

On December 23, 1863, a Vigilante posse of twenty-four men rode out of Nevada City on what Thomas Dimsdale would label as the "Deer Lodge Scout." To briefly summarize the achievements of this posse, after failing to find the men whom they sought to arrest (including those actually responsible for the murder of Nick Tbalt), the posse would take into custody George Brown and Erastus "Red" Yeager. It was believed these men had acted as road agents or, at the very least, had aided road agents. While at the Laurin stage station, en route to Virginia City, Yeager would subsequently give a confession which provided a surprisingly detailed account of an organized band of road agents under the general leadership of Henry Plummer, Sheriff of the Bannack Mining District. Yeager's confession would provide the justification—

and the individuals targeted—for most of the extra-legal activities of the Alder Gulch Vigilance Committee.

Neither Dimsdale nor Nathaniel Langford in their manuscripts identify Slade as a member of the Deer Lodge posse, but neither do they specifically name any other member; although it is widely acknowledged that the leader of the posse was the former wagon train Captain, James Williams. Author Art Pauley, however, also cites Slade as a key member of the posse and details his role in obtaining Yeager's confession and contributing—perhaps unintentionally—to the controversy which lingers to this day. More details on this episode are provided in the chapter profiling James Williams.

Corner of Jackson & Idaho Streets (Virginia City)

Despite his new surroundings, Slade retained an old and destructive habit. As he had in towns from Nebraska to Utah, Jack would occasionally fall into a bottle and then go on a rampage. Vigilante and lawman John X. Beidler (who also enjoyed his drink and had a reputation for fearlessness) considered Slade a friend, but readily acknowledged his deference to Jack's capacity for violence. Beidler opined that, "Slade was an honest man and did not like a thief, but was a very dangerous man when drinking." As previously, either Jack or Maria would come around to the aggrieved parties and pay for damages following Jack's drunken sprees, but the tolerance of the Virginia City community began to wear thin. Only the intervention of Paris Pfouts and Alexander

Davis seems to have sheltered Jack from retribution.[21]

On the morning of March 9, 1864, X. Beidler noted Slade's arrival at the Washington Billiard Hall where Jack began drinking. Throughout the day, Slade moved from one saloon to another, freely imbibing and collecting friends along the way; including Bill Fairweather. The band of revelers amused themselves by taking over various saloons and firing their guns "promiscuously up and down the streets." Their evening's raucous amusement included attending a theatre performance where Slade shocked the audience by loudly calling for the actress to remove her skirt, and concluded the following morning with the destruction of a milk wagon. It isn't certain whether he was genuinely unaware of Slade's binge—or just ignoring it—but with the dawn's early light, Sheriff Jeremiah M. Fox decided to take action and went to see Judge Alexander Davis, who had been recently elected as judge of the newly established People's Court of Virginia City. Depending upon which version of events one may chose to believe, Sheriff Fox obtained an arrest warrant against either (perhaps both) Jack Slade and/or Bill Fairweather.[22]

William Drannan wrote that Sheriff Fox managed—undoubtedly with very carefully chosen words—to induce the miscreants to appear before Judge Davis, "without knowing the reason." As the accused men stood before Judge Davis, the sheriff began to read the indictment and the situation quickly deteriorated. Although at least one account blames Slade, perhaps the most reliable source—Judge Davis—claimed that it was actually Bill Fairweather who grabbed the arrest warrant from the hands of Sheriff Fox and tore it into pieces. Regardless of who initiated the turmoil, Slade didn't hesitate to join in the fray that finally ended with Judge Davis directing Fairweather and Slade to "go home," and the defendants and their cronies backing out of the room with their hands on their guns.[23]

Bill Fairweather, more from the efforts of friends than of his own initiative, did leave town and went to his cabin to sober up. Slade, however, ignored the sagacious advice of Judge Davis. Meanwhile, news of the brazen defiance of the city court was quickly spreading through the awakening town. A small group of "leading citizens" soon gathered for an impromptu meeting at the mercantile store of Paris Pfouts and Samuel Russell on Wallace Street.

Although it is commonly thought that the events which followed were the actions of the Vigilance Committee, a careful reading of the contemporary accounts suggest otherwise. To begin with, as John Lott would recall, "little attention was paid to whether or not the men present [at the meeting] were members of the Vigilante organization or of the Virginia City Executive Committee." Lott, who was a member of the Executive Committee, further stated that "the meeting was peculiar and hasty…[and] in five minutes they settled the question." Lott acknowledged that he was selected to go to Nevada City for the purpose of convening a similar meeting to present the events which had occurred, and to "determine their attitude as to the punishment" of Slade. Lott's account of an open-air style of meeting, as well as the call for approval from another quarter regarding punishment was hardly in keeping with the Vigilante's precedent, and strongly suggests that this was not an "official" meeting of the Executive Committee, but also confirms a lack of resolve among the principals as to whether Slade's actions were a matter for the Vigilance Committee's consideration. Similarly, Thomas Dimsdale's version of this event clearly indicates that the Virginia City meeting had determined only to arrest Slade. Moreover, Dimsdale wrote that "[Slade's] execution had not been agreed upon, and at that time, would have been negatived, [sic] most assuredly." Nevertheless, events were set into motion by the "peculiar and hasty" meeting which would quickly gather a deadly momentum.[24]

While John Lott made his way to Nevada City, X. Beidler went looking for Slade. If not personally in attendance at Pfout's store, Beidler had obviously learned of the meeting and was anxious about the possible outcome. Probably without much effort, Beidler found Jack in one of his favorite watering holes and warned Slade that he was in great jeopardy and urged him to immediately leave town. Slade, however, casually dismissed Beidler's warning with the flaunting statement that the Vigilantes were "played out." Still determined to save Slade from himself, Beidler went to Jerry Sullivan, another of Slade's friends, and "asked him if he couldn't get Slade to go home." Beidler recalled that

Sullivan was aware of Slade's venomous mood, and initially begged off the mission by saying that, "he couldn't touch [Jack]."[25]

In the meantime, Judge Davis courageously went to visit Slade. Davis, a resolute anti-Vigilante, also urged Slade to leave Virginia City as quickly as possible. Slade responded to Davis' warning by drawing a derringer, placing its barrel against Davis' forehead, and "made a few maudlin remarks about holding the judge as a hostage for his own safety." After a few tense moments, Slade not only withdrew his gun but was also persuaded to surrender his weapons. Shortly thereafter, Slade apparently had an awakening of sober consciousness.[26]

Whether motivated by deepening remorse for his behavior toward Judge Davis, or whether he learned of the evolving situation outside the saloon isn't certain, but Jack left his drinking companions and sought out Judge Davis. Slade found Davis at the Pfouts & Russell store, and began to effusively apologize for his behavior. Davis told Slade that he accepted his apology, and he earnestly repeated his admonition that Jack should leave as quickly as possible. Slade left the store although, perhaps believing that the matter had been satisfactorily resolved, made the fateful decision to remain in town.

While these events were taking place in Virginia City, the meeting John Lott hastily organized in Nevada City had resulted in an angry and wide-spread response to the news of Slade's defiance. As James Williams (the Executive Officer of the Vigilante Committee) organized approximately 200 armed men for a march to Virginia City, Lott rode ahead and urgently assembled a meeting of the Vigilante's Executive Committee. Lott advised his colleagues of the tenor of the Nevada City contingent, and sought their formal approval for Slade's execution. Much to his surprise, Lott found that "the Virginia men were loath to act at all." All too aware of how quickly this critical situation was escalating, Lott forcefully reminded the committee that there was a large body of men already on its way to the city and that they "meant business." Lott fervently assured the committee that these men "would not stand in the street to be shot down by Slade's friends, but intended to "take [Slade] and hang him."[27]

Despite Lott's exhortations, the Executive Committee was "most unwilling to proceed to extremities," and remained paralyzed by indecision. Figuratively washing their hands of the situation, "it was finally agreed that if the whole body of the miners [from Nevada City] were of the opinion that [Slade] should be hanged, the Committee left it in their hands to deal with him." John Lott, perhaps a bit stunned from the realization that he did not have the support of the Executive Committee, rode back to meet the mob of men who were now approaching the lower end of Wallace Street.[28]

Although the source isn't certain, Jack Slade—who had been sitting in a saloon—had learned of the dramatic events taking place. In what would prove to be a fatally poor decision, Slade left the saloon and mounted his horse, but instead of riding out of town as quickly as possible, he returned to Pfouts & Russell's store. As Slade renewed his mea culpa to Judge Davis, the street outside the store was suddenly filled with a large crowd of men led by James Williams. The intention of the mob was unmistakable, and Williams entered the store and confronted Slade. In simple, direct terms Williams advised Slade that he was under arrest and would have to pay the ultimate penalty for his behavior. Author Hoffman Birney wrote that "it is possible that determined action at this juncture might have saved Slade's life, but the men who could have influenced the crowd were silent." Judge Davis would later claim, however, that he not only "talked to the leading men," but that he even offered to escort Slade to Salt Lake City if they would pardon him. Davis, however, was unable to turn the tide. Jack asked that Wilbur Sanders be brought to serve as his lawyer. Sanders, a member of the Vigilante's Executive Committee, was very aware of the situation—and presumably present at one or both of the earlier meetings—and had returned to his home where he explained to his wife that he "expected there would be a hanging and he did not wish to be present...." Mrs. Sanders would recall that shortly afterwards two men arrived at their house and "begged" Sanders to intervene, but that he told them "I can do nothing. It is too late." One of Slade's friends (whom Mrs. Sanders wrote was one of the same men who had visited her husband) jumped on his horse and rode hard to Spring Dale Ranche to inform Maria of her husband's predicament.[29]

Virtually all accounts agree that there was little delay in carrying out the execution of Slade, and it is commonly reported that in the interim the condemned man piteously begged for mercy and the chance to see his wife. While certainly understandable that anyone facing execution would lose their composure, it is interesting to note how frequently those chronicling such events would seem to emphasize this common theme of the "bad guy" dissolving into a whimpering puddle. Whether these are genuine accounts of the actual events, or an effort to cast a final measure of shame upon those executed, is worth consideration. It is also interesting to consider Langford's account in which—after writing that Slade "fell upon his knees...begging for his life," that he also noted "...there were a few men, even among those who had doomed this man to death, that would have given all they possessed to save his life...some of them...wept like children when they beheld him on his march to the scaffold."[30]

It was late afternoon when Jack Slade, with his hands tied behind his back, was led down the hill behind Pfouts & Russell's store to the Elephant Livery & Corral. After some moments of hesitation, during which time someone foolishly threatened to save Slade, Williams gave the fatal command and Jack was hanged on the cross-beam of the corral gate. Some sources dramatically—and inaccurately—report that Maria, riding hard in a futile effort to save her husband, was in sight of the corral as the box was pulled from beneath Jack's feet. Although unlikely that her earlier appearance may have actually resulted in a stay of execution at that late juncture, there were those who offered an alternative scenario. With a matter-of-fact detachment, some contemporaries expressed the opinion that, had Maria arrived in time, she would have shot and killed Jack herself rather than allow him to suffer the indignity of hanging.

John X. Beidler later wrote that he, with the help of a few friends, removed Slade's lifeless body, wrapped it in a blanket, and carried it back up the hill to the Virginia Hotel. Beidler noted that it was approximately ten minutes later that Maria Slade arrived. William Drannan claimed to have been one of those who had helped carry Jack's body to the hotel, and was among those men present when Maria arrived.

Drannan wrote that as Maria stood over Jack's lifeless body she repeatedly asked and on the third time "at the top of her voice, 'Who did this,' [but] no one answered her." Mollie Sheehan, who was acquainted with Maria, also recalled the dreadful aftermath: "I…determined to go and tell [Maria] how sorry I was for her. I found her sobbing and moaning, bowed over a stark form shrouded in a blanket. I stood beside her for a moment, trembling and choking, then I slipped away unnoticed."[31]

Jack's memorial services were conducted by Rev. A.M. Torbett, a Baptist minister. Among the large crowd which attended were Paris Pfouts, Alexander Davis, and Wilbur and Harriet Sanders. Harriet would write that: "It was the fashion at that time for ladies to wear white stockings [to funerals]. The day before the funeral Mrs. Slade sent a friend to me with the request that I loan her a pair of black stocking if I had them, to wear at the funeral, as she wished to dress entirely in black. It is needless to say that her wish was granted."[32]

Maria Slade was so embittered by the circumstances of her husband's death that she refused to have his remains stay in the land where people who had taken his life still lived. Maria arranged to have a zinc-lined coffin built and—with poignant irony—filled with alcohol in order to preserve Jack's body. Despite popular local lore, Jack's remains were not held in Virginia City but, rather, were taken to the toll house ranch property and buried in a shallow grave a few yards from the house. Once the roads were suitable for travel, Maria disinterred the remains and, by herself, transported the coffin to Salt Lake City for burial. Before leaving, Maria filed probate of Jack's Will on April 14th. Lest anyone believe that this brought closure to the matter of her husband's death, it should be noted that Maria had vowed to cut the heart from the man who placed the noose around Jack's neck—a threat taken very seriously. Several years later, X. Beidler revealed that it was "a noble German by the name of Brigham [who] adjusted the rope around Slade's neck," and that he had soon thereafter "left the Territory, being afraid [of retribution]."[33]

Maria returned to Montana following Jack's burial in Salt Lake City and moved into a small house in Virginia City, and soon learned that

Maria Virginia Slade (c1868)

much of Jack's estate had already been parceled out in her absence. Despite the Court being advised that Maria was in possession of Jack's Will, she found that the hearing on Jack's estate, an appraisal, and the appointment of a "Special Administrator," had been made. Moreover, matters were badly entangled by a bevy of questionable (opportunistic) claims against the estate; including a claim of $201.25 by the Idaho Billiard Hall for "liquor and breakage," and one by James Williams for "labor." Among Jack's personal effects that were being held by the court-appointed executor, George Parker, was a pair of ivory-handled Colts revolvers. Maria went to Parker and asked for the guns. Parker refused, citing that it may be necessary to sell the guns in order to help settle the estate. Maria quietly left Parker's store, but returned a short time later and told him: "You say you cannot give me my revolvers, perhaps I can persuade you to change your mind," whereupon, she placed the muzzle of a .45 Colts in his face. "George took no time to reason with the lady, but promptly handed her the revolvers which she coolly took possession of and left the store."[34]

Although Maria's recovery of Jack's guns would seem to be very

Maria's home in Virginia City

much in keeping with her reputation it is a bit more surprising that she would remarry and, even more so, whom she would choose for her second husband. One year past Jack's execution, Maria married James Kiskadden, a livery owner—and prominent Vigilante. The wedding ceremony took place on March 22, 1865, in Maria's Virginia City home and was officiated by Hezikiah Hosmer; the Chief Justice of the Territory. The Montana Post reported that the guests were served "two beautiful cakes...imbedded with two golden V's," and offered the wish that: "James, may you and your amiable bride enjoy many long years of happiness and content." One may be excused for thinking that blessing was a bit tongue-in-cheek.[35]

Soon after the wedding, James and Maria would move to Salt Lake City. It is interesting to speculate upon the motivation for this move. Kiskadden's brother was operating a mercantile business in Salt Lake, but James had a very successful business in Virginia City. Perhaps, as other Vigilantes, James wanted to distance himself from the lingering controversy regarding Jack's execution. Or, perhaps the move was initiated by Maria's lingering animosity for those involved with the execution of Jack and she wanted to be near his burial site. One thing is certain: life with Maria provided Kiskadden with neither happiness nor contentment. Kiskadden filed for divorce in March of 1868, citing her "desperate nature" as an irreconcilable grievance.[36]

One source cites that Maria later married James Reed, in St. Louis, Missouri, but the most definitively last-known whereabouts of Maria was in Chicago where, in 1890, her attorney (J. O'Brien Scobey) sent two letters of inquiry to Virginia City inquiring about the Slade estate—neither of which were apparently answered. In 1973, attorney John McClernan thoroughly researched the court records regarding Jack Slade's estate. McClernan's summary notes: "We must concede that the record indicates a conspiracy to pilfer and defraud the Slade estate," and cites as principals in this effort T. C. Jones (the Probate Judge) and Wilbur Fisk Sanders.[37]

Among the interesting footnotes to Slade's execution is one provided by author Art Pauley. Pauley wrote that the Deer Lodge posse split up at Laurin, and James Williams appointed Jack Slade to take temporary command of Red Yeager and George Brown while he—unaware that a united Vigilance Committee had been formed—rode to Virginia City to determine whether it was safe for the posse to appear with the prisoners. It was during his absence that Slade proceeded to refresh himself to the point of becoming intoxicated. Perhaps the memory of his battles with road agents during his Overland Stage Company days were rekindled by the whiskey, and Slade countermanded Williams' directive to hold the captives for transport to Nevada City and ordered the late-night execution of Yeager and Brown. Understandably, it would not have been an order that any posse member who valued his own life would have refused. Pauley wrote that James Williams was deeply embittered by Slade's defiance...and that he was not the sort of man who would forget or forgive such a transgression. Pauley's scenario certainly provides for an intriguing alternative version to the events which occurred that bitterly cold January night, and may easily explain why James Williams didn't hesitate to proceed with Slade's execution at the Elephant Corral.[38]

Nevertheless, there were many friends and former colleagues who held Jack in high regard and were outraged at the news of his execution.

One example of their outrage is found in the account of L.A. Fenner. Fenner, who was traveling on the Overland Stage, witnessed such an incident: "A day or two before we reached Virginia Dale [stage station], a badly battered man arrived from Virginia City. He had told that Slade had been hanged, and he was set upon by the [stage coach] drivers and the life nearly beaten out of him with champagne bottles."[39]

And, as evidence of the frightening—and lingering—reputation of Slade, there is this story: Soon after Jack's death, the legend spread that his spirit was living within the little cabin at Slade's "Ravenswood Ranch" in the Madison Valley. One evening, with approach of bad weather, two sheepherders decided to take refuge in the cabin. Sometime later, the men were found dead in the cabin of no apparent cause. "Travelers and curiosity seekers since then have not tarried there after nightfall."[40]

"Such was Captain J. A. Slade, the idol of his followers, the terror of his enemies and of all that were not within the charmed circle of his dependents.

Notes:

Opening Epigrams: Alexander Davis.

1. Illinois State Historical Society, "History of the Slade Family," 1903.

2. Ibid.

3. Discharge certificate of J.A. Slade; J.A.Slade mss. L. Callaway, Two Tales, pg 98, claims Slade killed a man in Carlyle using a rock. Service as a teamster per Cunningham.

4. Slade vertical file (MHS).

5. "She possessed...," Langford.

6. Davis quotes per *St. Louis Globe-Democrat*, appears in *Helena Herald* issue of July 18, 1878. Davis claims to have seen the marriage certificate of Jack & Maria.

7. "16 wagons" per Rottenberg. "the wagon boss...," Stuart. Site of murder also cited as "Ham's Fork." Stuart did not witness event, but wrote that he heard the shot and got story from witnesses.

8. "was easily the best...," Rottenberg. Sweetwater route essentially followed the course of present-day routes of I-80 and I-76.

9. Weiser: Pony Express lost $1,000.00 per day.

10. "was feared...," Dimsdale. Revenge of Dr. Bartholomew's murder per Callaway.

11. "vilest liquor...," per over-land.com/Julesburg. "Wickedest City," Fort Sedgwick Historical Society brochure.

12. Appears that Beni arranged for associates to steal horses and return them for a reward paid by the Company, which he would spilt with his accomplice.

13. Per Daems and Callaway, Slade cut both of Beni's ears, and nailed one to door of Julesburg station. Beni may have actually been captured at Cold Spring.

14. "rattled up...," Twain. Incident appears to have occurred in August, 1861.

15. Fort Halleck was located in present-day Wyoming. Dorothy Johnson wrote the event included Slade shooting another Overland

employee. Callaway and Birney mention spree at sutler's building at Ft. Halleck, but do not indicate any person being shot by Slade.

16. See profile on James Williams in this manuscript for details on his meeting with Slade.

17. Quotes per Callaway. Description of Spring Dale Ranche per notice of Probate Court, Montana Post, November 26, 1864.

18. John McClernan to Dabney Collins: Slade left "after September 24, and returned before Christmas."

19. Appears as "Tiebalt" per Langford; "Tbalt" per Dimsdate and W.F. Sanders.

20. Slade cited as a Vigilante in Langford and Pauley.

21. "Slade was…," Beidler.

22. "Promiscuously…," H. Birney, Vigilantes, ppg 328-9; "friends" included Dan Harding and Charley Edwards. Actress insulted was Kate Harper. Slade's entourage visited at least five saloons: Washington Billiard Hall, Idaho Billiard Hall, Gem Saloon (Stonewall Hall), Beaverhead Saloon, and the Pony Bar. While impressive, Langford (who was the Federal Revenue Collector) would report that the city had 25 hotels and 73 liquor dealers and that "one-third [of all territorial revenues] has been for the sale of liquor alone." Langford to William Doolitte, April 25, 1865.

23. "without knowing…," Drannan, Thirty-one Years on the Plains and in the Mountains, pg 388. "Slade tore…," Birney, pg 330. Langford, pg 372, cites Fairweather as one who tore warrant. Alexander Davis, Helena Herald, July 20, 1878, also stated that it was Fairweather who destroyed the warrant.

24. "little attention…," account of John Lott in Birney, ppg 331-33. "his execution…," Dimsdale.

25. "played out…asked him…Jerry said…," J.X. Beidler, X. Beidler: Vigilante, pg 99.

26. W. Davis mss. "made a few…," Birney, pg 332.

27. "the Virginia men…would not…meant business…," Dimsdale. Beidler and L. Callaway report 200 men were in the posse, while Langford and Dimsdale claim as many as 600. Drannan states that there were only 20 "vigilantes" who appeared to arrest Slade.

28. "most unwilling…it was finally…, Dimsdale.

29. L. Callaway writes that there was another meeting of leading men following Slade's arrest, at which time his fate was sealed. "it is possible…," Birney. "talked to leading men…," A. Davis interview, *Helena Herald,* op cit. "Reminiscences of Harriet Sanders," Harriet wrote that one of the men who visited their home rode to notify Maria Slade.

30. Quotes per Langford.

31. Beidler. "I slipped away…," M. Ronan, <u>Frontier Woman,</u> pg 25. "at the top…," Drannan, pg 392. Alexander Davis interview, op cit, states Maria arrived "not more than ten minutes" after body had been taken to hotel. James Kiskadden cited as one of those who carried Slade's body to hotel.

32. Torbett cited as the first Protestant minister, per G. Stuart. "It was the fashion…," per H. Sanders.

33. Langford and Birney give details of Slade's body being re moved to his ranch for temporary internment. Slade was buried at the "old Mormon cemetery" on July 20, 1864. "a noble German…," Beidler. Beidler also recalled that it was Charles Beehrer ("Dutch Charley") who selected the site for Slade's execution. Beehrer is quoted in Birney that it was Charley Brown, "a German man," responsible for cinching noose around Slade's neck.

34. Maria filed for probate on April 14, 1864; Probate Records Book A, pg 6.; additional related entries on May 2, May 4, May 13, and September 7. "you say…," Mrs. Granville Stuart; Maria Slade vertical file, MHS. The claim of the Idaho Hall would be paid, but not James Williams. Total claims against the estate from Virginia City saloons were in excess of $17,000 in present-day value.

35. "two beautiful…," per *Montana Post*, March 25, 1865. Annie Stanley and Oliver Sweet served as witnesses for the marriage.

36. Divorce per *Redstone Review*, June 10, 1927.

37. Maria's marriage to James Reed per <u>History of Erie County, Ohio.</u> "we must concede…," McClernan mss, in Slade vertical file (MHS)

38. Pauley, Art, <u>Henry Plummer, Lawman and Outlaw.</u>

39. Fenner mss.
40. "Travelers…," Towle.

Closing Epigram: "Such was…," Dimsdale.

Sources:

Beidler, John X. X. Beidler, Vigilante.
Birney, Hoffman. Vigilantes.
Callaway, Llewellyn. Two True Tales.
Carlyle Union Banner
Cunningham, Bob. "Slade: A Hard Case Study," Journal of the West, Vol 30, no. 4.
Daems, Henry B. "Tales of a Pioneer," from Pioneer Trails & Trials.
Fenner, L.A. mss (MC #64) Montana Historical Society.
Dimsdale, Thomas. Vigilantes of Montana.
Forney, Gary R. Dawn in El Dorado.
Gordon, Victoria. "Mollie Slade—Faithful Wife," The Montana Journal, July 1991.
Illinois State Historical Society.
Langford, Nathaniel mss (SC #215) MHS.
_____. Vigilantes Days & Ways.
McClernan, John B. "The Slade Estate File," Joseph Slade vertical file, (MHS)..
Montana Post
Pauly, Art. Henry Plummer, Lawman and Outlaw.
Probate Records, Madison County Recorder's Office, Virginia City, MT.
Rottenberg, Dan. "The Forgotten Gunfighter," Civilization Magazine, Vol 3, no. 2.
Sanders, Harriet P mss. (SC#1254, MHS)
Sanders, Wilbur F. mss (MC#53, MHS)
Joseph A. Slade vertical file, (MHS)
Joseph A. Slade mss (sc #749) MHS.

Virginia M. Slade vertical file, (MHS)

Stuart, Granville. <u>Forty Years on the Frontier, Vol. I.</u>; edited by Paul C. Phillips.

Towle, Virginia Rowe. <u>Vigilante Women</u>.

Twain, Mark. <u>Roughing It</u>.

Weiser, Kathy. "Ben Holladay," America Legends website.

<u>Photo credits:</u>

Freight wagon; Pace Archives.

Overland Stage route map; Wikipedia

Stone House at Spring Dale Ranche; Madisonian, October 1959.

Maria Virginia Slade; Denver Public Library.

Maria's home in Virginia City; author

Jack's tombstone; findagrave.com

James Williams
A Reluctant Ruffian

The legends of the Alder Gulch Vigilantes serve as an attraction for many of those who visit Virginia City while, for others, it becomes an obsession. Stories—entangled in fact and fiction—of Montana's first vigilante organization have been passed down for years through the writings of some contemporaries and many modern-day authors, at family gatherings and by often ill-informed tour guides and vendors. The most common error made by these storytellers is that they paint the men who participated as vigilantes as being either men with knightly hearts or cloven-footed villains. I would submit that the truth is a good bit more complicated and actually lies somewhere between those absolutes. And perhaps no better example of that can be found than in the life—and tragic death—of James Williams.

James Williams was born January 9, 1834, near Greensburg, Pennsylvania. His father, John M., and his mother, Mary 'Polly' [nee McCraken], were both natives of Pennsylvania and members of the Congruity Presbyterian Church. Six children born from this union are known to have survived infancy: Nancy (1830), Catharine M. (1832), James (1834), John (1836), Robert (1839), and Joseph (1844). Based upon surviving evidence we can assume that James attended a local school, but this author has not been able to obtain confirmation. In 1850, the Federal Census report listed James (age 18) residing with his parents and employed—as his father—as a "laborer." By his own account, James left home and headed West in the Spring of 1855. His first extended stop was at Rock Island, Illinois, where he remained for approximately 18 months, before moving to Leavenworth, Kansas. James left us no details of his time in Rock Island.[1]

Leavenworth was a bustling new frontier town in 1857, and was already embroiled in the contentious arguments which would lead to not only turmoil in Kansas, but help to propel the nation toward civil war. Williams' only comment upon his time in Leavenworth was that he "took no active part in the fights there at that time." There must have been plenty of opportunity for both fights and employment in that rapidly growing area but, in the fall of 1858, Williams continued his journey West. This time, his destination was the gold fields of Colorado, where he spent his first winter along the Platte River, "below Cherry Creek."[2]

Williams prospected until 1861, and was joined at some point during that time by his brother, John. The brothers were apparently successful enough to purchase, in partnership with two other men, a ranch located "four miles south of Pueblo." James sold his interest in the ranch in the Spring of 1863, with the intention of returning to Pennsylvania. Whether it was learning the news of a major new gold strike or discouraging news from back East isn't certain, but something caused James to change his plans. James (and John) joined a wagon train of miners headed West for the new gold fields of the Idaho Territory.[3]

As was the common practice among such trains, the members of the wagon train which James engaged with held an election to appoint one of the party as its "Captain." The responsibilities of a Captain typically included assigning camp tasks, serving as spokesperson, and adjudicating any disputes among the members. The word of the train's

Captain being law. Although frequently described by colleagues as shy and soft-spoken, James Williams had the reputation of showing good judgment and courage. Additionally, as his brother, John, would later point out: "if James got a chance to study a man for a short time, he seemed to know all about him." And although there is no evidence that he sought the position, those traits were undoubtedly significant factors in his election as "Captain." It would be a moniker he would carry for the rest of his life.[4]

En route to the area known as the Salmon River Mines in the Idaho Territory, the Williams' train came upon a freight train camped for the evening and it was decided to join them at this site. As the men of the two trains engaged in conversation, it quickly became consensus that the trains should travel together to provide a more formidable force against any possible attack. The parties also determined to appoint James Williams as Captain of the newly consolidated enterprise, but this was immediately challenged by the man who had been serving as Captain of the freight train…Joseph Albert (Jack) Slade.

Jack Slade was already known to many for his ruthless service in administering—with deadly force—the interests of the Overland Stage Company. In short, he was not a man who was accustomed to anyone challenging his authority. When someone in his party—no doubt with great trepidation—notified Slade that a new Captain had been elected, Slade defiantly declared he didn't much care for such an election and that he would be serving as Captain. Upon learning of this challenge, Williams confronted Slade and reportedly declared, "I want to say whoever is elected captain will be captain. Did you hear what I said?" After what must have been a few incredibly tense moments, Slade is said to have replied, with a little smile crossing his face, "All right, Cap, that suits me." To perhaps further diffuse the situation, Williams announced that he was appointing Slade as the train's Lieutenant and would later recall that he "never had a man with me that I got along with better [than Slade.]"[5]

The two trains separated at Soda Springs with the original Williams' headed toward a strike they had learned of along Grasshopper Creek. Williams and his group arrived at Bannack on June 20, 1863, where they quickly learned of the incredible new gold strike which had been made less than a month earlier. Williams remained in Bannack for approximately a week before moving to the Alder Gulch, arriving at Nevada City on July 1st. An acquaintance at the time would later recall that, at the time of his arrival in the Gulch, James was "29 years old, a strongly built, slow moving man, 5 feet 10 ½ inches tall, weighing about 190 pounds" and with "deep-set blue eyes." Mrs. Charles Metzel would also recall that "a constant article of [Williams'] dress was a plaid scarf worn around his neck."[6]

Unlike most of the new immigrants to the Gulch who sought to earn a living—if not their fortune—working as miners, James began work as a contractor building 16' x 20' cabins for $200. By autumn, James had acquired a herd of approximately 50 horses and began operating a pack-horse train between Elk City (Idaho) and Virginia City, and added a freighting operation between the Gulch and Salt Lake City. He also, with his brother, established a ranch South of Nevada City, and opened a corral and livery business in Nevada City. Had he done nothing more than maintained these enterprises he would have probably passed into history as a successful, but little-known pioneer. He was destined, however, to play an unforgettable role in the drama of early Montana.[7]

The discovery of gold at Bannack and in the Alder Gulch attracted an eclectic swarm of humanity, including some men who operated as "road agents." The modus operandi of the road agents, as depicted in scores of Hollywood films, was to surprise a small party of travelers and rob them of their valuables. Typically, the bandits would work together in gangs of three to six men and target stagecoaches, merchants, or miners known to be traveling with a generous supply of gold dust. As may be expected in the case of any armed robbery, circumstances often spiraled out of control and what began with simply threats of violence sometimes resulted in murder. With virtually no threat of pursuit by law enforcement, the road agents were essentially able to act with impunity. By December of 1863, several robberies had occurred on the roads between Bannack, the Alder Gulch camps, and the Salt Lake City route, and there was a growing outrage among the "honest folk." The catalyst which would turn seething outrage into a fire-storm of revenge would be the murder of Nicholas Tbalt.[8]

Commonly known as "the Dutchman," Nicholas Tbalt was a young man in the employ of George Butschy and William ("Bill") Clark who operated mining claims in Brown's Gulch; South of Nevada City. Tbalt is described as "a big, plodding, blue-eyed German...far, far from a mental giant, but as honest as Arizona sunshine, faithful as an old draft horse, and with the engaging friendliness of a bull-terrier puppy. Everybody knew him and liked him." Although there is some variation among sources regarding some of the details surrounding the demise of Tbalt, the version which rings most true is that Nicholas was sent to retrieve a pair of mules owned by his employers which were boarded at the ranch and stage station of Bob Dempsey; near present-day Sheridan. When he didn't return with the mules as expected, some disparagingly suggested that Nicholas had taken a turn of character and absconded with the mules and the gold which he had been provided to pay the bill for the boarding fees.[9]

Approximately 10 days after Tbalt's disappearance, William Palmer discovered the body of a man (whom he did not recognize) lying amid some willows near the road to Virginia City; East of Pete Daly's inn. The man had been shot in the head and badly disfigured by having been dragged through the brush. Palmer rode to a small camp he spotted nearby and asked the two men he found (John Franck and George Hilderman) to help him recover the body. The men refused, so Palmer returned to load the frozen body into his wagon by himself, drove to Nevada City, and parked the wagon in front of the Lott brothers store; a prominent location on the main thoroughfare. The body was soon identified as that of Nicholas Tbalt and his employers were notified. John X. Beidler was at Lott's store when the body arrived and went to Williams' corral and asked James to come to the wagon. After confirming the identity of the remains, Bill Clark also paid a visit to James Williams and declared that "this thing has been running on long enough and has got to be stopped." Clark obviously told James of his intention to form a posse, and Williams replied that he "had fifty or sixty head of horses and about twenty-five saddles and bridles and if that were of any use they could have them."[10]

Clark assembled a posse of twenty-five men, which did not include Williams, and rode out in search of Franck and Hilderman for further questioning. The posse would subsequently "arrest" these two men, as well as Jim Crowell and George Ives...whom Franck identified as the murderer of Tbalt. Upon their return to Nevada City, arrangements were made for an open-air trial (held December 20-21 at Nevada City), and resulted in George Ives being found guilty of the murder of Tbalt. Immediately after the judgment of the jury was read the lead prosecuting attorney, Wilbur Fisk Sanders, called for the execution of Ives; which was administered by hanging within 45 minutes of the verdict. With a noose cinched tight around his neck, Ives—who had maintained his innocence throughout the trial—declared once again: "I am innocent of this crime," and added "Alex Carter killed the Dutchman." The command, "Men do your duty" was shouted out and the box upon which Ives was standing was pulled from his feet. While he did not make any note of such, it is reasonable to assume that James Williams was an observer of the proceedings.[11]

Although this author is unaware of any direct evidence, one may easily be led to believe that the final words of Ives were the catalyst for some interesting discussions during the next couple of days among the men who had been principals in his arrest and execution. Subsequent events support the hypothesis that some of the posse came to believe that: (a) Ives was telling the truth in accusing Carter, (b) they realized that "this thing" was far from being settled, and (c) they needed to organize themselves to achieve the task—and, perhaps, to legitimize their efforts. Nathaniel Langford wrote that there was "consultation" between men of Nevada City and Virginia City in regard to those matters, but the recollections of other principals suggest that each community initially acted independently in taking their respective steps at organizing.

On the evening of December 23rd a meeting was held at the Lott brothers store in Nevada City. The meeting appears to have been organized principally by John Lott and Bill Clark. The known participants were 25 carefully selected men—including James Williams. Although no recored of the specific details of the meeting are known to exist, there are two remarkable surviving documents: a handwritten Oath and a bill of sale. The oath reads:

"We the undersigned uniting ourselves in a party for the Laudible purpos of arresting thievs & murderers & recovering stolen property do pledge ourselves upon our sacred honor each to all others & solemnly swear that we will reveal no secrets, violate no laws of right & never desert each other or our standard of justice. So help us God as witnessed our hand and seal this 23 of December AD 1863."

The oath was signed by 24 of the 25 men believed to have attended the gathering; with James Williams apparently being the first to sign the oath. The missing signature is believed to be that of John Lott, who is thought to have composed the oath and left space for his signature, but neglected to sign.

It is interesting to consider the motivation of Williams to join this vigilante organization. Certainly there is nothing in his personality or background to suggest he had a "blood lust," or that he had heretofore any personal connection with those who may have suffered at the hands of road agents. He did have a very deeply embedded sense of right and wrong and the courage to stand by his convictions and willing—if necessary—to step to the front when called upon. There is also the practical matter that he was a businessman who had a financial stake in the freight he transported and the livestock he used being safe from theft. Although there is no record of Williams sharing his thoughts on this question, it seems reasonable to assume that it was a combination of conviction, financial concern, and loyalty to friends which led him into this controversial chapter of his life...a role which he may not have embraced, but truly believed to be his duty.

The bill of sale, as previously noted, is headed: "Wm. Clark bot of Lott Brothers for the Vigilant Community." Following is a detailed list of items and their prices totaling $143.00, and signed for by James Williams. These items would clearly suggest the newly organized "party" had also determined to form another posse at their meeting, and that Williams was selected to serve as the leader of the expedition. Williams would self-effacingly later write of his appointment that "they had an idea I had some leather in me I guess." Twenty-four posse members were recruited and it appears they rode out of Nevada City by late afternoon of December 24th with the intention of arresting Alex Carter. Although Williams is known to have later taken part in other vigilante posses, this one also carries special significance with regard to not only the information which would allegedly be obtained, but the uncertainty of his role in the final outcome of the affair.[12]

Contemporary accounts of this second posse (called the "Deer Lodge Scout" by Dimsdale) do not provide the specific identity of the posse members who were involved, but there are some clues which provide direction. Accounts are similar in most regards, with one very significant exception. The common points agree that after enduring bitter cold and deep snow, the posse arrived at Deer Lodge only to learn that Alex Carter had received word of the posse's approach and escaped. They also learned the messenger had apparently been a man whom they had met en route, Erastus "Red" Yeager. The posse returned via the Beaverhead Rock, and while resting there they learned that Red— now a person of great interest to them-—was known to be at a camp called Rattlesnake Ranch. The posse split with a smaller number, led by James Williams, riding in search of Red Yeager while the remainder rode towards Dempsey's Ranch where they agreed to rendezvous.[13]

The group found Yeager at the Rattlesnake Ranch in the custody of two deputies of Bannack's Sheriff, Henry Plummer. The deputies had served a warrant for Red, on the charge of horse theft. Williams advised the deputies they wanted Red for questioning in connection with the murder of Nicholas Tbalt. The deputies agreed to let them have Red with the provision they would return him to Bannack once they finished their business with him, and Red was taken by the posse without trouble.[14]

The posse with Red Yeager rode to Dempsey's and, after a meal and some rest, "the captain" (presumably Williams) questioned Red about his involvement with Alex Carter. Red confessed he had delivered a message to Carter, but that the author of the note and the man who had requested him to do so was none other than George Brown—the barkeeper at Dempsey's. Brown was subsequently questioned and admitted he had written the note, but that Red had indicated he was "going to see the boys" at Deer Lodge and had asked if there were any messages he could deliver.

The information obtained from Red and Brown was shared with the full posse and a vote taken on the how to proceed. The posse voted unanimously that the culprits deserved to hang for their involvement, but that they should be returned to Nevada City before their execution. Williams ordered that the posse would again split and, on January 4th, one group of seven or eight men escorted Red and Brown to Laurin's Ranch, where the remainder of the posse (which seems probable to

215

have included Williams and the Rattlesnake group) agreed to meet them after having some additional rest at Dempsey's.[15]

As agreed, the posse in charge of the accused men arrived at Laurin and waited for the second group, which arrived "near sundown." In Langford's account as well as that of Art Pauley, there was a "brief consultation" between the two groups, and that the second group rode on to Nevada City. Pauley specifically cites that Williams appointed Jack Slade, his former wagon train "Lieutenant," to serve as leader of the group in charge of the accused men. Williams rode ahead with the group to Alder Gulch, presumably because there was an anxious uncertainty as to how they may be greeted upon arrival with their prisoners. Dimsdale wrote that "the trial of George Ives had demonstrated most unquestionably that no amount of certified guilt was sufficient to enlist popular sympathy exclusively on the side of justice." Both Dimsdale and Lew Callaway wrote that the posse "expected a battle on their arrival at Nevada." It would seem very plausible that, given the uncertainty of the situation, that Williams—as Captain of the posse—would have taken the responsibility to go forward. Nevertheless, it was at Laurin where events would take a deadly turn.[16]

Dimsdale and Langford write that it was approximately 10:00 p.m. when the ad hoc "Leader" of the Laurin posse group was awakened by another member of the posse who advised—presumably as result of conversation with the others—that "The hour has arrived. We mean business, and are waiting for you." The leader went to the room where Red and Brown were being held and the two men were separated. Red, who admitted taking part in road agent activities but never having committed murder, proceeded to offer a wide-ranging, very detailed account of an organized gang of road agents (including Brown) who were led by none other than Henry Plummer, the sheriff of Bannack. Red named 23 men who were active in the gang—who called themselves the "Innocents,"—and which also included Ned Ray and Buck Stinson (the deputies who had held Red under arrest just 24 hours earlier), Alex Carter, and George Ives.

Yeager reportedly not only willingly offered his confession without coercion or force, but acknowledged it would probably result in his execution; which he "merited years ago." Whether Red performed so honorably from a sense of duty or desperation seems open to discussion, but perhaps the greater—and unanswerable—question is who actually heard his confession and whether any of it was recorded. We are also left with the deliciously intriguing uncertainty of whether it was Williams or Slade who heard the confession. The consequences of Yeager's confession, however, is not in question.[17]

The leader called the posse together, shared information from Red's confession, and another vote was taken. This time, the posse determined that Yeager and Brown should be immediately executed. With little delay, the condemned men were led to a nearby grove of cottonwood trees where the execution was carried out. The lifeless bodies of Yeager and Brown were left hanging from the tree limbs which served as their gallows and with a note attached to Brown which read: *"Brown! Corresponding Secretary"* and to Yeager: *"Red! Road Agent and Messenger."*[18]

To conclude Pauley's version of events, he wrote that after consulting with other Vigilantes in Nevada City on the night of January 4, Williams knew that circumstances were favorable for the posse to bring Yeager and Brown to the Gulch for trial. Williams rode back to Laurin early the following morning, to find that Yeager and Brown had been hanged. And, although he was angry about this action, Williams did not confront those responsible because "there was more than enough dissension within the infant organization" at this point. Williams, however, may have understandably regarded the execution as an act of disobedience—and held a deep grudge against the man he held responsible.[19]

Although it isn't certain as to exactly when he learned, undoubtedly one of the first things of which James Williams was made aware of when he arrived in Nevada City was that a Vigilance Committee had been formally established in his absence, and that "the crisis was past." Williams also learned that he had been elected as Executive Officer of the nascent organization which now included men from Virginia City. At, or about, the same time as the Nevada City group was established and its posse left for Deer Lodge, a similar effort to organize was underway in Virginia City. Led by Paris Pfouts and Wilbur Fisk Sanders, the Virginia City committee of 5 or 6 men initially met in the hardware store of John Nye and quickly added new recruits to their ranks. This group soon merged with the Nevada City men to form the Alder Gulch Vigilance Committee; which branched out to other camps in the Gulch.[20]

Almost certainly influenced by (if not actually authored by) attorney Wilbur Sanders, the newly coordinated organization drafted a set of "Regulations and By-Laws" which included the creation of an Executive Committee of 17 men and the offices of President (Paris Pfouts), Secretary (Levinus Daems), Treasurer (John Lott), Official Prosecutor (Wilbur Sanders), and Executive Officer (James Williams). Membership on the Executive Committee was apportioned to each of the camps in the Gulch and a set of committees was also established. Interestingly, at the meeting when the officers were elected, Pfouts, Sanders, and Williams were absent. Each man, however, subsequently assumed the "honor" bestowed upon them.[21]

As the Executive Officer, Williams' duties were defined in the Vigilance Committee By-Laws as being responsible for apprehending those men judged to have committed high crimes, and administering the verdicts as determined by the Executive Committee; which was specifically defined "the only punishment that shall be inflicted by this Committee is death." In practice, however, punishment also came to include whipping and banishment. The question of how enthusiastically Williams embraced his role of Executive Officer is matter for speculation. Nevertheless, he would prove to be faithful to his pledge and unwavering in carrying out his assignments. Adriel B. Davis would later be quoted as stating, "I was with Captain Williams on some of his trips, and know him to be...a man of few words [but] he was obeyed implicitly." Several other sources would also acknowledge Williams' importance to the organization with the observation that "Captain Williams was the real head of the Vigilantes."[22]

Among the actions in which Williams would lead on behalf of the Vigilance Committee would be: the "Hell Gate Scout" (which captured and executed Alex Carter), the infamous "Hangman's Building" execution of 5 men, and the executions of Jack Slade, Jem Kelly, and Jacob Seachrist. Certainly, the execution of Slade was the most controversial in terms of whether it was truly authorized by the Vigilance Committee, how inappropriate it was in relation to Slade's "crime," and the declared purpose of the Vigilantes. Slade, however, may have been an execution which Williams didn't hesitate to carry out. Almost immediately following the execution of Slade, the Alder Gulch Vigilance Committee began to break apart from what appears to have been both internal and external pressures. Nathaniel Langford, Wilbur Sanders, and James Kiskadden resigned from the Executive Committee; John Lott resigned as Treasurer; and Paris Pfouts would later write, "I twice, at general meetings, handed in my resignation...but on both occasions was unanimously re-elected [as President]." Pfouts finally managed to terminate his membership by virtue of leaving the Territory.[23]

James Williams would remain active with the Alder Gulch Committee through the summer of 1865, when he responded to a request by X Beidler in early August to help execute Jacob Seachrist (and perhaps to help establish a Vigilance Committee) at Helena. Although some version of the Alder Gulch Vigilantes continued to operate for a short time afterwards, the Seachrist execution was the final action of James Williams as Executive Officer. James returned to the Ruby Valley seeking to resume a quiet life as a rancher and livery owner, but carrying the heavy weight of a his reputation. Upon learning that Thomas Dimsdale was writing a book about the Vigilantes, Williams paid him a visit and chillingly advised that "he was no longer a Vigilante and that Dimsdale should forget that he ever was." A friend later similarly observed that Williams "seldom talked of his connection with the [Vigilantes]." Poignantly, however, it seems that perhaps Williams was unable to forget—or forgive—himself.[24]

The mission of the Alder Gulch Vigilantes was formally rendered superfluous by the election of county sheriffs, the appointment of a United States Marshal, and with the arrival of the federally-appointed Chief Justice for the Montana Territory, Hezekiah Hosmer. Hosmer convened a Grand Jury into service shortly after his arrival and, in his opening remarks to the jurors, he stated: "On reference to the statute

RASCALS, RUFFIANS, AND REBELS

prescribing the nature and punishment of crime, I find nothing which requires me to charge you specially upon any of the offenses therein defined...[however] such societies [as the vigilantes], originating in necessity, have fulfilled their work. To go further is to commit crime... [the vigilantes] are no longer necessary. They should at once and forever be abandoned. Do not, I adjure you, disappoint the expectations of all good men." Perhaps not entirely by coincidence, among those receiving this lecture was James Williams.[25]

A more stinging rebuke would be delivered by the *Rocky Mountain Gazette* which opined, "The *[Montana] Post* has a right to eulogize the [Vigilantes] if it chooses. It is possible they are the immaculate beings which that journal has painted them...It is possible that human nature has soared above its surroundings, and ascended into a higher circle of humanity than it has been the privilege of the rest of frail mortality to know; but in our experience we have known many such panegyrics passed upon similar bodies, whose subsequent careers showed too many cloven feet to justify the conclusion."[26]

It is indisputable that because of the Vigilante organization some very bad men were eliminated from the Montana Territory, and incidents of highway robberies and murder were reduced—although certainly not eliminated. It must also be admitted, however, that some of those men executed by the vigilantes, had they been provided a fair and impartial trial, would have likely been found innocent of a capital crime. Whether the lives of those innocent men may have been the price necessary to obtain justice for those victims who were robbed or murdered remains the haunting question of the Vigilante story.

Williams found himself—as many others from the Alder Gulch communities—increasingly doing business, and/or living, in Helena. First established by a gold rush in the summer of 1864, Helena was rapidly surpassing Virginia City as the economic and population center of the Territory. It was during a visit there in early January of 1866, that James received an invitation to attend a birthday celebration for Elizabeth Ledford. James attended the gathering on January 9th, the same day as the anniversary of his own birthday, and was immediately love-struck with Elizabeth. "Lizzie" was 8 years younger than James, had worked as a teacher, and was a native of Audrain County, Missouri. Liz had traveled to Montana in 1863 with her widowed father (James) and two brothers; John and George. The coincidences of birth date, that both had a brother named John, and that both their mothers were named Mary may have seemed like an omen to James and Elizabeth that they belonged together.[27]

In the early summer of 1866, James and his brother, John, leased the Western Corral in Helena; perhaps as an attempt to franchise their livery business. The Helena enterprise was short-lived, and the Williams brothers returned to the Ruby Valley by autumn to manage their ranch, and to further acquaint themselves with their new neighbors; the Ledford family. The courtship between James and Liz continued to bloom and, in late December, the couple was married in Virginia City with Chief Justice Hosmer officiating.[28]

Certificate of marriage between James Williams and Elizabeth Ledford

The first child of James and Elizabeth, James, was born in 1867, and he would be steadily followed by 8 siblings: Mary, John, Maud, George, Rose, and Charles would survive childhood. Warren died as an infant and an unnamed child died as a newborn. The challenges of raising such a large family (and losing two children) must have been incredibly stressful. And while there doesn't seem to be any direct mention that Elizabeth was ever diagnosed as unstable, one close acquaintance did describe her as "an excellent woman [but with] a shrewish turn of mind." Whether this opinion was "code" to express concern for her mental health or simply as an expression of her personality is, perhaps, open to interpretation.[29]

While his brother, John, increasingly turned his attentions to mining, James would build a solid stock ranch operation on his Ruby Valley property. It appears, however, that it was in early 1868 when James made a well-intended, but fateful, commitment. Dr. Donald Byam (who had served as one of the judges at the trial of George Ives and doctor to the Williams family) decided to follow some other former Alder Gulch residents and move to the fertile Gallatin Valley and begin farming. Byam required a bank loan for adequate start-up capital and Williams agreed to co-sign on his note. Repeated crop failures, however, left Dr. Byam unable to meet payment on the note, which obligated Williams to cover the debt. James was forced to sell most of his stock in order to make good on his obligation, but he would determinedly set about the task of re-building.[30]

A part of the effort by Williams to financially recover may have served as his motivation to seek public office—and the guaranteed salary which it provided. In the autumn of 1871, James successfully ran for a position as Commissioner for Madison County. It appears from a review of the Minutes of the meetings of the Commissioners that Williams was regular in his attendance and would serve during his term with Henry H. Mood and three different men in the position of Chairman; J.M. Knight, D.C. Farrell, and W.G. Pfouts (brother of Paris). Perhaps buoyed by this experience, Williams decided to resign as Commissioner in 1873 and become a candidate for County Sheriff; an office which he—and others—may have considered a natural fit given his experience as a vigilante.[31]

Thomas Deyarmon, who had served the previous two years, had decided to not seek re-election, and Williams filed as a candidate for Sheriff of Madison County on the Republican Party ticket. Running against Williams was Thomas Farrell, a native of Ireland and successful rancher in the Madison Valley. Although the County leaned significantly toward Democrats at the time, Williams lost by only 20 votes. Williams would never again seek public office.[32]

Williams returned to the primary task of restoring his ranch and, although it was observed that "life must have been hard for the Williams family in the latter 1870's," he managed to "gradually get upon the upgrade." By 1880, Williams had restored his property and holdings to an assessed value of $7,000 and, the following year, went into partnership with James Callaway; an attorney and former Territorial Secretary. Callaway's son, Llewellyn ("Lew"), became a ranch hand and de facto member of the Williams family, and later wrote fondly—but candidly—of James and his family. Lew would write that James "was possessed of a whimsical sense of humor and at meal times frequently kept us laughing by telling stories, but seldom talked of himself." Perhaps this closing observation provides an insight to a man who was not so much modest in regard to his life, but one who had deeply imbedded regrets.[33]

Callaway also observed that Williams was developing a destructive habit: "Whenever he had anything important to do, he avoided strong liquor; but at other times he was fond of it and imbibed freely. As he grew older this tendency grew upon him, and it was difficult for him to maintain sobriety upon his visits to Virginia City...." Another oasis of temptation for Williams was an inn/saloon known as Puller Springs; located approximately three miles northwest of his ranch. In a letter which he wrote to James Callaway in late January of 1886, Williams noted that he had recently joined the Order of Knights Templar, and vowed that he "will never drink another drop of whiskey as long as I live unless I get snake bit [and] I will not look for a Snake either." Ominously, however, Williams also noted in the letter that there was "No snow on the range [but] have nearly all the feed on hand yet." The spring and summer of 1886 was very dry and, by September, Lew Callaway observed that the "range did not look good." That would prove to be a monumental understatement.[34]

Winter arrived in early November and was unrelenting. By December some ranches were recording temperatures of -63 degrees, and Williams was keenly aware of the increasingly desperate situation of his stock. And, with increasing frequency, he was again visiting Puller Springs; which must have been a source of great irritation to Lizzie. In early February of 1887, Williams' supply of hay was exhausted and he knew that he was facing the possibility of a complete loss of his stock. In desperation, he rode to Virginia City to meet with the local banker, Henry Elling, for the purpose of obtaining a loan to purchase hay. Elling, however, refused the loan. Before leaving Virginia City, Williams stopped by the City Drug Store to purchase a bottle of laudanum from his friend and former Vigilante, Dr. Levinus Daems.[35]

As if to add insult to injury, a heavy snowfall blanketed the Ruby Valley soon after Williams returned home from Virginia City. Without question, these conditions made a very desperate situation turn to one of hopelessness. On the morning of Monday, February 21, James told Lizzie he was going out to inspect his remaining herd. He was last observed—presumably hunting stray cattle—at approximately 4:00 p.m. by Will Maloney "going into the brush…known as the Murphy place." When he didn't return that evening, Lizzie assumed that his inspection route had included an extended stop at Puller Springs. When James had still not returned home by mid-morning of the 22nd she became anxious and sent the boys out to look for their father, but they were unsuccessful. Neighbors were called to help with the search on Wednesday, and the body of James Williams was found at 10 a.m. in a thick grove of willows…an empty bottle of laudanum at his side.[36]

James was buried in the cemetery plot on a butte overlooking the Ruby River where he had buried his infant son, Warren, and an unnamed child. Unfortunately, Lizzie and her family would come to endure even more sorrow. The oldest Williams son, James, committed suicide, and son, John, would attempt suicide and was sent to the asylum at Warm Springs. Another son, George, was also sent to Warm Springs in 1898. Daughter, Maud, was diagnosed as "mentally unstable" and sent to Warm Springs in 1914. James' brother, John, who never married, lived out his life in the Ruby Valley (last living with his youngest nephew, Charles) before his death in 1912.[37]

Elizabeth Williams would never remarry and continued to live at the ranch, primarily supported by her surviving children. After Maud was committed to Warm Springs, Elizabeth moved to the community of Sheridan, where she died the following year (April 26, 1915) at the age of 72. She was laid to rest beside her husband and near some of her deceased children and family members in the quiet little family cemetery above the Ruby River.

Principally through the efforts of Frank Bird Linderman, in 1907, the Montana Legislature approved an act "To commemorate the name and deeds of James Williams." The Legislature approved an expenditure of $250 to secure a bronze tablet honoring Williams to be displayed in the Montana capitol. Linderman, a former State Representative from Madison County who was serving as Assistant Secretary of State, made arrangements for the casting and authored the text that appears on the memorial tablet which reads:

> *To Commemorate the name and deeds of James Williams,*
> *Captain of the Vigilantes, through whose untiring efforts and*
> *intrepid daring, law and order were established in Montana*
> *and who, with his associates, brought to justice the*
> *most desperate criminals in the Northwest.*
>
> "The sluice was left unguarded
> When Williams' task was done,
> And trails were safe for honest men
> Through victories he won." [38]

Standing among the unmarked graves and sagebrush in the little cemetery now known as the Jack Creek Cemetery, one can easily imagine the heroic struggle of those early Montanans to carve out a new life in this challenging land. This was a place that demanded men and women be strong in body and spirit, fiercely resilient, to oftentimes find new ways to carve out a life, to face brutal conditions, and to live with—and sometimes rely upon—people from very different backgrounds and with very different values. And, perhaps most challenging for some, was to learn to live with their own demons. James Williams certainly wasn't the last of the early Montana settlers to pass away—not even the last of the Alder Gulch Vigilantes. He may have been the last, however, to have carried the staggering emotional weight of those "victories won."

Notes:

1. Birth year cited as 1832 in 1850 Census and Williams' autobiographical statement, but other sources (including 1880 Census) indicate birth in 1834, which is accepted by author as accurate. Mother, commonly known as "Polly," and John married at Congruity Church, November 19, 1829.

2. "took no…," "below Cherry Creek," Williams Reminiscences

3. "4 miles…," Callaway, "Cpt. Williams."

4. "if James got…," Callaway, Two True Tales.

5. Ibid.

6. Ibid. Daems in "Eyes of a Pioneer" wrote Williams was "6' tall, with blonde hair down to his shoulders."

7. Ibid.

8. Many variations of the young man's name appear; Tbalt most common. Letter of L.A. Fenner to Laura Howey of August 5, 1906: "deVault…is the name he was called when I knew him in Colorado, but as it was customary with every Irish and German name at that time, it was transformed." (MC 64, MHS)

9. Quote per Birney. Known as Cottonwood Ranch, Dempsey's enterprise included an inn and a saloon of some notoriety. Sanders, H.F., Vol. 1, account states that Tbalt went to ranch of George Ives on Wisconsin Creek. Pete Daly's camp, located near present-day Laurin, is better known today as "Robber's Roost."

10. Williams "Reminiscences".

11. Langford. Most sources indicate it was Wilbur Sanders who gave the fateful command, but in an interview with A.B. Davis, he stated that it was James Williams, Alder Gulch Times, September 15, 1899.

12. Oath and Bill of Sale copies in "Vigilantes" vertical file, MHS. "they had an idea…," Williams, op cit.

13. Accounts of Dimsdale, Langford and Birney.

14. Callaway, Two True Tales, cites Williams was with the Rattlesnake posse. Plummer was sheriff of the Bannack Mining District; deputies at Rattlesnake were Buck Stinson and Ned Ray.

15. Vote taken on the Stinkingwater Bridge, per Langford, Callaway (Two True) indicates Williams made the decision to split the posse at Dempsey's, but not afterwards. Birney describes the location of Laurin's ranch as being "on the opposite side of the Stinkingwater River from Dempsey's and near the mouth of California Creek."

16. Laurin commonly referred to in contemporary accounts as "Lorraine's."

17. Both Langford and Dimsdale write that Red urged that the names of his associates be written down. There is no surviving evidence that this was done.

18. Quotes per Dimsdale.

19. "there was more…," Pauley.

20. "crisis is past," Dimsdale. In the absence of the Deer Lodge posse, A.B. Davis stated that "companies" of Vigilantes had been established in the Alder Gulch camps of Summit, Pine Grove, Highland and Junction in addition to Virginia City and Nevada City. Sanders, "History of Early Montana."

21. Birney.

22. "I was with…," Davis quote per *Alder Gulch Times*, September 29, 1899. "Captain Williams…," Birney.

23. "I twice…," Pfouts.

24. "he was no…," Pauley. Silvie posse hanging per *Montana Post*, August 5, 1865. Although he was known in Montana as Jacob Seachrist, it was determined his actual name was Jack Silvie. "seldom talked…," Callaway, Two True.

25. Address to the Grand Jury," December 5, 1864, by Chief Justice Hezekiah Hosmer.

26. *Rocky Mountain Gazette*, August 25, 1866.

27. 1860 Federal Census of Audrain County, Missouri, shows James and wife (Mary) were both natives of Kentucky, and children: Elizabeth, Savilla, John, James, Jr., and George.

28. Callaway, Two Tales. James and Elizabeth married December 27, 1866.

29. Callaway, ibid.

30. *Park County Times*, March 8, 1936.

31. Madison County Commissions Journal, Books C, D, E.

32. Deyarmon would become editor of the *Madisonian*.

33. Quotes per Callaway, "Cpt. Williams." Property values per 1880 Census. Wilbur Sanders would offer a dramatically contrasting opinion of Williams, although it is very unlikely he knew Williams as well. In an unidentified news article, Sanders was quoted: "Williams was a gloomy and gruesome fellow." Llewellyn Callaway became an attorney, and was appointed to the Montana Supreme Court in 1922; Chief Justice 1923-34.

34. Quotes per Callaway, "Cpt. Williams."

35. Similar conditions to Williams' ranch conditions are poignantly illustrated by Charlie Russell's painting "Last of the Five Thousand." Various estimates report that at least 60% of Montana's cattle died during the winter of 1886-87. Situation led to end of open range. Laudanum was a mixture of cocaine with alcohol; a terribly addictive—and often deadly—concoction used as a pain-killer.

36. Quotes per Callaway, Two Tales.

37. Ren.

38. Memorial tablet is now in the care of the Virginia City Preservation Alliance.

Sources:

Alder Gulch Times

Beidler, John X. mss (SC #300), Montana Historical Society.

Birney, Hoffman. Vigilantes.

Burlingame, Merrill. "Montana's Righteous Hangmen," Montana Magazine of Western History, Vol. 28, no. 4.

Callaway, Llewellyn L. "Captain James Williams," an 8-part series which appeared in several Montana newspapers during 1933.

_____. Two True Tales of the Wild West. Oakland, 1973.

_____. Montana's Righteous Hangmen.

Daems, Henry B. "Eyes of a Pioneer." Madison Valley History Association.

Davis, A.B. interview in *Alder Gulch Times*, September 29, 1899.

Derry Area Historical Society, New Alexandria, PA.

Dimsdale, Thomas. Vigilantes of Montana.

Federal Census of Derry Township, Pennsylvania (1850).

Fenner, L.A. mss (MC 64) MHS.

Forney, Gary R. Dawn in El Dorado.

_____. "For the Laudible Purpos: The Alder Gulch Vigilantes," Nuggets in Time, Virginia City Preservation Alliance.

Hosmer, Hezekiah. "Declaration to the Grand Jury of the 1st Judicial District of Montana," Contributions to the Montana Historical Society, vol. 10.

Langford, Nathaniel P. Vigilante Days and Ways.

Madison County Commissioners Journals "C, D, E."

Madisonian

Opheim Observer

Park County Times

Pauley, Art. Henry Plummer: Lawman and Outlaw, Meagher County News (White Sulphur Springs, MT)

Pfouts, Paris S. Four Firsts for a Modest Hero.

Ren, Sue. All Should Be Remembered, Vol. 4.

Sanders, Helen F. History of Montana, Vol 1.

Sanders, Harriet F. and William H. Bertsche, Jr., editors. X. Beidler: Vigilante.

Sanders, Wilbur F. mss, "History of Early Montana" (MC 53), M.H.S.

Thomas, Jan. "Montana's Forgotten Man?" Virginia City Nugget Summer 2015.

United States Census records, 1850, 1860, 1870 Westmoreland County, PA; 1860 Audrain County, MO; 1870 Madison County, MT.

Vigilantes vertical file, MHS.

Williams, James. Reminiscences, (SC #975), Montana Historical Society.

_____. mss (SC #1418), MHS

_____. Vertical files, MHS.

Photo credits:

Portrait; Pace archives

Vigilante Oath; vertical file, Montana Historical Society.

Mhynnnarriage certificate; Madison County Clerk & Recorder's Archives

Williams gravesite; author.

www.ingramcontent.com/pod-product-compliance
Lightning Source LLC
Chambersburg PA
CBHW071322090426
42738CB00012B/2763